ANNOTATED TE

SADLIER

VOCABULARY WORKSHOP®

ENRICHED EDITION

Jerome Shostak

Senior Series Consultant

Vicki A. Jacobs, Ed.D.
Associate Director, Teacher Education Program
Lecturer on Education
Harvard Graduate School of Education
Cambridge, Massachusetts

Series Consultants

Louis P. De Angelo, Ed.D.
Associate Superintendent
Diocese of Wilmington
Wilmington, Delaware

John Heath, Ph.D.
Professor of Classics
Santa Clara University
Santa Clara, California

Sarah Ressler Wright, NBCT
English Department Chair
Rutherford B. Hayes High School
Delaware City Schools, Ohio

Carolyn E. Waters, JD, Ed.S.
ELA/Literacy 6–12 Supervisor
Cobb County School District
Marietta, Georgia

Reviewers

The publisher wishes to thank for their comments and suggestions the following teachers and administrators, who read portions of the series prior to publication.

Teresa Appleby
English Teacher
Paxon Hollow Middle School
Marple Newtown District
Broomall, Pennsylvania

Laura Braun
Assistant Principal
Sawyer School
Chicago Public Schools
Chicago, Illinois

Eileen Brosnahan
Language Arts Teacher
St. Rita Catholic School
Dallas, Texas

Colleen DeGonia
Reading/Language Arts Teacher
Worth Junior High School
Worth, Illinois

Karen Berlin Ishii
Academic and Test Prep Tutor
New York, New York

Susan W. Keogh
Associate Director
Curriculum and Instruction
Lake Highland Preparatory
Orlando, Florida

Carol H. Rohrbach
Director of Curriculum and Staff Development
School District of Springfield Township
Oreland, Pennsylvania

Scott L. Smith
Teacher
Whitewater Valley Elementary
Harrison, Ohio

Patricia Stack
English Teacher
South Park School District
South Park, Pennsylvania

Sally F. Waller
English Teacher
Loyola Blakefield Middle School
Towson, Maryland

Cover: Concept/Art and Design: MK Advertising and William H. Sadlier, Inc.; Cover pencil: Shutterstock/VikaSuh. **Photo Credits:** Blend/Jose Luis Pelaez Inc: T7 *right*, T1. iStockphoto LP/Alex Slobodkin: T7 *left*; Grady Reece: T3; Sean Locke: T4. Ken Karp: T6 *top*. Photodisc/Amos Morgan: T8 *center*. Punchstock/Image Source: T8 *right*. Veer/Corbis: T2.

Printed in the United States of America.
ISBN: 978-0-8215-8026-4/6 7 8 9 EB 20 19 18 17 16

For additional online resources, go to vocabularyworkshop.com and enter the Teacher Access Code: VW13TA63WQX7

CONTENTS

ENRICHED EDITION: NEW FEATURES *T12*
- QR Codes
- Reading Passages
- Writing Prompts
- Vocabulary in Context
- Word Study

VOCABULARY WORKSHOP AND THE COMMON CORE STATE STANDARDS *T14*

ENRICHED VOCABULARY APPROACH:
Systematic Vocabulary Instruction *T16*
- Grade Level Placements
- Word Lists
- "Sliding-Scale" Placement

PRINT COMPONENTS *T18*

DIGITAL COMPONENTS *T21*

IMPLEMENTING THE PROGRAM *T24*

BEST PRACTICES *T28*

ACADEMIC VOCABULARY AND READING COMPREHENSION *T31*

CLASSIC LITERATURE TO USE WITH THE PROGRAM *T33*

VOCABULARY STRATEGY: Roots and Affixes *T36*

DENOTATION, CONNOTATION, AND SHADES OF MEANING *T39*

FIGURATIVE LANGUAGE *T40*

ENRICHED EDITION: NEW FEATURES

Vocabulary Workshop has for more than five decades been the leading program for systematic vocabulary development for grades 6–12. It has been proven a highly successful tool in helping students expand their vocabularies, improve their vocabulary skills, and prepare for the vocabulary strands of standardized tests.

This Common Core Enriched Edition of **Vocabulary Workshop** preserves and improves key elements of the program that have made it so effective, and it introduces important new features that make the series more comprehensive in scope and more current in its approach to vocabulary instruction, especially with respect to standardized testing and the **Common Core State Standards** for English Language Arts.

QR Codes

New QR (Quick Response) codes appear on the **Reading Passage** and **Vocabulary in Context** pages. The code can be read with a smartphone camera. To read the QR code, users may download any free QR code application to a smartphone. Snapping this code links students directly to the relevant **Vocabulary Workshop** Web site, where they can listen to iWords and audio passages, or take an interactive vocabulary quiz.

Use a smartphone camera and a QR code application to snap this code to link to the **Vocabulary Workshop** home page.

Reading Passages

New Reading Passages open each Unit of **Vocabulary Workshop**. At least 15 of the 20 Unit vocabulary words appear in each Passage. Students read the words in context in informational texts to activate prior knowledge and then apply what they learn throughout the Unit, providing practice in critical-reading skills. Idioms, adages, and proverbs used in Passages provide exposure to figurative language. Passage topics are high-interest and represent a variety of genres, including expository texts, informational essays, historical nonfiction, and biographies. Snap the code or go to the **Vocabulary Workshop** home page to listen to iWords, and hear modeled reading of each Unit Passage.

UNIT 4

*Read the following passage, taking note of the **boldface** words and their contexts. These words are among those you will be studying in Unit 4. As you complete the exercises in this Unit, it may help to refer to the way the words are used below.*

Coyotes in Legend and Myth

<Informational Essay>

In some of the most **spirited** Native American myths and legends, the main character is a trickster figure named Coyote. In these tales, Coyote is nearly always **controversial**, inspiring both admiration and disapproval. Sometimes he is wily and ingenious, while at other times he plays the **buffoon**. At first glance, such paradoxes may seem **bewildering**.

But Coyote's great achievement as a mythical figure is to break the **orthodox** mold. In the end, he cannot be easily classified. It is usually **fruitless** to predict how Coyote will behave in any given situation. He is a **virtual** bundle of contradictions. He is simultaneously a clown, a rebel, and a **wayward** troublemaker.

In myths and legends, the character Coyote displays some clear resemblances to the behavior of the animal known as *Canis latrans*. Like coyotes in real life, the story character is nearly always hungry. One of his primary concerns is to **procure** food to fill his belly. To this end, he **scurries** around, often in disguise and more than willing to cheat others.

One amusing tale about Coyote and cheating involves the challenge of a trader. This man dares Coyote to beat him in a deal. Far from being **disheartened**, Coyote accepts the challenge. He tells the man, though, that he needs to return home to collect his "cheating medicine." Coyote will need to borrow the trader's horse. Also, to make the horse comfortable, he will need to borrow the trader's clothes. Eagerly, the trader gives in to these requests. As Coyote rides off into the distance, the trader, who had hoped to **inflict** a defeat on Coyote, is left **mortified** and **wincing** with shame.

In another tale, an opponent turns the tables on Coyote, bearing out the truth of the old adage "set a thief to catch a thief." As often in trickster tales, Coyote has forged an **alliance** with his friend Iktome, or Spider. The two friends admire a beautiful rock named Iya. Coyote places his own blanket on the rock as a gift. When the weather turns colder, however, Coyote reclaims the blanket, despite Iktome's warnings. After Coyote refuses to return the blanket, Iya turns **hostile**. Rolling through the woods, he pursues the two friends. Finally, Iktome dashes down a hole to escape, abandoning Coyote. Iya then rolls over Coyote, flattening him out like a rug. The trickster has been beaten. At least, so it appears.

Coyote is never permanently defeated, however. In Native American legends and myths, he always has the power to return to life. In fact, many of these stories present Coyote as the creator of the world. In these tales, he fashions the universe from the **void** and makes people out of mud. Coyote is also featured as a culture hero who steals fire and gives it to human beings. This dimension of Coyote parallels the most famous deed of the Greek mythological hero Prometheus, who was punished by the gods for his theft of fire.

In fact, Coyote as a trickster resembles many of the best-known figures of world mythology, such as Loki in northern Europe, the fox Reynard in medieval France, the Japanese kitsune or seven-tailed fox, and the trickster/creator figure of Raven, who is also a hero in many Native American tales.

Audio

For iWords and audio passages, snap the code, or go to vocabularyworkshop.com.

50 ▪ Unit 4

Unit 4 ▪ 51

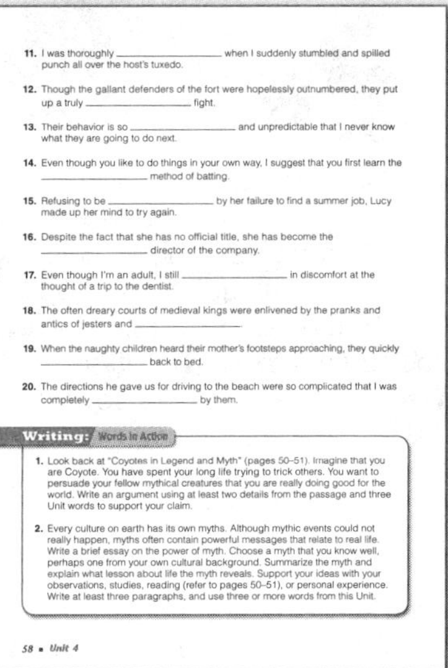

11. I was thoroughly ____________ when I suddenly stumbled and spilled punch all over the host's tuxedo.

12. Though the gallant defenders of the fort were hopelessly outnumbered, they put up a truly ____________ fight.

13. Their behavior is so ____________ and unpredictable that I never know what they are going to do next.

14. Even though you like to do things in your own way, I suggest that you first learn the ____________ method of batting.

15. Refusing to be ____________ by her failure to find a summer job, Lucy made up her mind to try again.

16. Despite the fact that she has no official title, she has become the ____________ director of the company.

17. Even though I'm an adult, I still ____________ in discomfort at the thought of a trip to the dentist.

18. The often dreary courts of medieval kings were enlivened by the pranks and antics of jesters and ____________.

19. When the naughty children heard their mother's footsteps approaching, they quickly ____________ back to bed.

20. The directions he gave us for driving to the beach were so complicated that I was completely ____________ by them.

Writing: Words in Action

1. Look back at "Coyotes in Legend and Myth" (pages 50–51). Imagine that you are Coyote. You have spent your long life trying to trick others. You want to persuade your fellow mythical creatures that you are really doing good for the world. Write an argument using at least two details from the passage and three Unit words to support your claim.

2. Every culture on earth has its own myths. Although mythic events could not really happen, myths often contain powerful messages that relate to real life. Write a brief essay on the power of myth. Choose a myth that you know well, perhaps one from your own cultural background. Summarize the myth and explain what lesson about life the myth reveals. Support your ideas with your observations, studies, reading (refer to pages 50–51), or personal experience. Write at least three paragraphs, and use three or more words from this Unit.

58 ▪ Unit 4

Writing Prompts

Students practice writing responses to two types of prompts. The first prompt refers to the Passage that introduced the Unit and encourages close reading of the text. The second prompt is modeled on those that appear on standardized tests, such as the SAT® and ACT®.*

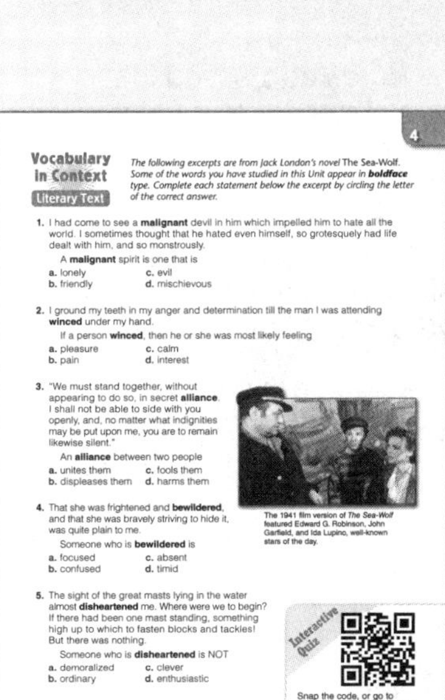

4

Vocabulary in Context
Literary Text

The following excerpts are from Jack London's novel The Sea-Wolf. *Some of the words you have studied in this Unit appear in* ***boldface*** *type. Complete each statement below the excerpt by circling the letter of the correct answer.*

1. I had come to see a **malignant** devil in him which impelled him to hate all the world. I sometimes thought that he hated even himself, so grotesquely had life dealt with him, and so monstrously.

   A **malignant** spirit is one that is
   a. lonely c. evil
   b. friendly d. mischievous

2. I ground my teeth in my anger and determination till the man I was attending **winced** under my hand.

   If a person **winced**, then he or she was most likely feeling
   a. pleasure c. calm
   b. pain d. interest

3. "We must stand together, without appearing to do so, in secret **alliance**. I shall not be able to side with you openly, and, no matter what indignities may be put upon me, you are to remain likewise silent."

   An **alliance** between two people
   a. unites them c. fools them
   b. displeases them d. harms them

4. That she was frightened and **bewildered**, and that she was bravely striving to hide it, was quite plain to me.

   Someone who is **bewildered** is
   a. focused c. absent
   b. confused d. timid

The 1941 film version of *The Sea-Wolf* featured Edward G. Robinson, John Garfield, and Ida Lupino, well-known stars of the day.

5. The sight of the great masts lying in the water almost **disheartened** me. Where were we to begin? If there had been one mast standing, something high up to which to fasten blocks and tackles! But there was nothing.

   Someone who is **disheartened** is NOT
   a. demoralized c. clever
   b. ordinary d. enthusiastic

Interactive Quiz

Snap the code, or go to **vocabularyworkshop.com**

Unit 4 ▪ 59

Vocabulary in Context

The **Vocabulary in Context** pages contain excerpts from classic literature. Each excerpt uses one of the vocabulary words from the Unit and provides students with exposure to the vocabulary in the context of authentic literature. Multiple-choice questions give practice in standardized-test format. An interactive quiz using the Unit words is accessible by snapping the QR code on the page or by visiting **vocabularyworkshop.com**.

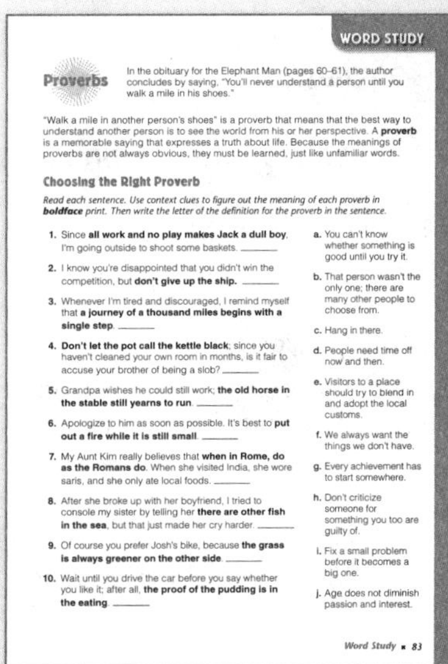

WORD STUDY

Proverbs

In the obituary for the Elephant Man (pages 60–61), the author concludes by saying, "You'll never understand a person until you walk a mile in his shoes."

"Walk a mile in another person's shoes" is a proverb that means that the best way to understand another person is to see the world from his or her perspective. A **proverb** is a memorable saying that expresses a truth about life. Because the meanings of proverbs are not always obvious, they must be learned, just like unfamiliar words.

Choosing the Right Proverb

Read each sentence. Use context clues to figure out the meaning of each proverb in ***boldface*** *print. Then write the letter of the definition for the proverb in the sentence.*

1. Since **all work and no play makes Jack a dull boy**, I'm going outside to shoot some baskets. ______
2. I know you're disappointed that you didn't win the competition, but **don't give up the ship.** ______
3. Whenever I'm tired and discouraged, I remind myself that **a journey of a thousand miles begins with a single step**. ______
4. **Don't let the pot call the kettle black**; since you haven't cleaned your own room in months, is it fair to accuse your brother of being a slob? ______
5. Grandpa wishes he could still work; **the old horse in the stable still yearns to run**. ______
6. Apologize to him as soon as possible. It's best to **put out a fire while it is still small**. ______
7. My Aunt Kim really believes that **when in Rome, do as the Romans do**. When she visited India, she wore saris, and she only ate local foods. ______
8. After she broke up with her boyfriend, I tried to console my sister by telling her **there are other fish in the sea**, but that just made her cry harder. ______
9. Of course you prefer Josh's bike, because **the grass is always greener on the other side**. ______
10. Wait until you drive the car before you say whether you like it; after all, **the proof of the pudding is in the eating**. ______

a. You can't know whether something is good until you try it.
b. That person wasn't the only one; there are many other people to choose from.
c. Hang in there.
d. People need time off now and then.
e. Visitors to a place should try to blend in and adopt the local customs.
f. We always want the things we don't have.
g. Every achievement has to start somewhere.
h. Don't criticize someone for something you too are guilty of.
i. Fix a small problem before it becomes a big one.
j. Age does not diminish passion and interest.

Word Study ▪ 83

Word Study

In accordance with the Common Core State Standards, the **Word Study** pages address figurative language with instruction and practice using idioms, adages, and proverbs, as well as provide instruction on determining and applying denotation and connotation. This new section appears every three Units, after the Review.

*SAT is a registered trademark of the College Board which was not involved in the production of, and does not endorse, this product. ACT is a registered trademark of ACT, Inc. which was not involved in the production of, and does not endorse, this product.

Vocabulary Workshop and the Common Core State Standards

The Common Core Enriched Edition of **Vocabulary Workshop** is aligned with and supports relevant and applic able standards contained in the Common Core State Standards for English Language Arts. The program is fully aligned with the Vocabulary Acquisition and Use standards and supports them with the kind of instruction, modeling, and practice that promote and cultivate corresponding vocabulary skills. Additionally, the Common Core Enriched Edition of **Vocabulary Workshop** addresses several Common Core Reading and Writing standards—in particular those associated with the role of vocabulary both in determining meaning and nuance within the broader context of reading, and in refining usage and expression in written and oral communication.

In this Teacher's Edition, the Common Core State Standards addressed in the form of instruction and/or practice in any given section of the Student Edition are indicated at the bottom of the corresponding page or pages. The standards are identified in an abbreviated notation. For example, "CCSS Vocabulary 4.c, 4.d" indicates that the vocabulary skill or skills represented on that page support Vocabulary Acquisition and Use standards 4.c and 4.d. Similarly, "CCSS Reading (Informational Text) 4, 6" is shorthand for Reading Standards for Informational Text 4, 6, and "CCSS Writing 1.c, 2.d" stands for Writing Standards 1.c and 2.d.

The full language of the corresponding Vocabulary, Reading (both Informational Text and Literature), and Writing standards for grade 6 is provided below. Note that in some instances, text is highlighted to show specific correlations between a particular skill and a more general standard. (A full correlation of the **Vocabulary Workshop Common Core Enriched Edition** program to the Common Core State Standards is available at **vocabularyworkshop.com**.)

Common Core State Standards for English Language Arts

Language Standards

(Grade 6)

Vocabulary Acquisition and Use

4. Determine or clarify the meaning of unknown and multiple-meaning words and phrases based on *grade 6 reading and content,* choosing flexibly from a range of strategies.

- **a.** Use context (e.g., the overall meaning of a sentence or paragraph; a word's position or function in a sentence) as a clue to the meaning of a word or phrase.
- **b.** Use common, grade-appropriate Greek or Latin affixes and roots as clues to the meaning of a word (e.g., *audience*, *auditory*, *audible*).
- **c.** Consult reference materials (e.g., dictionaries, glossaries, thesauruses), both print and digital, to find the pronunciation of a word or determine or clarify its precise meaning or its part of speech.
- **d.** Verify the preliminary determination of the meaning of a word or phrase (e.g., by checking the inferred meaning in context or in a dictionary).

5. Demonstrate understanding of figurative language, word relationships, and nuances in word meanings.

  a. Interpret figures of speech (e.g., personification) in context.

  c. Distinguish among the connotations (associations) of words with similar denotations (definitions) (e.g., *stingy*, *scrimping*, *economical*, *unwasteful*, *thrifty*).

6. Acquire and use accurately grade-appropriate general academic and domain-specific words and phrases; gather vocabulary knowledge when considering a word or phrase important to comprehension or expression.

Reading Standards for Literature

(Grade 6)

Craft and Structure

4. Determine the meaning of words and phrases as they are used in a text, including figurative and connotative meanings; analyze the impact of a specific word choice on meaning and tone.

Reading Standards for Informational Text

(Grade 6)

Key Ideas and Details

2. Determine a central idea of a text and how it is conveyed through particular details; provide a summary of the text distinct from personal opinions or judgments.

Craft and Structure

4. Determine the meaning of words and phrases as they are used in a text, including figurative, connotative, and technical meanings.

6. Determine an author's point of view or purpose in a text and explain how it is conveyed in the text.

Writing Standards

(Grade 6)

Text Type and Purposes

1. Write arguments to support claims with clear reasons and relevant evidence.

  c. Use words, phrases, and clauses to clarify the relationships among claim(s) and reasons.

2. Write informative/explanatory texts to examine a topic and convey ideas, concepts, and information through the selection, organization, and analysis of relevant content.

  d. Use precise language and domain-specific vocabulary to inform about or explain the topic.

3. Write narratives to develop real or imagined experiences or events using effective technique, relevant descriptive details, and well-structured event sequences.

  d. Use precise words and phrases, relevant descriptive details, and sensory language to convey experiences and events.

Production and Distribution of Writing

4. Produce clear and coherent writing in which the development, organization, and style are appropriate to task, purpose, and audience. (Grade-specific expectations for writing types are defined in standards 1–3 above.)

ENRICHED VOCABULARY APPROACH: Systematic Vocabulary Instruction

The **VOCABULARY WORKSHOP** program focuses on the words, their meanings, their ranges of application, and their uses in context. The approach is systematic because it begins with and builds upon a word list drawn from vocabulary that students will encounter in their reading. It provides students with the vocabulary skills they will need to achieve higher-level reading proficiency and to succeed at standardized tests.

With the introduction of reading passages and literary text, the Enriched Edition goes further than previous editions in integrating vocabulary instruction in the context of reading. (For a discussion of the importance of vocabulary in reading comprehension, see pages T31–T32. For more on how **VOCABULARY WORKSHOP** can be used to complement a literature program, see pages T33–T35.)

A cornerstone of the **VOCABULARY WORKSHOP** approach is intensive practice through varied and abundant "hands-on" exercises. This method provides both exposure to different meanings of the key words studied and coverage of the range of each key word through its appearance in many different contexts. The aim of the pattern of intensive practice is to embed the words in the students' active, daily-use vocabulary.

Grade-Level Placements

The chart below shows suggested grade placement for each Level of **VOCABULARY WORKSHOP**. In determining proper placement of a particular Level, consider the following:

- Grade placements are based on teacher experience and recommendations.
- Differences in grade are reflected in the difficulty of the words presented, the maturity of the sentences, and other contexts in which those words are used.
- Grade levels should not be taken too literally. Experimentation and the use of the program's online diagnostic materials will establish the correct placement of a particular Level in a given situation.

Grade Placements			
Average Students		**Above-Average Students**	
Level	**Grade**	**Level**	**Grade**
A	6	A	5
B	7	B	6
C	8	C	7

Word Lists

Each Student Level presents 300 vocabulary words organized into 15 Units. Mastering these words will help students understand academic texts and increase their everyday language abilities.

For a discussion by Vicki A. Jacobs of the importance of academic vocabulary to reading comprehension, see pages T31–T32.

Criteria for Selection: The selection of **Vocabulary Workshop** words is based on four criteria: currency in and usefulness for present-day American oral or written communication; frequency on recognized high-utility and academic vocabulary lists; applicability to standardized tests; current grade-placement research.

General Sources: The lists of key words were developed from many sources: traditional, classic, and contemporary literature, including novels, short stories, essays, newspaper and magazine articles, plays, and films. Spelling and vocabulary lists recognized as valid bases for teaching language skills at the middle and secondary levels are used, as well as current subject-area textbooks, glossaries, and ancillary materials (especially for general, nontechnical terms).

Dictionary and Reference Sources: The following were the primary dictionary resources used for word (and definition) selection:

- *Webster's Third International Dictionary of the English Language* (unabridged)
- *Merriam-Webster's Collegiate Dictionary* (Ninth, Tenth, and online editions)
- *The American Heritage Dictionary of the English Language* (editions 1–4)
- *The Random House Dictionary of the English Language* (unabridged editions)
- *The Compact Edition of the Oxford English Dictionary*

Standard Word-Frequency Sources: Standard word-frequency studies were conducted to evaluate and revise the word list.

- *Primary* Dale-O'Rourke: *The Living Word Vocabulary*, Carroll-Davies-Richman: *The American Heritage Word Frequency Book*
- *Supplementary* Harris-Jacobsen: *Basic Reading Vocabularies*, Thorndike-Lorge: *The Teacher's Word Book of 30,000 Words*, Zeno-Ivens-Millard-Duvvuri: *The Educator's Word Frequency Guide*

"Sliding-Scale" Placement

Each word list works on a sliding scale based on the following principles: Any word that according to Dale-O'Rourke is known in a given grade is not presented in that grade. It is presented two or three grades earlier. Each grade level contains mostly words not known (according to Dale-O'Rourke) two or three grades later, with an admixture (in decreasing numbers) of words not known four or more grades later. The higher the grade, the larger the percentage of more difficult words contained in the word list.

Professional development papers discussing the research supporting the instructional approach of **Vocabulary Workshop** may be found in the Teacher Center of **vocabularyworkshop.com**.

PRINT COMPONENTS

This Enriched Edition of **VOCABULARY WORKSHOP**, Levels A–C, consists of an integrated array of print and digital components. Print materials for each Level include:

- Student Texts
- Teacher's Annotated Editions
- Test Booklets with Combined Answer Keys (Forms A and B)
- SAT-Type TEST PREP Blackline Masters (answers included)

Student Texts/Teacher's Annotated Editions

Each of the three Student Texts (Levels A–C) presents 300 key words and is organized in the same way: 15 Units of 20 words each and 5 Reviews following Units 3, 6, 9, 12, and 15. Preceding the first Unit is a section on types of questions students will find throughout the program. Concluding each Student Text is a Final Mastery Test.

In the Teacher's Annotated Editions, answers are shown for each student page. Correlations to Common Core State Standards are also noted on each page.

Reading Passages

New nonfiction Reading Passages open each Unit of **VOCABULARY WORKSHOP**. At least 15 of the Unit vocabulary words, as well as examples of figurative language such as idioms, adages, or proverbs, are used in each Passage. Students read the words in context to activate prior knowledge, and then they apply what they learn throughout the Unit and the Review.

Definitions

DEFINITIONS The definitions provided are clear, useful, and informal. The intent is to give students a reasonably good core idea of what each word means without extensive detail or secondary connotations. Generally, only a single meaning of maximum usefulness is given.

PART OF SPEECH Simple abbreviations give the part of speech with each definition. When a word functions as several parts of speech, the appropriate abbreviation appears before the corresponding definition.

PRONUNCIATION Only one pronunciation is given for each word, except when a word changes its pronunciation in accordance with its use as different parts of speech (*ob′ ject* and *ob ject′*).

Students may utilize the **Online iWords Audio Program** for each Unit. Available at **vocabularyworkshop.com**, this program provides nearly four hours of spoken material per Student Text, including pronunciation and examples of usage.

ILLUSTRATIVE SENTENCE Concluding each key entry is an illustrative sentence. These sentences provide a context that clarifies the meaning of each word. By writing the word in such contextual settings, students begin to see how the word can be used effectively in their own writing.

SYNONYMS AND ANTONYMS Each word has a list of synonyms and/or antonyms if there is one or more of either for the word. By studying the given synonyms and antonyms, students will better understand the denotational family of words of which each key word is part; and by comparing specific usages of key words and their synonyms, students can better appreciate appropriate contexts for these words. Note that the lists of synonyms and antonyms are not exhaustive.

Choosing the Right Word

In this activity, students choose one of a pair of words that most satisfactorily completes the sentence. Completing this activity requires a thorough understanding of a range of a word's definitions.

Synonyms and Antonyms

In this section, students read phrases that include synonyms or antonyms for the Unit words. Students must choose the Unit word that matches the given synonym or antonym. In addition to reinforcing meanings, this exercise provides students with further examples of usage and context.

Completing the Sentence

This activity provides a simple completion exercise in which students choose and write the word that logically and meaningfully fits into a blank in a given sentence.

When using this activity in the classroom, the teacher should bear in mind the following considerations:

- The sentences in this activity call for the literal or direct (as opposed to the metaphorical or extended) meaning of the words involved.
- The sentences are designed so that only one of the words fits in the given blank. Context clues have been placed in each sentence.
- The words are to be used as the part of speech given in Definitions. The only exceptions are: Nouns given in the singular in Definitions may be plural in the sentences; verbs given in the base form in Definitions may be used in any tense or form (including participial) required by the sentence.

Writing: Words in Action

New prompts provide practice with writing responses to two modes of writing. The first prompt is a text-dependent question that asks students to respond to the Reading Passage at the beginning of the Unit. The second prompt is modeled on those that appear on standardized tests. Students write their responses on a separate sheet of paper. Teachers should grade the responses using a rubric of their choice.

PRINT COMPONENTS *cont.*

Vocabulary in Context/Literary Text

This activity provides Unit vocabulary words used in classic literature, which:

- gives examples of usage for the selected words,
- offers an opportunity to derive meaning from context, and
- provides practice in the sort of vocabulary exercises found on standardized tests.

Refer students to Student Text page 7 for an introduction to the strategies involved in studying vocabulary in context.

Review

A Review follows every three Units.

- Vocabulary for Comprehension: This section is designed to help students prepare for the critical-reading sections of standardized tests. Students read a Passage and then answer vocabulary-in-context and comprehension questions related to the texts.
- Two-Word Completions: Students practice with word-omission (cloze) exercises that appear on typical standardized tests, including the SAT.

Word Study

A Word Study section follows every Review. Exercises include instruction and practice with figurative language and relationships in meaning:

- Choosing the Right Idiom/Adage/Proverb
- Writing with Idioms/Adages/Proverbs
- Denotation and Connotation/Shades of Meaning
- Building with Classical Roots

The Final Mastery Test

The Final Mastery Test in the Student Text is a practice test of 70 items that gives students and teachers fair insight into how much progress has been made during the year and what kind of additional work is in order.

The purpose of the Final Mastery Test is threefold.

- It can serve as a dry run in preparation for the more formal (and secure) tests available as optional components of this program.
- It can serve as an informal evaluation of achievement to date.
- It can serve as a reinforcement activity.

Test Booklets (Optional)

Two Test Booklets (Form A and Form B) may be used to reduce the risk of answers being passed on. Though the formats of the Test Booklets are the same, the items tested in any given section are completely different. The contents are: a list of the 300 tested vocabulary words; a Warm-Up Test; 15 Unit Tests, each consisting of 25 items focusing on pronunciations, parts of speech, spelling, definitions, synonyms, antonyms, and sentence completions; and 5 Cumulative Tests of 52–110 items each.

TEST PREP Blackline Masters (Optional)

The TEST PREP component provides practice with SAT-type test questions and formats and also with review tests covering the corresponding Student Text. Prep Tests approximate the word-omission sections of the SAT and provide practice in the vocabulary-in-context strand with brief reading passages as well. Answer sheets in SAT-type test format develop student ease and familiarity with standardized testing materials. Mastery Tests are used when students have completed the corresponding group of three Units in the Student Text. Each test covers basic meanings, synonyms, antonyms, and sentence completions. Answer keys, including selected answer rationales, are provided for all tests.

DIGITAL COMPONENTS

Digital resources for each Level are available at **vocabularyworkshop.com** and include:

- iWords Audio Program
- Audio of Unit Passages
- Online Interactive Games
- Vocabulary in Context: Informational Text
- Diagnostic Tests and Cumulative Reviews
- Professional Development Videos
- Interactive Quizzes

The components have been designed for use in an integrated year-long vocabulary program, as suggested in the chart on pages T24–T26.

PDFs of the following materials may be found online for each level:

- Correlations to the Common Core State Standards
- Vocabulary in Context: Informational Text
- SAT and ACT Practice Worksheets
- Additional Practice and Quiz pages for each lesson
- Greek and Latin Roots Reference Guide
- Diagnostic Tests and Cumulative Reviews
- Pacing Guides
- Pronunciation Key

DIGITAL COMPONENTS *cont.*

iWords™ Audio Program

The VOCABULARY WORKSHOP iWords Audio Program provides students with pronunciations, definitions, and examples of usage for all program vocabulary words and word meanings. Students can visit **vocabularyworkshop.com** to listen to each word or download files of the words.

- The audio program is ideal for English Language Learners (ELL) and ELL classrooms.
- Students hear the recommended pronunciation of each word at least six times and are given two opportunities to pronounce each word themselves.
- Pronunciations are followed by brief definitions and examples of the word used in complete sentences.
- For recommendations on when to use iWords, see pages T24–T30.

Online Interactive Vocabulary Games

For each Level, students are provided interactive word games using the vocabulary presented in the Units. These activities include flashcards, crossword puzzles, word searches, "hangman," Roots Matching Challenge, and Test Your Vocabulary questions. Additional Practice and Quiz pages including Interactive Quizzes provide more possibilities for academic assessment.

Vocabulary in Context: Informational Text

A Reading Passage that uses key Unit words provides another opportunity to read vocabulary in context. Each Passage is followed by multiple-choice questions for extra practice with nonfiction texts, the Unit vocabulary words, and question types found on standardized tests.

Diagnostic Test and Cumulative Reviews

- A **Beginning-of-Year Diagnostic Test** contains a sampling of words from the program to assess students' prior knowledge.
- After Units 3, 6, 9, 12, and 15, students can complete **Cumulative Review Tests**. Questions on Choosing the Right Meaning and Two-Word Completions provide practice on SAT-style questions. Activities on analogies and vocabulary enrichment are also included.

SAT and ACT Practice Worksheets

For teachers who wish to offer their students extra practice for the SAT or ACT, 45 standardized-test worksheets are available online for each Level. These practice worksheets are accessible only to teachers.

For each Level, there are 15 worksheets in standardized-test format for each of the following:

- comprehension and vocabulary skills assessed on the SAT and ACT,
- multiple-choice grammar and usage items included in the Writing section of the SAT and in the ACT, and
- step-by-step guidance in crafting a timed essay of the kind that is required on the SAT (and is optional on the ACT).

Teacher Resources

Available in PDF format:

- Correlations to the Common Core State Standards
- Pacing Guides
- Greek and Latin Roots Reference Guide
- Graphic Organizers
- Pronunciation Key

Online Student Assessment System (Optional)

The Web-based **Vocabulary Workshop** Online Student Assessment System allows teachers quickly and easily to create secure, interactive Unit practice and assessment pages that are automatically scored and provide students with immediate, prescriptive feedback. With a database of nearly 4,000 test items per Level, teachers have the option to individualize tests.

The Online Student Assessment System provides:

- the ability to create and edit question sets and tests,
- the ability to scramble answer choices and/or questions so that multiple versions of the same test can be administered securely,
- a wide assortment of question types: pronunciation, part of speech, spelling, definitions, synonyms, antonyms, sentence completions, sentence framing,
- formatted Unit tests, ready for immediate use,
- a secure portal to assign practice/test pages, with the option to print these pages,
- immediate feedback on each question,
- a detailed end-of-assignment report to help the teacher know exactly how students are progressing,
- the ability to track student progress through a comprehensive reporting system,
- a way to create detailed reports on class and individual student results, and
- the option to send practice/test pages and student results to learning management systems.

The **Vocabulary Workshop** Online Student Assessment System is a convenient and secure source of assessment and/or extra practice. The Online Student Assessment System is easy to use, either as needed or more systematically, as an integral part of the **Vocabulary Workshop** series. See pages T24–26 for recommendations on how it may be used in conjunction with the Student Text and other components.

IMPLEMENTING THE PROGRAM

Vocabulary Workshop not only provides vocabulary instruction but also teaches students a variety of other essential Language Arts skills. Teachers have many options for pacing **Vocabulary Workshop's** activities to best meet the needs of their students and classes.

Planning and Pacing of Instruction

The charts on pages T24–T26 offer sample plans for weekly scheduling and for daily implementation of all components of the **Vocabulary Workshop** program. The charts are constructed to reflect the coverage of the Units in the Student Text and associated online resources on a 5-day and on a 10-day basis, and the Reviews on a 5-day basis. (Full-year schedules for both 5-day and 10-day plans are available at **vocabularyworkshop.com**.)

Weekly Schedules (5 days per unit and 10 days per unit)

5-Day Schedule	10-Day Schedule	Student Text and Online Resources	Implementation Plan
Week 1	**Weeks 1–2**	**Unit 1**	Complete **Vocabulary Workshop** activities in the book and online (see the "How to Use **Vocabulary Workshop** Exercises" charts on the following pages). Examine Best Practices on pages T28–T30 for further vocabulary activities. Additional Assessment: Assign Unit 1 Test from Test Booklets or from Online Assessment.
Week 2	**Weeks 3–4**	**Unit 2**	Follow procedure shown for Unit 1. Testing Options: Assign Unit 2 Test from the Test Booklets or from Online Assessment, and review Unit 1 Test to encourage deeper recall of all words.
Week 3	**Weeks 5–6**	**Unit 3**	Follow procedure shown for Unit 1. Testing Options: Assign Unit 3 Test from the Test Booklets or from Online Assessment, and review Units 1–2 Tests to encourage deeper recall of all words.
Week 4	**Week 7**	**Review Units 1–3**	Complete Review Units 1–3 activities, and ensure knowledge of all 60 vocabulary words as well as the mastery of other essential English skills. Mastery Tests Units 1–3 available as Test Prep Blackline Masters.

Note: For suggestions for the integration of the Diagnostic Test and Final Mastery Test into a full-year schedule, see the sample weekly schedules at **vocabularyworkshop.com**.

Daily Activities for Each Unit (5 Days)

How to Use the Student Text and Online Resources (at vocabularyworkshop.com) in 5 Sessions/Periods (See page T26 for a 10-Day Planner)

Assignment	Day 1	Day 2	Day 3	Day 4	Day 5
Class work	**1.** Review previous Unit's test results. **2.** Review word meaning and usage in context in the Unit's Reading Passage. **3.** Present any words not used in the Reading Passage.	**1.** Review Choosing the Right Word. **2.** Assign online SAT/ ACT Practice Worksheets.	**1.** Review Synonyms and Antonyms and also Completing the Sentence. **2.** Assign the first prompt for Writing: Words in Action.	**1.** Share excerpts (with vocabulary usage) from Writing: Words in Action. **2.** Assign Vocabulary in Context: Literary Text.	**1.** Assign Unit Test (Test Booklet or Online Assessment).
Homework	**1.** Download and listen to iWords. **2.** Assign Choosing the Right Word.	**1.** Assign Synonyms and Antonyms; Completing the Sentence. **2.** Assign online Unit games.	**1.** Assign the second prompt of Writing: Words in Action.	**1.** Assign online interactive quiz.	**1.** Have students read the next Unit's Reading Passage.

Daily Activities for the Review and Word Study Sections

How to Use the Student Text and Online Resources (at vocabularyworkshop.com) in 5 Sessions/Periods

Assignment	Day 1	Day 2	Day 3	Day 4	Day 5
Class work	**1.** Review previous Unit's test results. **2.** Assign Vocabulary for Comprehension.	**1.** Review SAT/ACT Worksheets and Two-Word Completions. **2.** Present Idioms/Adages/Proverbs.	**1.** Review Idioms/ Adages/ Proverbs. **2.** Present Denotation/ Connotation.	**1.** Review Denotation/ Connotation. **2.** Present Building with Classical Roots.	**1.** Assign Mastery Test (Test Prep Blackline Masters).
Homework	**1.** Assign online SAT/ ACT Practice Worksheets. **2.** Assign Two-Word Completions.	**1.** Assign Idioms/ Adages/ Proverbs. **2.** Assign online Unit games.	**1.** Assign Denotation/ Connotation. **2.** Assign online Unit games.	**1.** Review Building with Classical Roots.	**1.** Assign the next Unit's Reading Passage.

Daily Activities for Each Unit (10 Days)

How to Use the Student Text and Online Resources (at vocabularyworkshop.com) in 10 Sessions/Periods

Assignment	Day 1	Day 2	Day 3	Day 4	Day 5
Class work	**1.** Introduce vocabulary in context of the Unit's Reading Passage. **2.** Discuss two Unit words and their definitions.	**1.** Discuss two Unit words and their definitions.	**1.** Discuss two Unit words and their definitions.	**1.** Discuss two Unit words and their definitions. **2.** Have students play online Unit games and/ or introduce an activity from Best Practices (T28-30).	**1.** Discuss two Unit words and their definitions. **2.** Assign the Interactive Unit Quiz.
Homework	**1.** Download and listen to iWords. Flashcards. **2.** Complete the Definitions.	**1.** Assign Choosing the Right Word.	**1.** Assign Synonyms and Antonyms.	**1.** Assign Completing the Sentence.	**1.** Have students play online Unit games.

Assignment	Day 6	Day 7	Day8	Day 9	Day 10
Class work	**1.** Discuss two Unit words and their definitions **2.** Introduce one of the two Writing: Words in Action prompts	**1.** Discuss two Unit words and their definitions.	**1.** Discuss two Unit words and their definitions.	**1.** Discuss two Unit words and their definitions. **2.** Have students play online Unit games and/ or introduce an activity from Best Practices.	**1.** Discuss two Unit words and their definitions. **2.** Assign Unit Test (Test Booklet or Online assessment).
Homework	**1.** Complete Writing: Words in Action prompt assignment.	**1.** Assign Vocabulary in Context: Literary Text.	**1.** Assign online Practice Worksheets.	**1.** Assign online SAT/ ACT Practice Worksheets	**1.** Assign audio passage and have students note context clues in margins.

Implementing the Weekly and Daily Schedules

The following may prove helpful when adapting the foregoing schedules to specific situations.

- As appropriate, review activities to monitor student progress (whole class or individual).
- Students need to recognize the value of learning vocabulary and completing the vocabulary exercises. Simply assigning words and the exercises for class work or homework does not provide intrinsic value for those who are learning new vocabulary. Teachers should model vocabulary usage and encourage students to learn the words to improve their speaking, writing, reading comprehension, and test scores (see "Best Practices" T28–T30 for suggestions).
- Activity order and timings are to some extent hypothetical. Teachers may switch items around and adjust timings as needed. Similarly, items may be modified or deleted.
- **Vocabulary Workshop** Units may also be adapted so that only 10 words are studied each week. The Online Assessment allows teachers to easily create quizzes for the first or second 10 words of a Unit, if desired. Students completing the exercises in **Vocabulary Workshop** can either wait until the second week to work on the activities, or they can identify the words they know and complete only those blanks that relate to the week's words being studied.

Student Study Guides

When students employ a review system for their vocabularies, they tend to learn the words and their meanings more thoroughly. Students may create flashcards or a vocabulary chart as two simple review methods. However, what students write down on their flashcards or charts may vary among learning styles.

For Basic Vocabulary Learners: Students should write the vocabulary word on one side of a flashcard (or in the first chart box), then a mnemonic device, synonym/brief definition of the word, and a short, student-created phrase incorporating the word on the back of the flashcard (or in chart boxes two, three, and four). Students then review by looking only at the word side of the flashcard or the first column of the chart (folding the paper so the other information is behind the first column) and seeing if they can remember the mnemonic device or phrase that enables them to recall the word's meaning.

For Kinesthetic Learners: Students may create a motion that goes with a vocabulary word definition, when possible. Students then write the word on one side of a flashcard (or in the first chart box), then the motion and a synonym/brief definition on the back of the flashcard (or in the second and third chart boxes). Students may review in the same way as is described above for basic learners.

For Visual/Artistic Learners: Students draw a picture that goes with each vocabulary word definition. Students may write the word on one side of a flashcard (or in the first chart box) and then draw the associated picture and write the synonym/brief definition on the back of the flashcard (or in the second and third chart boxes). Students then review in the same way as described above for basic and kinesthetic learners.

For Auditory Learners: In addition to the Basic Vocabulary Learner review sheet, teachers may strongly encourage these learners to review iWords on a daily basis to recall definitions.

BEST PRACTICES FOR USING VOCABULARY WORKSHOP IN THE CLASSROOM

Classroom experience and research have shown that repeated exposure to and varied application of vocabulary words embed meaning in students' minds. The more teachers and students utilize vocabulary in the Language Arts class period, the more likely students are to understand and use new vocabulary themselves.

Classroom Environment

Depending on the reading proficiencies of their students, teachers may differentiate and/or scaffold instruction to accommodate varying learning styles and modalities—for example, by reading aloud or having students read aloud the passages that introduce the Units.

To encourage students' use of vocabulary, teachers may post vocabulary words in the classroom—on bulletin boards, walls, or chalkboards/whiteboards. Students and teachers may bring in examples of vocabulary from print sources to be displayed in the classroom. Additionally, students may create visual representations or drawings of vocabulary words that can be posted in the classroom. Discuss which visual representations are the most appropriate and accurate representations of the vocabulary words.

Differentiation may be achieved through choice. Create a vocabulary choice menu of extension activities, such as using vocabulary words to write a poem or create an interactive presentation, that appeal to different learning modalities.

Recognition of Vocabulary Discovery and Usage

Students may share experiences in which they hear or use vocabulary outside of the classroom. Whether it is another teacher who said a vocabulary word, a television show or movie that incorporated vocabulary, or the student him- or herself who embedded a word in an assignment, it is important to recognize the use of academic vocabulary.

Daily Discussion and Review

Teachers may model vocabulary usage by including vocabulary words in their instructions or conversations with students. The more frequently the teacher uses a word, the easier it becomes for students to understand its meaning and usage.

Teachers can have "Words of the Day" that students must incorporate into classroom activities. Whoever correctly uses the words the most might receive a reward.

During debates, discussions, or other times when students are conversing, teachers should require them to use the learned vocabulary words. A set minimum number of words can be established, and students who go above the minimum should be recognized for their efforts.

Any videos, songs, or art that students created to illustrate or act out the vocabulary words could be reviewed with the whole class.

When there is extra time, the class may review vocabulary words. See the following "Vocabulary Projects and Games" section for suggested activities.

Categorizing Vocabulary

When reviewing vocabulary words, students may categorize words as they relate to current events. By creating meaningful associations with each word, students more easily recall word meaning. Post the categories around the room and have students add to them during the year. Students can also create sentence strips for vocabulary words. Have students manipulate the strips to generate rankings and groupings. For an extra challenge, have students rank the words on a continuum.

Students can also learn vocabulary by creating more general categories. These categories can be as simple as "praise" or "insult" or as elaborate as students want (travel words, food words, etc.). When students learn new words, they can place them in the categories they have created.

Writing with Vocabulary

Students should incorporate at least one or two vocabulary words into their daily writing prompts, reading journals, or other forms of informal communication. Use pictures or photographs from magazines as an inspiration for writing.

Whenever students write formally for class (essays, stories, etc.), teachers may require a set minimum number of vocabulary words to be used, check to make sure that the usage is appropriate, and provide feedback. Students should highlight the vocabulary words in the writing. Read aloud essays and review the use of vocabulary for correct usage. Point out instances where the form of the words has been changed or a secondary meaning is used. Suggest ways for students to check their usage, such as replacing the vocabulary word in the sentence with its definition to see if it makes sense.

Teachers may also:

- Have students create puns that incorporate vocabulary. Example: "It's not clear" Tom said **ambiguously**.
- Ask students to write poems for individual words. Example: "There once was a word called _____."
- Ask students to write a "Where I'm From" poem that explains both a word's origins and use, and that also traces its genealogy to related words.
- Have students write myths about the origins of individual words or groups of words.

Vocabulary Projects and Games

Students may create advertisements for a word to "sell" its uses. Example: "Race to your local dictionary and pick up the word _____. Whether frustrated with your social life or unhappy with a school assignment, this word can be used in a variety of ways. . . ." Alternatively, teachers may have students sell a product, but have them use as many vocabulary words as possible to describe the item's attributes.

Students often learn words best when setting them to music. Students may write lyrics incorporating all (or most) of a Unit's vocabulary words/definitions and then perform, videotape, or record their finished products. Create a library of the videos and recordings for future classes to use.

Do a round-robin review of the words and their definitions. This activity can be teacher-directed or student-led. Begin with one student naming a vocabulary word, a second student defines it, then another gives the kinesthetic gesture the class gave the word, a fourth student puts the definition in his or her own words or provides a synonym or antonym. Another student uses the word in a sentence, and then another student finishes the activity by giving feedback on how the word was used in the sentence. Allow time after the activity for follow-up questions.

Create a "deck" of review cards, consisting of the word, the definition, a sentence with a blank where the vocabulary word would go, and the image for the word selected by the class. Have teams go head-to-head to see who can complete the sentence with the correct vocabulary word first.

Groups of students can act in skits or pantomimes that demonstrate a word's meaning; the rest of the class must guess the word being enacted.

Student groups may tell stories using vocabulary words. Groups should be created according to the ability and level of students.

Alternative Assessment

The following types of assessment may be used in addition to or in lieu of the objective-scoring materials provided in **Vocabulary Workshop**, Levels A–C.

- Teachers may have students write a story, song, poem, or essay incorporating vocabulary words (word list provided by the teacher). They can assign a topic or allow students to write about a topic they find interesting. Teachers should explain to students the rubric they will use to evaluate student writing before beginning the exercise.

- Teachers can write a series of true/false statements, each concerning a vocabulary word, and then have students decide whether the statements are true or false based on their understanding of the words.

- Students can use vocabulary words in conversations throughout the week. Students may either write down their statements or collect signatures from peers or adults who heard the student using each word. Students turn in their sheets at the end of the week. Teachers should review for correct usage for an assessment grade.

- Teachers should consider using a suggestion from "Writing with Vocabulary" or "Vocabulary Projects" as a final assessment.

ACADEMIC VOCABULARY AND READING COMPREHENSION

by Vicki A. Jacobs
Senior Series Consultant

As students advance to the higher grades, reading becomes more and more a matter of comprehending concepts that represent relationships among facts and information. At the same time, learning the academic vocabulary that represents those concepts becomes more critical to comprehension.

For example, to understand literature, students must read to understand more than a narrative's simple sequence of events. They need to know how to inquire about a text—about why an author chooses particular events or how an author uses characterization, imagery, and plot to develop a thematic statement. Students can memorize the definitions of the vocabulary of literature; but, more importantly, they need to be able to apply their understanding of the concepts that the vocabulary of literature represent.

Similarly, comprehension of content-area text requires more than locating and memorizing specific information; it also requires students to make meaning of the concepts, represented by disciplinary vocabulary, that relate facts to each other. To make conceptual connections among facts, readers first need to activate and organize the background knowledge and experience that they have gained from real-word experience (the "given") that will be relevant to understanding the "new" information and concepts that the text offers. Comprehension then becomes a complex matter of confirming or disconfirming the relationship between the students' "given" and the text's "new" and of resolving any differences. Successful readers skillfully identify relationships among facts and information, analyze and synthesize often-conflicting facts and points of view, and consolidate their learning by testing the validity of what they have comprehended and thus learned.

To comprehend increasingly sophisticated content-specific texts, students typically draw upon their knowledge of three kinds of vocabulary. The first is the language of everyday experience, the concrete words commonly used in conversation. The second is the academic language that content areas share (e.g., *argument*, *persuasion*, *analysis*, *synthesis*, *comparison*, and *contrast*)—although such words may represent different meanings depending on subject-matter (e.g., *conflict*, *resolution*, and *analysis* represent different concepts in the study of literature and history). The third kind of vocabulary represents the highly specialized concepts that are particular to particular content (e.g., *allegory*, *mitosis*, *sine*, *colonialism*).

Vocabulary also plays an integral role in both inquiry-based learning and reading comprehension. Both are cognitive processes that roughly involve the same three instructional stages: preparation, strategic guidance, and consolidation. An abbreviated description of these stages is given on the following page.

Stage I:

Preparation for Learning/Reading

Teachers:

- provide students with instructional means by which they can activate, extend, amend, and organize the "given"—the background knowledge (including vocabulary knowledge) and experiences that will be relevant to learning new concepts and the vocabulary that represents those concepts; and
- explain to students how their background knowledge and experience will be relevant to understanding a lesson or text's "new" central concepts and vocabulary.

Stage II:

Strategic Guidance of Learning/Reading

Teachers facilitate inquiry/comprehension by providing instructional means by which students can:

- investigate, enrich, deepen, and revise their understanding of a reading's key vocabulary and central concepts; and
- practice skills, including their understanding of new vocabulary.

Stage III:

Consolidation of Learning/Reading

Teachers provide students with the means to consolidate their learning/comprehension by:

- providing means by which they can probe the validity of their understanding (learning/comprehension) of new concepts and vocabulary; and
- preparing students to demonstrate their learning/comprehension (e.g., through the application of new concepts and vocabulary to novel contexts, comparison and contrast, and argument).

Above all, the comprehension and vocabulary strategies teachers use must support the kind of learning that their instructional goals require. For example, the strategies that teachers might use to help students memorize facts and information are very different from those they might use to support students' deep comprehension and understanding.

To become independent learners/readers, students depend on their teachers to be explicit with them about *what* instructional strategies they are learning, *how* they could use those strategies most effectively given varied purposes, and *why* such strategies work. Students need to know how to monitor the success of their learning/reading, recognize when learning or comprehension has broken down, have a ready store of learning/reading strategies, and be able to choose the most expedient strategy to correct their course. In other words, students need to learn how to learn as well as learn how to comprehend if they are to become independent, ongoing students of an academic discipline who are not only prepared to graduate from high school but also, in the language of the Common Core State Standards, to be "college and career ready."

CLASSIC LITERATURE TO USE WITH THE PROGRAM

Levels A–C

Lloyd Alexander *The Book of Three*

Laurie Halse Anderson *Speak*

William Armstrong *Sounder*

Natalie Babbit *Tuck Everlasting*

Ray Bradbury *Dandelion Wine*

Pearl S. Buck *The Good Earth*

Sheila Bumford *The Incredible Journey*

Frances Hodgson Burnett *The Secret Garden*

Sandra Cisneros *The House on Mango Street*

Sook Nyul Choi *Year of Impossible Goodbyes*

Robert Cornier *The Chocolate War*

Karen Cushman *The Midwife's Apprentice*

Daniel Defoe *Robinson Crusoe*

Elizabeth B. De Trevino *I, Juan de Pareja*

Sir Arthur Conan Doyle *The Hound of the Baskervilles*

Esther Forbes *Johnny Tremain*

Paul Gallico *The Snow Goose*

Jean Craighead George *Julie of the Wolves*

William Goldman *The Princess Bride*

Rosa Guy *The Friends*

Virginia Hamilton *The House of Dies Drear* and *M.C. Higgins, the Great*

Jean Wakatsuki Houston and James D. Houston *Farewell to Manzanar*

Norton Juster *The Phantom Tollbooth*

Rudyard Kipling *Just So Stories*

E.L. Konigsburg *The View from Saturday*

Harper Lee *To Kill a Mockingbird*

Madeline L'Engle *A Wrinkle in Time*

Julius Lester *Long Journey Home*

Lois Lowry *The Giver* and *Gathering Blue*

Daniel P. Mannix *The Fox and the Hound*

Nicholasa Mohr *Going Home*

Walter Dean Myers *Hoops*

Mary Norton *The Borrowers*

George Orwell *Animal Farm*

Katherine Paterson *Jacob Have I Loved*

Ann Petry *Harriet Tubman: Conductor on the Underground Railroad*

Marjorie Kinnan Rawlings *The Yearling*

Jack Schaefer *Shane*

George Selden *The Cricket in Times Square*

Antoine de Saint-Exupéry *The Little Prince*

Elizabeth George Speare *The Sign of the Beaver*

Rex Stout *Fer-de-Lance* and *The Golden Spiders*

Yoshiko Uchida *Journey Home*

H.G. Wells *War of the Worlds*

Laura Ingalls Wilder *Little House on the Prairie*

Laurence Yep *Dragon's Gate*

Additional Titles and Enrichment

Louisa May Alcott *Little Women*

Lewis Carroll *Alice's Adventures in Wonderland*

Willa Cather *My Antonia*

James Fenimore Cooper *The Deerslayer*

Charles Dickens *Oliver Twist, A Tale of Two Cities* and *A Christmas Carol*

Carson McCullers *The Member of the Wedding*

To coordinate reading and vocabulary study, the following may prove helpful:

- Students may devote a notebook to vocabulary. As they encounter key words in their reading, they should head a page of the notebook with the word; copy the title of the work; and then indicate (a) the definition used in that sentence, (b) its part of speech, and (c) whether it is used in a literal or figurative sense.
- Students may then be instructed to check *Bartlett's Familiar Quotations* for other famous examples of the use of the key word in question. These quotations may be copied into the notebook and shared with others in the class.

Vocabulary in Context

VOCABULARY WORKSHOP uses excerpts from classic literature to show how a Unit's vocabulary words are used in context.

Level A Vocabulary in Context Literary Selections

Unit 1	Johann David Wyss	*The Swiss Family Robinson*
Unit 2	Walt Whitman	*Leaves of Grass*
Unit 3	Jules Verne	*Twenty Thousand Leagues Under the Sea*
Unit 4	Edgar Rice Burroughs	*A Princess of Mars*
Unit 5	H.G. Wells	*The First Men in the Moon*
Unit 6	Mark Twain	*The Prince and The Pauper* and "The Celebrated Jumping Frog of Calaveras County"
Unit 7	Charles Dickens	*Oliver Twist*
Unit 8	Sir Arthur Conan Doyle	*The Adventures of Sherlock Holmes*
Unit 9	L.M. Montgomery	*Anne of the Island*
Unit 10	Edgar Allan Poe	"The Gold-Bug," "The Unparalleled Adventure of One Hans Pfaall," "Ms. Found in a Bottle," and "The Murders in the Rue Morgue"
Unit 11	Jack London	*White Fang*
Unit 12	Sir Arthur Conan Doyle	*Tales of Terror and Mystery*
Unit 13	L.M. Montgomery	*Anne of Green Gables*
Unit 14	Charles Dickens	*The Life and Adventures of Nicholas Nickelby*
Unit 15	Washington Irving	"The Legend of Sleepy Hollow"

Level B Vocabulary in Context Literary Selections

Unit 1	Edgar Allan Poe	"The Balloon Hoax," "The Mystery of Marie Roget," "Ms. Found in a Bottle," and "The Gold-Bug"
Unit 2	O. Henry	"The Cop and the Anthem," "The Coming-out of Maggie," "The Green Door," "Springtime á la Carte," and "Man About Town"
Unit 3	Sir Arthur Conan Doyle	*The Lost World*

Unit 4	Jack London	*The Sea-Wolf*
Unit 5	Charles Dickens	*Oliver Twist*
Unit 6	Sir Arthur Conan Doyle	*The Adventures of Sherlock Holmes*
Unit 7	Mark Twain	*A Connecticut Yankee in King Arthur's Court*
Unit 8	Jules Verne	*A Journey to the Center of the Earth*
Unit 9	Bram Stoker	*Dracula*
Unit 10	Victor Hugo	*The Hunchback of Notre Dame*
Unit 11	Mary Wollstonecraft Shelley	*Frankenstein*
Unit 12	Victor Hugo	*Les Misérables*
Unit 13	Jules Verne	*Around the World in 80 Days*
Unit 14	Hans Christian Andersen	*Andersen's Fairy Tales*
Unit 15	Sir Arthur Conan Doyle	*The Adventures of Sherlock Holmes* and *The Hound of the Baskervilles*

Level C Vocabulary in Context Literary Selections

Unit 1	Baroness Orczy	*The Scarlet Pimpernel*
Unit 2	O. Henry	"Brickdust Road," "Two Thanksgiving Day Gentlemen," "The Trimmed Lamp"
Unit 3	Henry David Thoreau	*Walden*
Unit 4	Edgar Allan Poe	"A Descent into the Maelström," "The Premature Burial," "The Pit and the Pendulum," "William Wilson"
Unit 5	Charles Dickens	*A Christmas Carol*
Unit 6	Jack London	*The Call of the Wild* and *White Fang*
Unit 7	Louisa May Alcott	*Little Women*
Unit 8	Stephen Crane	*The Monster and Other Stories* and *The Red Badge of Courage*
Unit 9	Mark Twain	*Life on the Mississippi*
Unit 10	Edgar Rice Burroughs	*Tarzan of the Apes*
Unit 11	E.M. Forster	*Where Angels Fear to Tread*
Unit 12	Sir Arthur Conan Doyle	*The Lost World*
Unit 13	George Eliot	*Silas Marner* and *The Mill on the Floss*
Unit 14	Robert Louis Stevenson	*Strange Case of Dr. Jekyll and Mr. Hyde*
Unit 15	Henry James	*The Turn of the Screw*

VOCABULARY STRATEGY: Roots and Affixes

One important way students build vocabulary is to learn the meaning of Greek and Latin word parts that make up many English words. These word parts consist of **prefixes**, **suffixes**, and **roots**, or bases. A useful strategy for determining the meaning of an unknown word is to "take apart" the word and think about those parts.

Following is a list of common prefixes. Knowing the meaning of a prefix can help students determine the meaning of a word in which the prefix appears.

Prefix	Meaning	Sample Words
bi-	two	bicycle
com-, con-	together, with	compatriot, contact
de-	down, away from, not	devalue
dis-/di-	apart, opposite	disloyal, diverse
fore-, pre-	before, ahead of time	forewarn, preplan
il-, im-, in-, ir, non-, un-	not	illegal, impossible, inactive, irregular, nonsense, unable
in-, im-	in, into	inhale, import
mid-	middle	midway
mis-	wrongly, badly	mistake, misbehave
re-	again, back	redo, repay
sub-, sup-	under, less than	submarine, subzero, support, supplant
super-	above, greater than	superimpose, superstar
tri-	three	triangle

Following is a list of common suffixes. Knowing the meaning and grammatical function of a suffix can help students determine the meaning of a word.

Noun Suffix	Meaning	Sample Nouns
-acy, -ance, -ence, -hood, -ity, -ment, -ness, -ship	state, quality, or condition of, act or process of	adequacy, attendance, persistence, neighborhood, activity, judgment, brightness, friendship
-ant, -eer, -ent, -er, -ian, -ier, -ist, -or	one who does or makes something	contestant, auctioneer, resident, banker, comedian, financier, dentist, doctor
-ation, -ition, -ion	act or result of	organization, imposition, election

Verb Suffix	Meaning	Sample Verbs
-ate	to become, produce, or treat	validate, salivate, chlorinate

-en	to make, cause to be	weaken
-efy, -ify, -ize	to cause, make	liquefy, glorify, legalize

Adjective Suffix	Meaning	Sample Adjectives
-able, -ible	able, capable of	believable, incredible
-al, -ic	relating to, characteristic of	natural, romantic
-ful, -ive, -ous	full of, given to, marked by	beautiful, protective, poisonous
-ish, -like	like, resembling	foolish, childlike
-less	lacking, without	careless

A root is the main part of a word to which prefixes and suffixes may be added. Many roots come to English from Latin. Knowing Greek, Latin, and even Anglo-Saxon roots can help students determine the meaning of a word.

In the Building with Classical Roots sections of this book students will learn more about some of these Latin and Greek roots and about the English words that derive from them.

Greek Root	Meaning	Sample Words
-aster-, -astro-	star	asteroid, astronaut, disaster
-auto-	self	autograph
-bio-	life	biography
-chron-, chrono-	time	chronic, chronological
-cosm-, -cosmo-	universe, order	microcosm, cosmopolitan
-cryph-, -crypt-	hidden, secret	apocryphal, cryptographer
-dem-, -demo-	people	epidemic, democracy
-dog-, -dox-	opinion, teaching	dogmatic, orthodox
-gen-	race, kind, origin, birth	generation, genetic
-gnos-	know	diagnostic
-graph-, -graphy-, -gram-	write	graphite, autobiography, telegram
-log-, -logue-	speech, word, reasoning	logic, dialogue
-lys-, -lyt-	break down	analysis, electrolyte, catalytic
-metr-, -meter-	measure	metric, kilometer
-micro-	small	microchip
-morph-	form, shape	amorphous
-naut-	ship	nautical

-phon-, -phone-, -phono-	sound, voice	phonics, telephone, phonograph
-pol-, -polis-, -polit-	city, state	police, metropolis, political
-scop-, -scope-	watch, look at	microscopic, telescope
-tele-	far off, distant, end	television, teleological
-the-	put or place	parentheses

Latin Root	**Meaning**	**Sample Words**
-cap-, -capt-, -cept-, -cip-	take	captive, concept, recipient
-cede-, -ceed-, -ceas-, -cess-	happen, yield, go	precede, proceed, decease, cessation
-cred-	believe	incredible
-dic-, -dict-	speak, say, tell	indicate, diction
-duc-, -duct-	lead, conduct, draw	educate, conduct
-fac-, -fact-, -fect-, -fic-	make	faculty, artifact, defect, beneficial
-ject-	throw	eject
-mis-, -miss-, -mit-, -mitt-	send	promise, missile, transmit, intermittent
-note-, -not-	know, recognize	denote, notion
-pel-, -puls-	drive	expel, compulsive
-pend-, -pens-	hang, weigh, set aside	pendulum, pension
-pon-, -pos-	put, place	component, position
-port-	carry	portable
-rupt-	break	bankrupt
-scrib-, -scribe-, -script-	write	scribble, describe, inscription
-spec-, -spic-	look, see	spectator, conspicuous
-tac-, -tag-, -tang-, -teg-	touch	contact, contagious, tangible, integral
-tain-, -ten-, -tin-	hold, keep	contain, tenure, retinue
-temp-	time	tempo
-ven-, -vent-	come	intervene, convention
-vers-, -vert-	turn	reverse, invert
-voc-, -vok-	call	vocal, invoke

DENOTATION, CONNOTATION, AND SHADES OF MEANING

The ***denotation*** of a word is its specific dictionary meaning. Here are a few examples:

Word	Denotation
amiable	friendly
irk	to annoy
data	information

The ***connotation*** of a word is its **tone**—that is, the emotions or associations it normally arouses in people using, hearing, or reading it. Depending on what these feelings are, the connotation of a word may be *favorable* (*positive*) or *unfavorable* (*negative, pejorative*). A word that does not normally arouse strong feelings of any kind has a *neutral* connotation. Here are some examples of words with different connotations:

Word	Connotation
amiable	favorable
irk	unfavorable
data	neutral

Every Word Study section of **Vocabulary Workshop** has two pages of instruction on and practice with the denotation and connotation of words. The exercises in this section will prepare students to meet the Craft and Structure requirements of the Common Core State Standards.

FIGURATIVE LANGUAGE

After every three Units of VOCABULARY WORKSHOP, there is a Review and a Word Study section, for a total of five Word Study sections per book. Each Word Study section contains a two-page lesson on idioms, proverbs, or adages. These three types of figurative language, especially problematical for ELL students, are important in light of the Common Core State Standards, which require students in grades 6–8 to demonstrate an understanding of figurative language by interpreting figures of speech in context and analyzing their role in the text. The Common Core directive that students read texts (both literary and informational) of increasing complexity means that students are more likely to encounter figurative expressions in their reading. Furthermore, these three types of figurative language frequently appear in standardized test items.

- An **idiom** is an informal expression whose literal meaning does not help the reader or listener figure out what the expression means. English is particularly rich in idioms and idiomatic expressions, such as "raining cats and dogs," "the apple of my eye," or "a dark horse."
- An **adage** expresses a common experience, often in the form of a phrase or sentence, such as "Time flies when you're having fun."
- A **proverb** is a statement that provides a lesson or a moral, such as "A stitch in time saves nine" and "A rolling stone gathers no moss."

Teachers may note with students that every language has its own idioms, proverbs, and adages. Students may find or think of examples from other cultures, especially if another language is spoken at home. Understanding the meaning of common English idioms, adages, and proverbs will improve reading ability and enrich students' writing.

How to Use the Word Study Lessons

The first page of each lesson refers to one of the introductory Reading Passages in the three preceding Units. An idiom, adage, or proverb is embedded in the Passage, where it is used in context. Students next encounter the idiom (or adage or proverb) on the first page of the Word Study section. Following instruction and examples of these figures of speech, students are given ten sentences containing different idioms (or adages or proverbs) in context and are asked to match each with its definition. The second page is a **writing exercise** in which students are required to write original sentences using twelve additional idioms (or adages or proverbs).

Enriching the Word Study Lessons

Teachers may suggest that students draw a cartoon that uses a proverb or an adage as a caption, or they might write brief narratives or fables with a proverb or adage as the moral. Standardized tests, such as the SAT, might use a proverb as a writing prompt; students are then asked to discuss the proverb, drawing from their personal experiences, observations, and reading. Students will practice writing such essays in the **Writing: Words in Action** activities during the course of the school year.

SADLIER

VOCABULARY WORKSHOP®

ENRICHED EDITION

Jerome Shostak

Senior Series Consultant

Vicki A. Jacobs, Ed.D.
Associate Director, Teacher Education Program
Lecturer on Education
Harvard Graduate School of Education
Cambridge, Massachusetts

Series Consultants

Louis P. De Angelo, Ed.D.
Associate Superintendent
Diocese of Wilmington
Wilmington, Delaware

John Heath, Ph.D.
Professor of Classics
Santa Clara University
Santa Clara, California

Sarah Ressler Wright, NBCT
English Department Chair
Rutherford B. Hayes High School
Delaware City Schools, Ohio

Carolyn E. Waters, JD, Ed.S.
ELA/Literacy 6–12 Supervisor
Cobb County School District
Marietta, Georgia

Reviewers

The publisher wishes to thank for their comments and suggestions the following teachers and administrators, who read portions of the series prior to publication.

Teresa Appleby
English Teacher
Paxon Hollow Middle School
Marple Newtown District
Broomall, Pennsylvania

Laura Braun
Assistant Principal
Sawyer School
Chicago Public Schools
Chicago, Illinois

Eileen Brosnahan
Language Arts Teacher
St. Rita Catholic School
Dallas, Texas

Colleen DeGonia
Reading/Language Arts Teacher
Worth Junior High School
Worth, Illinois

Karen Berlin Ishii
Academic and Test Prep Tutor
New York, New York

Susan W. Keogh
Associate Director
Curriculum and Instruction
Lake Highland Preparatory
Orlando, Florida

Carol H. Rohrbach
Director of Curriculum and Staff Development
School District of Springfield Township
Oreland, Pennsylvania

Scott L. Smith
Teacher
Whitewater Valley Elementary
Harrison, Ohio

Patricia Stack
English Teacher
South Park School District
South Park, Pennsylvania

Sally F. Waller
English Teacher
Loyola Blakefield Middle School
Towson, Maryland

Cover: Concept/Art and Design: MK Advertising and William H. Sadlier, Inc.; Cover pencil: Shutterstock/VikaSuh. **Photo Credits:** A'Lelia Bundles/Madam Walker Family Archives/madamcjwalker.com, 174, 175 *inset*. akg-images/British Library: 103; Jean-Pierre Verney: 71 *bottom*; Universal Images Group: 32, 33 *top*, 33 *bottom*. Alamy/AF Archive: 69, 107; Archive Images: 141; Classic Image: 21; Everett Collection Inc.: 93, 169; INTERFOTO: 17, 79; LatitudeStock: 27; Lebrecht Music and Arts Photo Library: 31, 75, 179; Moviestore Collection Ltd: 173; National Geographic Image Collection/Edward Herbert Miner: 184; Photos 12: 97; Pictorial Press Ltd: 129 *inset*; Pictorial Press Ltd: 135; Picture Press/Detlev van Ravenswaay: 61 *top*; Wild Places Photography/Chris Howes: 55; World History Archive: 155. Art Resource, NY/Alinari: 51 *bottom*; HIP: 99. The Bridgeman Art Library/*I Want You for the U.S. Army*, 1917 (colour litho) by James Montgomery Flagg (1877–1960) Private Collection/Peter Newark Pictures: 71 *top*; Look and Learn: 41; Medicine man of the Mandan tribe in the costume of the Dog Dance, 1834 (colour litho) by Karl Bodmer (1809–93) Private Collection/Peter Newark American Pictures: 50. Corbis: 60 *top*, 61 *bottom*; Bettmann: 131, 189; Frans Lanting: 185 *bottom*; Hulton-Deutsch Collection: 59; PoodlesRock: 165 *left*; Science Faction/Steven Kazlowski: 164; SuperStock: 129 *background*; Terra/Marilyn Angel Wynn: 88; Tim Davis: 165 *right*. Digital Vision: 60 *background*, 60 *bottom*. Getty Images/De Agostini/DEA/F. Galardi: 137; Dorling Kindersley: 164 *inset*; Michael Ochs Archives: 128; Moviepix/Paramount Pictures: 89 *top*; NY Daily News: 175; Science Source: 37; Stone+/Tim Flach: 185 *top*; The Bridgeman Art Library/Jonathan Barry: 145; Time & Life Pictures: 113, 151. The Granger Collection, New York/ullstein bild: 108. The Image Works/Lebrecht Music and Arts Photo Library: 193; Marilyn Kingwill/ArenaPAL/Topham: 183; Mary Evans Picture Library: 51 *top*. Kobal Collection/RKO: 117. Lebrecht Music & Arts/*A Christmas Carol*, by Charles Dickens/Illustration by Harold Copping: 65. Mary Evans Picture Library/ONSLOW AUCTIONS LIMITED: 70. NASA: 89 *bottom*, 109 *bottom*. © National Portrait Gallery, London: 98. Photodisc: 175 frame. Punchstock/Blend Images: 22. Shutterstock/alphaspirit: 60 frame; emo_O: 99 border; Fotokor77: 108 *background*; Ice-Storm: 32 *background*; Iwona Grodzka: 128 frame; Jeff Metzger: 98 frame; Kompaniets Taras: 146 frame, 147 frame; Lina_S: 146 *background*; Marc Dietrich: 51 *background*; MaxyM: 70 *background*; More Trendy Design Here: 60 banner; Olivier Le Moal: 22 *inset*, 23 *background*; Pola36: 129 frame; Thirteen: 164 pin, 165 pin; Valentyn Volkov: 88 *background*. SuperStock/All Canada Photos/Wayne Lynch: 136 *bottom*; Ambient Images, Inc.: 22; Stockbroker/Purestock: 23. Wikipedia: 109 *top*, 136 *top*.

Illustration Credits: Britt Spencer/Illustration Ltd: 146–147. Sally Wern Comport/Shannon Associates, Inc.: 12–13. Tim Haggerty: 46, 84, 122, 160, 198.

Address inquiries to Permissions Department,
William H. Sadlier, Inc.,
9 Pine Street, New York, New York 10005-4700.

Printed in the United States of America.
ISBN: 978-0-8215-8006-6
4 5 6 7 8 9 10 EB 20 19 18 17 16

For additional online resources, go to vocabularyworkshop.com and enter the Student Access Code: VW13SAHND88Y

ENRICHED EDITION: New Features

For more than five decades, **Vocabulary Workshop** has proven to be a highly successful tool for guiding systematic vocabulary growth and developing vocabulary skills. It has also been shown to help students prepare for standardized tests.

New in this edition are the **Reading Passages, Writing, Vocabulary in Context,** and **Word Study** activities. Nonfiction, high-interest passages use 15 or more of the Unit vocabulary words in context. Two writing prompts require a response to the reading and provide practice in writing for standardized tests. New Vocabulary in Context activities present words from the Unit as they are used in classic works of literature. After every three Units, Word Study activities, developed in conjunction with Common Core State Standards requirements, provide practice with idioms, adages, and proverbs, as well as denotation and connotation and classical roots.

Look for the new **QR** (Quick Response) codes on the **Reading Passage** and **Vocabulary in Context** pages. Codes can be read with a smartphone camera by downloading any free QR code application to a smartphone. Snap the code to listen to iWords and an audio of the Reading Passage for the Unit or take an interactive quiz. With iWords you can listen to one word at a time or download all of the words in a Unit to listen to them at your convenience.

***The new structure of* Vocabulary Workshop** is made up of 15 Units. Each Unit consists of the following sections: a **Reading Passage, Definitions, Choosing the Right Word, Synonyms and Antonyms, Completing the Sentence, Writing,** and **Vocabulary in Context**. Together, these exercises provide multiple and varied exposures to the taught words—an approach consistent with and supportive of research-based findings in vocabulary instruction.

Five **Reviews** cover Vocabulary for Comprehension and Two-Word Completions. Vocabulary for Comprehension is modeled on the reading sections of standardized tests, and as in those tests, it presents reading comprehension questions, including specific vocabulary-related ones, that are based on a reading passage.

A **Final Mastery Test** assesses a selection of words from the year with activities on Synonyms, Antonyms, Analogies, Two-Word Completions, Supplying Words in Context, Word Associations, and Choosing the Right Meaning.

In each level of **Vocabulary Workshop**, 300 key words are taught. The words have been selected according to the following criteria: currency and general usefulness; frequency of appearance on recognized vocabulary lists; applicability to, and appearance on, standardized tests; and current grade-level research.

ONLINE COMPONENTS

vocabularyworkshop.com

At **vocabularyworkshop.com** you will find iWords, an audio program that provides pronunciations, definitions, and examples of usage for all of the key words presented in this level of **Vocabulary Workshop**. You can listen to one word at a time or download all of the words of any given Unit. You will then be able to listen to the audio program for that Unit at your convenience.

At **vocabularyworkshop.com** you will also find **Audio Passages**, **interactive vocabulary quizzes, flashcards, games and puzzles** that will help reinforce and enrich your understanding of the key words in this level of **Vocabulary Workshop**.

CONTENTS

ENRICHED EDITION: New Features ... *iii*

VOCABULARY STRATEGY: Using Context ... *7*

VOCABULARY STRATEGY: Word Structure ... *8*

VOCABULARY AND READING ... *9*

WORKING WITH ANALOGIES ... *11*

UNIT 1 **Vocabulary:** apparel, besiege, compress, denounce, dispatch, douse, expressly, famished, forsake, gainful, immense, inept, ingenious, instantaneous, irk, libel, misgiving, oaf, recede, repast

- **Passage: City of Gold** <First-Person Narrative> ... *12*
- **Definitions and Exercises** ... *14–20*
- **Vocabulary in Context: Literary Text** (Johann David Wyss) ... *21*

UNIT 2 **Vocabulary:** adverse, arid, assailant, billow, confront, constrain, contemporary, depict, disinterested, encompass, groundless, hypocrite, incomprehensible, manipulate, maximum, mimic, ruffle, serene, sheepish, stamina

- **Passage: West End School Has Comestible Curriculum** <Interview> ... *22*
- **Definitions and Exercises** ... *24–30*
- **Vocabulary in Context: Literary Text** (Walt Whitman) ... *31*

UNIT 3 **Vocabulary:** barrage, bigot, designate, diversity, enigma, gloat, global, illusion, infuriate, motivate, pacifist, queue, restrict, sage, slake, terrain, vocation, vow, waylay, wither

- **Passage: This Day in 1923: The *Olympic*'s the Thing!** <Archived Newspaper Article> ... *32*
- **Definitions and Exercises** ... *34–40*
- **Vocabulary in Context: Literary Text** (Jules Verne) ... *41*

REVIEW UNITS 1–3

- **Vocabulary for Comprehension** ... *42*
- **Two-Word Completions** ... *44*

WORD STUDY

- **Idioms** ... *45*
- **Denotation and Connotation** ... *47*
- **Classical Roots** ... *49*

UNIT 4 **Vocabulary:** acquit, deem, devastate, discredit, elusive, generate, idolize, ingratitude, keepsake, mortal, ovation, petty, plight, repent, reverie, revocation, scan, strand, strife, topple

- **Passage: The Art and Science of Traditional Healing** <Expository Essay> ... *50*
- **Definitions and Exercises** ... *52–58*
- **Vocabulary in Context: Literary Text** (Edgar Rice Burroughs) ... *59*

UNIT 5 **Vocabulary:** acute, bluster, bungle, commentary, duration, eerie, facet, fidelity, fray, headstrong, inhabitant, numb, pacify, ravenous, refute, remorse, setback, smug, synopsis, tarry

- **Passage: Continue Space Exploration, Now!** <Persuasive Speech> ... *60*
- **Definitions and Exercises** ... *62–68*
- **Vocabulary in Context: Literary Text** (H.G. Wells) ... *69*

UNIT 6 **Vocabulary:** agenda, amiable, befuddle, blight, boisterous, clarity, compliant, conserve, debut, gory, gross, induce, leeway, limber, maze, oracle, partisan, reimburse, vacate, vagabond

Passage: **The Fine Art of War: WWI Propaganda Images** <Textbook Entry> ... 70
Definitions and Exercises ... 72–78
Vocabulary in Context: Literary Text (Mark Twain) ... 79

REVIEW UNITS 4–6
Vocabulary for Comprehension ... 80
Two-Word Completions ... 82

WORD STUDY
Idioms ... 83
Denotation and Connotation ... 85
Classical Roots ... 87

UNIT 7 **Vocabulary:** authorize, culprit, dawdle, dissect, expend, fatality, gullible, illicit, immerse, inflammatory, memorandum, pathetic, persevere, prevaricate, quash, relish, reminisce, scour, testimonial, writhe
Passage: **Made for the Shade** <Informational Essay> ... 88
Definitions and Exercises ... 90–96
Vocabulary in Context: Literary Text (Charles Dickens) ... 97

UNIT 8 **Vocabulary:** affluence, arrears, cascade, cringe, crotchety, immobile, impassable, innovation, jovial, manacle, martial, minimum, nimble, onset, partition, perishable, retrieve, sinister, taut, template
Passage: **From Big Dream to Big Top** <Interview> ... 98
Definitions and Exercises ... 100–106
Vocabulary in Context: Literary Text (Sir Arthur Conan Doyle) ... 107

UNIT 9 **Vocabulary:** avenge, cede, deluge, discretion, giddy, impact, intimidate, liberate, logical, misrepresent, optional, outright, rendezvous, rotund, saunter, sluggish, subordinate, tint, variable, verge
Passage: **From Fire Arrows to Space Flight: A History of Rockets** <Informational Essay> ... 108
Definitions and Exercises ... 110–116
Vocabulary in Context: Literary Text (L.M. Montgomery) ... 117

REVIEW UNITS 7–9
Vocabulary for Comprehension ... 118
Two-Word Completions ... 120

WORD STUDY
Adages ... 121
Denotation and Connotation ... 123
Classical Roots ... 125

UNIT 10 **Vocabulary:** abominable, bumbling, consequence, delude, dole, engulf, foil, formulate, initiative, memento, nonconformist, null and void, panorama, posterity, pry, refurbish, resourceful, rigorous, subsequent, unerring
Passage: **Farewell, Blue Yodeler** <Obituary> ... 126
Definitions and Exercises ... 128–134
Vocabulary in Context: Literary Text (Edgar Allan Poe) ... 135

UNIT 11 **Vocabulary:** alias, amble, burly, distort, dogged, dumbfounded, extinct, grit, inevitable, ingrained, meteoric, parody, prevail, relic, rend, replenish, rummage, skimp, sleuth, vandalism
Passage: **Here I Am: Galápagos Log** <Log> ... 136
Definitions and Exercises ... 138–144
Vocabulary in Context: Literary Text (Jack London) ... 145

UNIT 12 **Vocabulary:** abduct, ambiguous, balk, compact, confer, earmark, frigid, implement, incalculable, indisputable, intensive, maneuver, sabotage, scant, stealthy, strapping, strident, thrive, titanic, valiant

Passage: Vampires We Have Known <Humorous Essay> *146*

Definitions and Exercises *148–154*

Vocabulary in Context: Literary Text (Sir Arthur Conan Doyle) *155*

REVIEW UNITS 10–12

Vocabulary for Comprehension *156*

Two-Word Completions *158*

WORD STUDY

Idioms *159*

Denotation and Connotation *161*

Classical Roots *163*

UNIT 13 **Vocabulary:** adhere, affirm, atrocity, cope, deter, disquieting, empower, fluent, lag, mangle, misapprehension, optimist, prowl, recitation, stupefy, sulky, supplement, surge, trait, unscrupulous

Passage: Polar Opposites <Compare and Contrast Essay> *164*

Definitions and Exercises *166–172*

Vocabulary in Context: Literary Text (L.M. Montgomery) *173*

UNIT 14 **Vocabulary:** abstain, accommodate, allegiance, amalgamate, append, commemorate, enumerate, exalt, extort, far-fetched, glum, replica, responsive, sanctuary, self-seeking, submissive, tally, taskmaster, transform, upheaval

Passage: Madam C.J. Walker and Her Wonderful Remedy <Biographical Sketch> ... *174*

Definitions and Exercises *176–182*

Vocabulary in Context: Literary Text (Charles Dickens) *183*

UNIT 15 **Vocabulary:** beacon, berserk, celestial, chasten, confiscate, data, detract, encounter, epic, pantomime, pessimist, precaution, prosecute, puncture, retaliate, sham, uncouth, underscore, wholesome, wistful

Passage: Running With the Big Dogs <Magazine Article> *184*

Definitions and Exercises *186–192*

Vocabulary in Context: Literary Text (Washington Irving) *193*

REVIEW UNITS 13–15

Vocabulary for Comprehension *194*

Two-Word Completions *196*

WORD STUDY

Proverbs *197*

Denotation and Connotation *199*

Classical Roots *201*

FINAL MASTERY TEST *202*

INDEX *207*

VOCABULARY STRATEGY: Using Context

The **context** of a word is the printed text of which that word is part. By studying the word's context, we may find **clues** to its meaning. We might find a clue in the immediate or adjoining sentence or phrase in which the word appears; in the topic or subject matter of the passage; or in the physical features—such as photographs, illustrations, charts, graphs, captions and headings—of a page itself.

The **Vocabulary in Context**, **Vocabulary for Comprehension**, and **Choosing the Right Meaning** exercises that appear in the Units, the Reviews, and Final Mastery Test provide practice in using context to decode unfamiliar words.

Three types of context clues appear in the exercises in this book.

A ***restatement clue*** consists of a *synonym* for or a *definition* of the missing word. For example:

The ______________, stubborn horse refused to go down the path his rider chose and instead turned and headed for home.

a. headstrong **b.** eerie **c.** numb **d.** ravenous

In this sentence, *stubborn* is a synonym of the missing word, *headstrong*, and acts as a restatement clue for it.

A ***contrast clue*** consists of an *antonym* for or a phrase that means the opposite of the missing word. For example:

"It seems to me that my plan is plausible," I said,

"while yours seems too (**far-fetched, responsive**)."

In this sentence, *plausible* is an antonym of the missing word, *far-fetched*. This is confirmed by the presence of the word *while*, which indicates that the answer must be the opposite of *plausible*.

An ***inference clue*** implies but does not directly state the meaning of the missing word or words. For example:

Like any ______________, my brother always expects the worst and thinks that any good news is actually a carefully disguised ______________.

a. epic . . . pantomime
b. pantomime . . . precaution
c. beacon . . . encounter
d. pessimist . . . sham

In this sentence, there are several inference clues: (a) the phrase *expects the worst* suggests *pessimist*; (b) the words *carefully disguised* suggest the word *sham*. These words are inference clues because they suggest or imply, but do not directly state, the missing word or words.

VOCABULARY STRATEGY: Word Structure

Prefixes, **suffixes**, and **roots**, or **bases**, are word parts. One strategy for determining an unknown word's meaning is to "take apart" the word and think about the parts. Study the prefixes and suffixes below to help you find out the meanings of words in which they appear.

Prefix	**Meaning**	**Sample Words**
com-, con-	together, with	compatriot, contact
de-,	down, away from, not	devalue
dis-, di-	apart, opposite	disloyal, dichromatic
il-, im-, in-, ir, non-, un-	not	illegal, impossible, inactive, irregular, nonsense, unable
sub-, sup-	under, less than	submarine, support
super-	above, greater than	superimpose, superstar

Noun	**Suffix Meaning**	**Sample Nouns**
-acy, -ance, -ence, -hood, -ity, -ment, -ness, -ship	state, quality, or condition of, act or process of	adequacy, attendance, persistence, neighborhood, activity, judgment, brightness, friendship
-ant, -eer, -ent, -er, -ian, -ier, -ist, -or	one who does or makes something	auctioneer, contestant, resident, banker, comedian, financier, dentist, doctor
-ation, -ition, -ion	act or result of	organization, imposition, election

Verb Suffix	**Meaning**	**Sample Verbs**
-ate	to become, produce, or treat	validate, salivate, chlorinate
-efy, -ify, -ize	to cause, make	liquefy, glorify, legalize

Adjective Suffix	**Meaning**	**Sample Adjectives**
-able, -ible	able, capable of	believable, incredible
-al, -ic	relating to, characteristic of	natural, romantic
-ful-, -ive, -ous	full of, given to, marked by	beautiful, protective, poisonous
-ish, -like	like, resembling	foolish, childlike
-less	lacking, without	careless

A **base** or **root** is the main part of a word to which prefixes and suffixes may be added. On the Classical Roots page of the Word Study section, you will learn more about Latin and Greek roots and the English words that derive from them. The following lists may help you figure out the meaning of new or unfamiliar words.

Greek Root	**Meaning**	**Sample Words**
-cryph-, -crypt-	hidden, secret	apocryphal, cryptographer
-dem-, -demo-	people	epidemic, democracy
-gen-	race, kind, origin, birth	generation
-gnos-	know	diagnostic
-lys-, -lyt-	break down	analysis, electrolyte, catalytic

Latin Root	**Meaning**	**Sample Words**
-cap-, -capt-, -cept-, -cip-	take	captive, concept, recipient
-cede-, -ceed-, -ceas- -cess-	happen, yield, go	precede, proceed, decease, cessation
-fac-, -fact-, -fect-, -fic-	make	faculty, artifact, defect, beneficial,
-tac-, -tag-, -tang-, -teg-	touch	contact, contagious, tangible, integral
-tain-, -ten-, -tin-	hold, keep	contain, tenure, retinue

For more prefixes, suffixes, and roots, visit **vocabularyworkshop.com**.

VOCABULARY AND READING

Word knowledge is essential to reading comprehension. Your knowledge of word meanings and ability to think carefully about what you read will help you succeed in school and on standardized tests, including the SAT, the ACT, and the PSAT.

New **Reading Passages** provide extra practice with vocabulary words. Vocabulary words are boldfaced to draw your attention to their uses and contexts. Context clues embedded in the passages encourage you to figure out the meanings of words before you read the definitions provided on the pages directly following the passages.

You will read excerpts from classic literature in the **Vocabulary in Context** exercises. Each excerpt includes one of the Unit vocabulary words as it is used in the original work. You may use what you learn about the word from its use in context to answer questions on the definition.

The **Vocabulary for Comprehension** exercises in each review consist of a nonfiction reading passage followed by comprehension questions. The passages and questions are similar to those that you are likely to find on standardized tests.

Kinds of Questions

Main Idea Questions generally ask what the passage as a whole is about. Often, but not always, the main idea is stated in the first paragraph of the passage. You may also be asked the main idea of a specific paragraph. Questions about the main idea may begin like this:

- The primary or main purpose of the passage is . . .
- The passage is best described as . . .
- The title that best describes the content of the passage is . . .

Detail Questions focus on important information that is explicitly stated in the passage. Often, however, the correct answer choices do not use the exact language of the passage. They are instead restatements, or paraphrases, of the text.

Vocabulary-in-Context Questions check your ability to use context to identify a word's meaning. Use line references to see how and in what context the word is used. For example:

- **Testimonial** (line 8) is best defined as . . .
- The meaning of **dawdle** (line 30) is . . .

Use context to check your answer choices, particularly when the vocabulary word has more than one meaning. Among the choices may be two (or more) correct meanings of the word in question. Choose the meaning that best fits the context.

Inference Questions ask you to make inferences or draw conclusions from the passage. These questions often begin like this:

- It can be inferred from the passage that . . .
- The author implies that . . .
- Evidently the author feels that . . .

The inferences you make and the conclusions you draw must be based on the information in the passage. Your own knowledge and reasoning come into play in understanding what is implied and in reaching conclusions that are logical.

Questions About Tone show your understanding of the author's attitude toward the subject of the passage. Words that describe tone, or attitude, are "feeling" words, such as *bored*, *unsure*, *scornful*, *amazed*, *respectful*. These are typical questions:

- The author's attitude toward . . . is best described as . . .
- Which word best describes the author's tone?

To determine the tone, pay attention to the author's word choice. The author's attitude may be positive (respectful), negative (scornful), or neutral (distant).

Questions About Author's Technique focus on the way a text is organized and the language the author uses. These questions ask you to think about structure and function. For example:

- The final paragraph serves to . . .
- The author cites . . . in order to . . .

To answer the questions, you must demonstrate an understanding of the way the author presents information and develops ideas.

Strategies

Here are some general strategies to help you as you read each passage and answer the questions.

- Read the introduction first if there is one. The introduction will provide a focus for the passage.

- Be an active reader. As you read, ask yourself questions about the passage—for example: What is this paragraph about? What does the writer mean here? Why does the writer include this information?

- Refer to the passage when you answer the questions. In general, the order of the questions mirrors the organization of the passage, and many of the questions include paragraph or line references. It is often helpful to go back and reread before choosing an answer.

- Read carefully, and be sure to base your answer choices on the passage. There are answer choices that make sense but are not based on the information in the passage. These are true statements, but they are incorrect answers. The correct answers are either restatements of ideas in the text or inferences that can be drawn from the text.

- Consider each exercise a learning experience. Keep in mind that your ability to answer the questions correctly shows as much about your understanding of the questions as about your understanding of the passage.

WORKING WITH ANALOGIES

A verbal analogy expresses a relationship or comparison between sets of words. Normally, an analogy contains two pairs of words linked by a word or symbol that stands for an equal (=) sign. A complete analogy compares the two pairs of words and makes a statement about them. It asserts that the relationship between the first—or key—pair of words is the same as the relationship between the second pair.

In the **Analogies** exercises in the Final Mastery Test, you will be asked to complete analogies—that is, to choose the pair of words that best matches or parallels the relationship of the key, or given, pair of words. Here are two examples:

1. maple is to **tree** as
a. acorn is to oak
b. hen is to rooster
c. rose is to flower
d. shrub is to lilac

2. joyful is to **gloomy** as
a. cheerful is to happy
b. strong is to weak
c. quick is to famous
d. hungry is to starving

In order to find the correct answer to exercise 1, you must first determine the relationship between the two key words, **maple** and **tree**. In this case, that relationship might be expressed as "a maple is a kind (or type) of tree." The next step is to select from choices a, b, c, and d the pair of words that best reflects the same relationship. The correct answer is c; it is the only pair whose relationship parallels the one in the key words: A rose is a kind (or type) of flower, just as a maple is a kind (or type) of tree. The other choices do not express the same relationship.

In exercise 2, the relationship between the key words can be expressed as "joyful means the opposite of gloomy." Which of the choices best represents the same relationship? The answer is b: "strong means the opposite of weak."

Here are examples of some other common analogy relationships:

Analogy	Key Relationship
big is to **large** as **little** is to **small**	**Big** means the same thing as **large**, just as **little** means the same thing as **small**.
brave is to **favorable** as **cowardly** is to **unfavorable**	The tone of **brave** is **favorable**, just as the tone of **cowardly** is **unfavorable**.
busybody is to **nosy** as **klutz** is to **clumsy**	A **busybody** is by definition someone who is **nosy**, just as a **klutz** is by definition someone who is **clumsy**.
cowardly is to **courage** as **awkward** is to **grace**	Someone who is **cowardly** lacks **courage**, just as someone who is **awkward** lacks **grace**.
visible is to **see** as **audible** is to **hear**	If something is **visible**, you can by definition **see** it, just as if something is **audible**, you can by definition **hear** it.
liar is to **truthful** as **bigot** is to **fair-minded**	A **liar** is by definition not likely to be **truthful**, just as a **bigot** is by definition not likely to be **fair-minded**.
eyes are to **see** as **ears** are to **hear**	You use your **eyes** to **see** with, just as you use your **ears** to **hear** with.

There are many different kinds of relationships represented in the analogy questions you will find in the Final Mastery Test, but the key to solving any analogy is to find and express the relationship between the two key words.

UNIT 1

Note that not all of the 20 Unit words are used in this passage. *Compress*, *denounce*, *forsake*, and *libel* are not included.

Read the following passage, taking note of the ***boldface*** *words and their contexts. These words are among those you will be studying in Unit 1. It may help you to complete the exercises in this Unit if you refer to the way the words are used below.*

CCSS Vocabulary: 4; Reading (Informational Text): 4, 6. (See pp. T14–15.)

City of Gold

<First-Person Narrative>

Long ago in western Africa, bands of traders traveled to the city of Timbuktu to buy goods in exchange for gold. The following account is given by a boy describing his first trip to the famous city. He is with a group of friends in the year 1450.

My father has been carrying gold from our land to sell in Timbuktu since he was young. His father was a gold trader before him, and now I've joined him and my brothers. We joined other travelers with their goods and camels in a caravan. We brought gold to Timbuktu to sell, and now I've come home. I'll tell you about that city of gold, because soon you'll be old enough to go there with your fathers, too. I'm **famished**—I haven't eaten since morning. Let's enjoy this small **repast** together while I talk.

I'll start at the end: What a **gainful** expedition! You saw the great load of goods we brought home. **Immense** packages of salt, some **expressly** for our own use, but most for trade here and to the south. We brought back kola nuts to chew on, some palm oil for cooking, and fine cloth for clothing. We profited more than usual, because the buyers of gold wanted more than was available. One man even offered to lend my father gold at interest so we could trade more before having to leave. Father refused, saying, "Lend your money and lose a friend."

Before the journey, I had imagined that we would take our bags to Timbuktu and trade a handful here and there. What an **inept** trader I would become, if not for the wisdom of my father! My father is an **ingenious** man who knows his way

around the world. Before we even entered the city, we stopped to rest by the river. We washed and set up a cooking fire. My father left and returned with a wealthy merchant and his men. They brought us much salt in exchange for our gold. My father and this merchant, who's a big man in Taghaza up north, chewed kola nuts and spoke like old friends. Then, the merchant **dispatched** his men, ordering them back to their camp. Their compliance was **instantaneous**, and I watched them **recede** into the distance, carrying gold this time instead of salt. **Irked** by my idling, my father told me to stop gawking like an **oaf** and start packing the salt.

We ate a quick meal and **doused** the fires. At last, I entered the city of Timbuktu. There are people in Timbuktu of every shape, size, and color; and they come from everywhere, wearing all sorts of **apparel** and speaking many languages. Many speak Arabic, and many speak Mande, like us. There are thousands of people in that city. It's a busy place, but exciting, with massive mosques and palaces and markets.

We exchanged the rest of our gold in the marketplaces. Because there was so much happening, our time in the city went quickly. Now that I am home, I confess that I had some **misgivings** before I went. I feared thieves would attack our caravan. I wondered if the city might be raided or **besieged** while we were there. But everything went smoothly on my first visit. What a place, that busy city—I can hardly wait till we return!

Audio

For iWords and audio passages, snap the code, or go to **vocabularyworkshop.com**.

Note the spelling, pronunciation, part(s) of speech, and definition(s) of each of the following words. Then write the appropriate form of the word in the blank spaces in the illustrative sentence(s) following. Finally, study the lists of synonyms and antonyms.

1. apparel (ə par′ əl)

(*n.*) clothing, that which serves as dress or decoration; (*v.*) to put clothes on, dress up

Winter **apparel** should be warm and cozy.

Let's **apparel** our cats for the party.

SYNONYMS: (*n.*) attire, garments; (*v.*) deck out
ANTONYMS: (*v.*) undress, unclothe, strip, denude

2. besiege (bi sēj′)

(*v.*) to attack by surrounding with military forces; to cause worry or trouble

If troops **besiege** their stronghold, the rebel forces may be forced to surrender.

SYNONYMS: blockade, encircle, pressure, hound

3. compress (*v.*, kəm pres′, *n.*, käm′ pres)

(*v.*) to press together; to reduce in size or volume; (*n.*) a folded cloth or pad applied to an injury

The editor helped **compress** my rambling 25-page mystery into an 8-page thriller.

A cold **compress** may soothe headache pain.

SYNONYMS: (*v.*) condense, shrink, shorten
ANTONYMS: (*v.*) enlarge, swell

4. denounce (di nau̇ns′)

(*v.*) to condemn openly; to accuse formally

The United Nations decided to publicly **denounce** the tyrant's crimes.

SYNONYMS: criticize, censure
ANTONYMS: hail, acclaim

5. dispatch (dis pach′)

(*v.*) to send off or out for a purpose; to kill; (*n.*) an official message; promptness, speed; the act of killing

We'll **dispatch** a repair crew right away.

He approved the request with **dispatch**.

SYNONYMS: (*v.*) slay; (*n.*) report, communication
ANTONYMS: (*v.*) recall, withhold

6. douse (dau̇s)

(*v.*) to plunge into a liquid, drench; to put out quickly, extinguish

I'll **douse** the flames with the hose.

SYNONYMS: submerge, soak, dunk, immerse
ANTONYMS: dry out, dehydrate, kindle, ignite

CCSS Vocabulary: 4.c., 4.d. (See pp. T14–15.)

7. expressly
(ek spres′ lē)

(*adv.*) plainly, in so many words; for a particular purpose

At the meeting, parents **expressly** stated their approval of students wearing school uniforms.

SYNONYMS: pointedly, explicitly
ANTONYMS: implicitly, accidentally

8. famished
(fam′ isht)

(*adj., part.*) suffering severely from hunger or from a lack of something

The Vietnamese immigrants, new to a strange American city, were **famished** for news of home.

SYNONYMS: hungry, starving, ravenous
ANTONYMS: well fed, full, satisfied, satiated

9. forsake
(fôr sāk′)

(*v.*) to give up, renounce; to leave, abandon

I will never **forsake** my children, no matter what they do or say.

SYNONYMS: desert, disown
ANTONYMS: keep, hold on to, stand by

10. gainful
(gān′ fəl)

(*adj.*) profitable; bringing in money or some special advantage

I hope to find **gainful** employment that is pleasing to me.

SYNONYMS: moneymaking, paying
ANTONYMS: unprofitable, unrewarding, nonpaying

11. immense
(i mens′)

(*adj.*) very large or great; beyond ordinary means of measurement

Alaska enjoys **immense** natural resources, but its severe climate makes those resources difficult to use.

SYNONYMS: vast, immeasurable, gigantic
ANTONYMS: small, tiny, minute, infinitesimal

12. inept
(in ept′)

(*adj.*) totally without skill or appropriateness

The scientist is brilliant in the research laboratory but is **inept** at dealing with people.

SYNONYMS: clumsy, unskilled, incompetent
ANTONYMS: skillful, accomplished, adroit

13. ingenious
(in jēn′ yəs)

(*adj.*) showing remarkable originality, inventiveness, or resourcefulness; clever

The students found an **ingenious** solution to the math problem.

SYNONYMS: imaginative, resourceful
ANTONYMS: unimaginative, unoriginal, uninventive

CCSS Vocabulary: 4.c., 4.d. (See pp. T14–15.)

14. instantaneous (in stən tā′ nē əs)

(*adj.*) done in an instant; immediate

Most computer software is designed so that users can obtain nearly **instantaneous** responses.

SYNONYMS: prompt, quick, speedy
ANTONYMS: delayed, slow, gradual

15. irk (ərk)

(*v.*) to annoy, trouble, make weary

Questions that show a student's lack of attention **irk** the teacher.

SYNONYMS: bother, irritate, vex
ANTONYMS: please, delight, cheer

16. libel (lī′ bəl)

(*n.*) a written statement that unfairly or falsely harms the reputation of the person about whom it is made; (*v.*) to write or publish such a statement

The young celebrity accused her unauthorized biographer of **libel**.

It is a crime to **libel** others, no matter how you feel about them.

SYNONYMS: (*n.*) slur; (*v.*) smear, defame

17. misgiving (mis giv′ iŋ)

(*n.*) a feeling of fear, doubt, or uncertainty

They had **misgivings** about joining the chorus because of its demanding schedule.

SYNONYMS: worry, qualm, hesitation
ANTONYMS: feeling of confidence, assurance

18. oaf (ōf)

(*n.*) a stupid person; a big, clumsy, slow individual

He generally moved like an **oaf**, so I was surprised to see how graceful he was on the dance floor.

SYNONYMS: bonehead, dunce, clod, lout

19. recede (ri sēd′)

(*v.*) to go or move backward; to become more distant

The town residents must wait for the flood waters to **recede** before they can deal with the terrible mess left behind.

SYNONYMS: retreat, go back, back up
ANTONYMS: advance, come closer

20. repast (ri past′)

(*n.*) a meal, food

Let's get together after the show at Callie's Café for a late-night **repast**.

SYNONYM: victuals

CCSS Vocabulary: 4.c., 4.d. (See pp. T14–15.)

Choosing the Right Word

*Select the **boldface** word that better completes each sentence. You might refer to the passage on pages 12–13 to see how most of these words are used in context.*

1. His notebooks show that Leonardo da Vinci was not only a masterful artist but an (**inept, ingenious**) inventor as well.

2. We can (**compress, besiege**) the message of the sermon into one short sentence: "Do unto others as you would have others do unto you."

In the fifteenth century, da Vinci drew a design for the first armored tank, which had guns and was powered by men turning crankshafts.

3. He may claim that we have (**libeled, doused**) him, but we have facts to back up every statement made in the column about him.

4. The beauty of the Grand Canyon is so (**immense, instantaneous**) that it is absolutely impossible to capture its grandeur on film.

5. Which job would you take—one that is more (**ingenious, gainful**) right now or one that pays a small salary but offers a chance for valuable training?

6. Her conscience forced her to (**denounce, libel**) the conspirators to the authorities.

7. Tom may not be as polished and clever as some of the other boys, but I think it is unfair of you to call him an (**apparel, oaf**).

8. The story I am reading features a(n) (**inept, doused**) detective who cannot solve a case and continually loses things.

9. We were pleasantly surprised to see that she completed the difficult task we had given her with neatness and (**irk, dispatch**).

10. As soon as she took over the office of Mayor, she was (**besieged, dispatched**) by dozens of people eager to get city jobs.

11. (**Famished, Compressed**) for a chance to see her work in print, the young writer begged the magazine editor to publish her story.

12. His conceit is so (**immense, gainful**) that he cannot imagine anyone voting against him in the election for class president.

13. I will never (**recede, forsake**) the people who helped me in my hour of need!

14. After all the bad things he has done, I feel no (**dispatches, misgivings**) about telling him that I don't want him to be my "friend" anymore.

15. My sister is learning French, taking cooking classes, and participating in other (**inept, gainful**) pursuits that will allow her to become a master chef.

CCSS Vocabulary: 4.d. (See pp. T14–15.)

16. You may criticize the roads and the lights, but the fact is that (**inept, immense**) drivers are the cause of most car accidents.

17. I always feel sad at the end of the autumn, when the trees lose their beautiful (**repast, apparel**) of leaves.

18. As soon as he began his long, boring speech, our excitement died down, as though we had been (**denounced, doused**) with cold water.

19. Our puppy's paws and legs are much larger than her body, but she looks adorable as she lumbers around the yard like a huge (**libel, oaf**).

20. Where did he ever get the curious idea that we set up this volleyball court (**expressly, instantaneously**) for him and his friends?

21. We are working hard to improve conditions in our community, but we cannot expect (**famished, instantaneous**) results.

22. Each day, after she finishes her homework, she enjoys a light (**repast, misgiving**) of the detective stories she loves so well.

23. Instead of feeling (**forsaken, irked**) because you did poorly on the exam, why don't you make up your mind to study harder in the future?

24. When I realized that I was thoroughly prepared for the final exams, my fears quickly (**receded, irked**).

25. Hold the (**repast, compress**) on your ankle until the swelling goes down.

*Choose the word from this Unit that is the same or most nearly the same in meaning as the **boldface** word or expression in the phrase. Write that word on the line. Use a dictionary if necessary.*

1. compelled to **ditch** the leaky boat — forsake
2. had to fire the **bungling** carpenter — inept
3. thought the article **tarnished** her reputation — libeled
4. **inventive** use for lumber scraps — ingenious
5. using a machine to **squash** the cans — compress
6. fashionable hand-me-down **outfits** — apparel
7. waiting until the crowds **ebb** — recede
8. **bad feelings** about the leading candidate — misgivings
9. is **clearly** forbidden for use by minors — expressly
10. **expressed disapproval of** the protestors' actions — denounced

CCSS Vocabulary: 5. (See pp. T14–15.)

The synonyms and antonyms here do not appear on the Definitions page.

Antonyms

*Choose the word from this Unit that is most nearly opposite in meaning to the **boldface** word or expression in the phrase. Write that word on the line. Use a dictionary if necessary.*

1. writes a **compliment** ____libel____
2. likes to **support** all causes ____forsake____
3. **expand** the bundle to fit ____compress____
4. was certain to **gladden** the passengers ____irk____
5. reasons to **validate** the winner ____denounce____

Completing the Sentence

From the words in this Unit, choose the one that best completes each of the following sentences. Write the correct word form in the space provided.

1. How can we hope to ____besiege____ a city that is surrounded by such strong walls and has ample supplies of everything it needs?
2. Don't allow yourself to be ____irked____ by every small trouble that may arise during the day.
3. Let's make certain to ____douse____ the fire before leaving camp.
4. Some of life's rewards are ____instantaneous____; others are a long time in coming.
5. Some people hailed the man as a genius; others ____denounced____ him as a quack.
6. You had no right to call me a clumsy ____oaf____ just because I spilled some water on you.
7. As it was well past their lunchtime by the time we arrived home, the children were ____famished____ and demanding food.
8. You will be able to get everything into a single suitcase if you ____compress____ all the items as much as possible.
9. On my first baby-sitting job, I found that one must have ____immense____ patience to take care of young children.
10. When you play tennis for the first time, you are going to find that your attempts to hit the ball are very ____inept____.

CCSS Vocabulary: 4.a., 5. (See pp. T14–15.)

11. As an inexperienced sailor, I had more than a few ___**misgivings**___ about taking out the small boat in such rough weather.

12. The laws of this land do not shield public figures from just criticism, but they do protect them against ___**libel**___.

13. A(n) ___**dispatch**___ will be sent to all our representatives in Latin America advising them how to handle the problem.

14. While all true vegetarians ___**forsake**___ animal meats, some do eat dairy products, such as milk and yogurt.

15. Far away on the horizon, we saw the tiny figures of a lonely traveler and his mule ___**recede**___ into the sunset.

16. None of us could figure out how the ___**ingenious**___ magician had managed to escape from the trunk submerged in the tank of water.

17. When you are really hungry, even the simplest foods, such as a slice of buttered bread, will be a delicious ___**repast**___.

18. Your ___**apparel**___ can be neat and attractive without being expensive.

19. Because I have reached an age at which I am unwilling to depend on my parents, I am out to find a(n) ___**gainful**___ occupation.

20. The terms of our agreement ___**expressly**___ forbade us to take any of the goods for our own use.

Writing: Words in Action

Answers to both prompts will vary.

1. Look back at "City of Gold" (pages 12–13). Suppose you will be traveling soon with the traders. You wonder what your trip will be like when you arrive in Timbuktu. Write a journal entry, describing what excites you about the trip and what worries you. Use at least two details from the passage and three Unit words.

2. Like the traders from the 1400s, countries continue to trade gold, salt, clothing, and other goods in the world market. How is trading in the 1400s different from how people trade in modern times? What goods are most valued today? Write a brief essay in which you support your observations with specific examples, studies, and the reading (refer to pages 12–13). Write at least three paragraphs, and use three or more words from this Unit.

Writing prompt #2 is modeled on that of standardized tests.

CCSS Vocabulary: 6; Writing: 1.c., 2.d., 3.d., 4. (See pp. T14–15.)

Vocabulary in Context: Informational Text for Unit 1 is available online at **vocabularyworkshop.com**.

The following excerpts are from the novel The Swiss Family Robinson *by Johann David Wyss. Some of the words you have studied in this Unit appear in* **boldface** *type. Complete each statement below the excerpt by circling the letter of the correct answer.*

1. I found Ernest busily engaged in weaving a basket in which to catch fish: he had devised it **ingeniously**, with a funnel-shaped entrance; through which the fish passing would not easily find their way out.

When something is created **ingeniously**, it requires

a. feelings **c.** imagination
b. payment **d.** patience

2. On her work-table [were] fishing-lines of all sorts, and knives and other tools.

These latter she told me were, with a chest of wearing **apparel**, almost the only things washed ashore after the wreck.

A chest packed with **apparel** is filled with

a. clothing **c.** jewels
b. books **d.** food

The classic novel *The Swiss Family Robinson* tells of the adventures of a family that becomes shipwrecked on a deserted island.

3. We found the whole family in a state of the greatest excitement, and I felt it necessary to calm them down as much as possible, for neither could I answer the questions with which I was **besieged,** nor could I conceal the fact that the visit of the vessel might not prove so advantageous as they expected.

Someone who is **besieged** with questions feels

a. angry **c.** pleased
b. overwhelmed **d.** calm

4. By this time the sun was sinking beneath the horizon, and the poultry, which had been straying to some little distance, gathered round us, and began to pick up the crumbs of biscuit which had fallen during our **repast**. My wife hereupon drew from her mysterious bag some handfuls of oats, peas, and other grain, and with them began to feed the poultry.

A **repast** is a

a. meal **c.** hike
b. gathering **d.** bucket

5. I heard [Ernest] loudly calling: "Father, father! I've caught a fish! An **immense** fellow he is. I can scarcely hold him, he drags the line so!"

A fish that is **immense** is NOT

a. massive **c.** large
b. significant **d.** small

UNIT 2

Note that not all of the 20 Unit words are used in this passage. *Assailant*, *constrain*, *incomprehensible*, *serene*, and *sheepish* are not included.

*Read the following passage, taking note of the **boldface** words and their contexts. These words are among those you will study in Unit 2. It may help you to complete the exercises in this Unit if you refer to the way the words are used below.*

CCSS Vocabulary: 4; Reading (Informational Text): 4, 6. (See pp. T14–15.)

West End School Has Comestible Curriculum

<Interview>

The Scrumptious Schoolyard is a grassroots program that transforms concrete playgrounds into functional farmland. Part of the Scrumptious Schoolyard Project, it is the brainchild of **contemporary** food-education pioneer Clarissa Z. Ochoa. Students explore the connection between what they eat and where it comes from through hands-on organic gardening and cooking classes. The "comestible curriculum" **encompasses** math, science, history, geography, social studies, and more.

Interviewer: Rosa, you're a sixth grade student gardener in the Scrumptious Schoolyard at T.R. Middle School in West End. Have you tried growing anything before?

Rosa: No, this is my first time, and now I have a green thumb. I might become a farmer or a chef, or both!

Interviewer: I heard that the Scrumptious Schoolyard concept was somewhat controversial in the beginning.

Rosa: It **ruffled** a few feathers. Some people were **disinterested**, while others were suspicious, **depicting** it as playing instead of learning. I think their complaints are **groundless**, and they really don't know what they're missing. It's amazing to watch something grow from a tiny seed. It takes a lot of **stamina** and enthusiasm to keep the gardens growing, but everyone works together.

Interviewer: What are some favorite experiences and things you've learned?

Rosa: I was excited when the blossoms on the squashes and pumpkins appeared. We made pumpkin pancakes and sauteed zucchini blossoms, so I actually cooked and ate a flower! Rule number one for gardeners is smart planning, and we need to get **maximum** use from our plot. Have you heard of companion planting? Plants are like people—some exist together better than others, so we **manipulate** the plants, materials, and space to get the best harvest. We also extend the natural growing seasons by **mimicking** Mother Nature with grow lights and mini-greenhouses.

Scrumptious Schoolyard student gardeners plant, tend, harvest, cook, and eat what they grow.

Interviewer: **Have you encountered any stumbling blocks so far?**

Rosa: We develop tools and strategies for overcoming **adverse** conditions. Our climate isn't extremely **arid**, but sometimes it's pretty dry, so we practice water conservation by using rain barrels. Also, the first time we tried to make compost, it was unbelievably smelly. You have to get the ingredients and layers right. The second time, it turned out great. One of our teachers calls compost "black gold."

One of the best parts of the Scrumptious Schoolyard program is eating what you've grown.

Interviewer: **Do you have a secret for attracting butterflies and bees to the garden?**

Rosa: We grow flowers that draw beneficial insects. Honeybees pollinate our plants, but the bees are in trouble because of Colony Collapse Disorder, so we try to do our part. Since our gardens are organic, we would be **hypocrites** if we used pesticides, so we're studying all-natural pest control. One raised bed has a *koinobori*, a Japanese fish kite that **billows** in the breeze and scares off scavengers.

Interviewer: **What would you say to other schools or kids interested in the program?**

Rosa: **Confront** obstacles and go for it! You may think one kid can't do much to help the environment or change how people eat, but working in the Scrumptious Schoolyard has made me believe we *can* make a big difference.

Interviewer: **Finally, I have to ask—do you really eat *all* the vegetables you're growing? I thought kids were supposed to hate vegetables.**

Rosa: There's no way I'm going to eat turnips. But it's good to try new things, according to my science teacher. We're still waiting to see *him* try turnips!

Audio

For iWords and audio passages, snap the code, or go to **vocabularyworkshop.com**.

Note the spelling, pronunciation, part(s) of speech, and definition(s) of each of the following words. Then write the appropriate form of the word in the blank spaces in the illustrative sentence(s) following. Finally, study the lists of synonyms and antonyms.

1. adverse (ad vərs′)

(*adj.*) unfavorable, negative; working against, hostile

Some people suffer an ____**adverse**____ reaction if they eat peanut butter or anything with peanuts.

SYNONYMS: difficult, trying
ANTONYMS: favorable, positive, helpful, beneficial

2. arid (ar′ id)

(*adj.*) extremely dry; uninteresting, dull

Although California leads the nation in farming, crops won't grow in its most ____**arid**____ regions.

SYNONYMS: waterless, parched, boring, unimaginative
ANTONYMS: waterlogged, soggy, fertile, lush

3. assailant (ə sa′ lənt)

(*n.*) a person who attacks violently (with blows or words)

The jogger was injured by an unknown ____**assailant**____, who left him immobile at the side of the road.

SYNONYMS: assaulter, mugger
ANTONYMS: victim, prey

4. billow (bil′ o)

(*n.*) a large wave; (*v.*) to rise or swell like a wave

The ocean ____**billows**____ rose and fell, attracting the most daring surfers.

Fans cheered enthusiastically when they saw their team's flags ____**billow**____ over the stadium.

SYNONYMS: (*n.*) breaker; (*v.*) surge, bulge, balloon
ANTONYMS: (*n.*) trough; (*v.*) deflate, collapse

5. confront (kən frənt′)

(*v.*) to meet face-to-face, especially as a challenge; come to grips with

In court, defendants can ____**confront**____ their accusers in a controlled setting.

SYNONYMS: face, encounter
ANTONYMS: avoid, evade, sidestep

6. constrain (kən strān′)

(*v.*) to force, compel; to restrain, hold back

You can't ____**constrain**____ me against my will.

SYNONYMS: pressure, confine, limit
ANTONYMS: loosen, liberate, unfetter, relax

CCSS Vocabulary: 4.c., 4.d. (See pp. T14–15.)

7. contemporary (kən tem′ pə rer ē)

(*adj.*) belonging to the same period of time as oneself; (*n.*) a person of the same time

His novel used a **contemporary** style but had a historical setting.

Rather than ask parents for help, teens often turn to a **contemporary** for advice.

SYNONYMS: (*adj.*) present-day, modern, current; (*n.*) peer
ANTONYMS: (*adj.*) ancient, prehistoric, antique, antiquated

8. depict (di pikt′)

(*v.*) to portray; to represent or show in the form of a picture

The painter chose to **depict** a plain prairie landscape using bold colors and shadows.

SYNONYMS: sketch, draw, picture, illustrate

9. disinterested (dis in′ trəst id)

(*adj.*) fair-minded, free from selfish motives; indifferent

A judge must remain **disinterested** in order to render an evenhanded and logical decision.

SYNONYMS: impartial, unbiased, apathetic
ANTONYMS: partial, biased, prejudiced

10. encompass (en kəm′ pəs)

(*v.*) to encircle, go or reach around; to enclose; to include with a certain group or class

Oceans **encompass** about three-fourths of the surface of our planet.

SYNONYMS: surround, envelop, comprise
ANTONYMS: leave out, omit, exclude

11. groundless (graůnd′ ləs)

(*adj.*) without any good reason or cause, unjustified

Kate's **groundless** fear of hurting herself during exercise has left her weak and out of shape.

SYNONYMS: baseless, unsupported
ANTONYMS: well-founded, reasonable, justified

12. hypocrite (hip′ ə krit)

(*n.*) a person who pretends to be what he or she is not or better than he or she really is; a two-faced person

The speaker who said one thing but did something else entirely was regarded as a **hypocrite**.

SYNONYMS: phony, charlatan, fraud

13. incomprehensible (in käm pri hen′ sə bəl)

(*adj.*) impossible to understand

Our school's intercom system is so old that this morning's announcements were almost **incomprehensible**.

SYNONYMS: baffling, confusing, bewildering
ANTONYMS: understandable, plain, intelligible

CCSS Vocabulary: 4.c., 4.d. (See pp. T14–15.)

14. manipulate (mə nip′ yə lāt)

(*v.*) to handle or use skillfully; to manage or control for personal gain or advantage

Scientists should not ___**manipulate**___ data.

SYNONYMS: work, maneuver, exploit, influence

15. maximum (mak′ sə məm)

(*n.*) the greatest possible amount or degree; (*adj.*) reaching the greatest possible amount or degree

This postage scale can weigh a ___**maximum**___ of only five pounds.

To ease the patient's suffering, the doctor prescribed the ___**maximum**___ dosage of painkillers.

SYNONYMS: highest, utmost
ANTONYMS: least, lowest, minimum, smallest

16. mimic (mim′ ik)

(*n.*) a person who does imitations; (*v.*) to imitate; to make fun of

The comedy troupe needs to hire a ___**mimic**___.

Troy can ___**mimic**___ any accent he hears.

SYNONYMS: (*n.*) copycat, impersonator; (*v.*) parrot, impersonate

17. ruffle (rəf′ əl)

(*v.*) to wrinkle, make uneven; to annoy, upset; to flip through; (*n.*) material used for trimming edges; a ripple; a low drumbeat

His wisecracks always ___**ruffle**___ my feelings.

My favorite pillow has a velvet ___**ruffle**___.

SYNONYMS: (*v.*) disturb; (*n.*) frill
ANTONYMS: (*v.*) smooth out, soothe

18. serene (sə rēn′)

(*adj.*) peaceful, calm; free of emotional upset; clear and free of storm; majestic, grand

She stayed ___**serene**___ in the face of chaos.

SYNONYMS: composed, fair, august
ANTONYMS: agitated, troubled, inclement

19. sheepish (shēp′ ish)

(*adj.*) embarrassed; resembling a sheep in meekness, timid

His ___**sheepish**___ grin made the crowds cheer all the more for his unlikely victory.

SYNONYMS: shamefaced, meek
ANTONYMS: bold, saucy, brazen

20. stamina (stam′ ə nə)

(*n.*) the strength needed to keep going or overcome physical or mental strain; staying power

Marathon runners need a great deal of ___**stamina**___ to cover the many miles.

SYNONYM: endurance

CCSS Vocabulary: 4.c., 4.d. (See pp. T14–15.)

Choosing the Right Word

*Select the **boldface** word that better completes each sentence. You might refer to the passage on pages 22–23 to see how most of these words are used in context.*

1. After many stormy years in the service of his country, George Washington retired to the (**serene, adverse**) life of his beloved Mount Vernon.

2. His decision not to accept our sincere offer of assistance is completely (**disinterested, incomprehensible**) to me.

3. We expected the lecture on the energy crisis to be exciting, but it turned out to be a(n) (**ruffled, arid**) rundown of well-known facts and figures.

George Washington's home, Mount Vernon

4. After giving a few (**sheepish, serene**) excuses, the swimmers packed up and left the private beach.

5. Anyone who has ever sailed a small boat knows how thrilling it is to feel the spray in your face while the sails (**billow, encompass**) overhead.

6. After the storm, residents were (**constrained, depicted**) to stay in their homes, as all roads were impassable.

7. The big-league shortstop (**manipulates, constrains**) his glove like a magician, snaring every ball hit within reach.

8. After living for many years in that roomy old farmhouse, I felt awfully (**arid, constrained**) in that small apartment.

9. While some find her smile comical, I have always found the Mona Lisa's smile to be (**serene, sheepish**) and mysterious.

10. If you (**billow, confront**) your problems honestly and openly, instead of trying to hide them, you will have a better chance of solving them.

11. Do you think it would be a good idea to set a (**maximum, contemporary**) figure for the amount of homework any teacher is allowed to assign?

12. A good scientist must have a keen mind, an unquenchable curiosity, and a (**groundless, disinterested**) desire to discover the truth.

13. She has gained success as a writer who knows how to (**confront, depict**) in a lifelike way the hopes, fears, and problems of young people today.

14. She has many interesting ideas, but she seems to lack the physical and mental (**stamina, assailant**) to make good use of them.

15. The man was trying to (**depict, manipulate**) the young woman as a troublemaker, simply because she had dyed her hair purple and dressed in an unusual manner.

CCSS Vocabulary: 4.d. (See pp. T14–15.)

16. My idea of a(n) (**assailant, hypocrite**) is a person who gives advice that he or she is not willing to follow.

17. The (**adverse, sheepish**) publicity that he received during the investigation was probably the cause of his defeat in the next election.

18. Instead of working so hard to (**mimic, ruffle**) popular TV stars, why don't you try to develop an acting style of your own?

19. It was (**groundless, incomprehensible**) to think that our grandparents had to spend sweltering summers without air-conditioning.

20. The science program in our school (**depicts, encompasses**) biology, chemistry, physics, earth science, and other related courses.

21. I didn't want to (**ruffle, manipulate**) the feelings of the hotel manager, but I felt that I had to complain about the miserable service.

22. Despite the fact that she was in shock, the victim gave a clear description of her (**hypocrite, assailant**).

23. Martin Luther King, Jr. and Robert F. Kennedy were (**contemporaries, mimics**), born within a few years of each other.

24. What a relief to learn that my parents had been delayed by a storm, and that all my fears about an accident were (**groundless, maximum**)!

25. Report any (**sheepish, adverse**) side effects to your doctor immediately.

Choose the word from this Unit that is the same or most nearly the same in meaning as the ***boldface*** *word or expression in the phrase. Write that word on the line. Use a dictionary if necessary.*

1. possesses **determination** for the walkathon ____stamina____
2. the **largest** quantity available ____maximum____
3. always remembered the **attacker's** voice ____assailant____
4. able to **replicate** a bird's call ____mimic____
5. ran away with a **humiliated** look ____sheepish____
6. confused by the child's **puzzling** behavior ____incomprehensible____
7. mistrustful of that **impostor** ____hypocrite____
8. a **tranquil** expanse of clear blue sky ____serene____
9. tried to **restrict** the patient ____constrain____
10. to serve as a **neutral** witness ____disinterested____

CCSS Vocabulary: 5. (See pp. T14–15.)

The synonyms and antonyms here do not appear on the Definitions pages.

Choose the word from this Unit that is most nearly opposite in meaning to the ***boldface*** *word or expression in the phrase. Write that word on the line. Use a dictionary if necessary.*

1. exhibits a **confident** attitude ____sheepish____
2. hopes to **release** the prisoner soon ____constrain____
3. trying to control his **stormy** emotions ____serene____
4. protecting the **injured party** ____assailant____
5. rules that are quite **clear** ____incomprehensible____

Completing the Sentence

From the words in this Unit, choose the one that best completes each of the following sentences. Write the correct word form in the space provided.

1. As you become a more skillful driver, you will be able to ____manipulate____ all the controls of the car while keeping your eyes on the road.

2. This basic textbook ____encompasses____ all the information you will have to master for the entrance examination.

3. The jury found the defendant "not guilty" because they were convinced that the charges against her were ____groundless____.

4. You and Lucy will never settle your quarrel unless you ____confront____ each other directly and listen to what the other person has to say.

5. The brisk breeze caused the sheets on the line to ____billow____ like the sails on a yacht that is running with the wind.

6. Under the law, the ____maximum____ number of people who may ride in this bus is seventy-five.

7. For a long time, I thought that he was a good and sincere person, but I finally saw that he was no more than a(n) ____hypocrite____.

8. I was so embarrassed by my blunder that I could do nothing but grin in a(n) ____sheepish____ and self-conscious way.

9. The hot, ____arid____ climate of Arizona is favorable for many people suffering from various diseases, such as arthritis.

10. Since Tom is both smart and ____disinterested____, I think he is just the person to decide which of us is right in this long and bitter quarrel.

11. The skyscraper is one of the best-known and widely admired forms of **contemporary** architecture.

12. A breeze sprang up and began to **ruffle** the smooth and tranquil surface of the water.

13. You talk so fast and in such a low tone of voice that you are going to be completely **incomprehensible** to most people.

14. Although I may hurt your feelings, my conscience **constrained** me to tell you exactly what is on my mind.

15. Held back by **adverse** winds, the plane arrived at the airport two hours late.

16. Fortunately, I was able to fight off my **assailant**, even though his attack took me by complete surprise.

17. Parrots and a few other kinds of birds can **mimic** sounds, particularly human speech.

18. The **serene** expression on her face showed that she was totally undisturbed by the confusion and turmoil around her.

19. Using the entire east wall of the new post office building, the painter tried to **depict** the founding of our city.

20. Very few starting pitchers have the **stamina** to pitch consistently well for nine innings.

Writing: Words in Action

Answers to both prompts will vary.

1. Look back at "West End School Has Comestible Curriculum" (pages 22–23). Suppose you have been asked to speak to your classmates about starting a similar program at your school. You have to persuade them that a Scrumptious Schoolyard is a great idea. Write a speech using at least two details from the passage and three Unit words to support your position.

2. There is much discussion these days about eating healthy, organic foods. Some people associate healthy and organic diets with bland-tasting, expensive food and preparation that is too complicated and time-consuming. Can healthy foods be tasty? Do you think a healthy diet requires too much effort? Write a brief essay in which you support your opinion with specific examples, personal experience, and, if relevant, the reading (refer to pages 22–23). Write at least three paragraphs, and use three or more words from this Unit.

Writing prompt #2 is modeled on that of standardized tests.

CCSS Vocabulary: 6; Writing: 1.c., 2.d., 3.d., 4. (See pp. T14–15.)

Vocabulary in Context: Informational Text for Unit 2 is available online at **vocabularyworkshop.com**.

The following excerpts are from Leaves of Grass, *a collection of poems by Walt Whitman. Some of the words you have studied in this Unit appear in* **boldface** *type. Complete each statement below the excerpt by circling the letter of the correct answer.*

1. Thou ever-darting Globe! through Space and Air!
Thou waters that **encompass** us!
Thou that in all the life and death of us, in action or in sleep!
Thou laws invisible that permeate them and all,
Thou that in all, and over all, and through and under all, incessant!

Waters that **encompass** the Globe

a. cover it
b. expose it
c. widen it
d. seep into it

2. Those that look carelessly in the faces of Presidents and governors, as to say Who are you?
Those of earth-born passion, simple, never **constrain'd**, never obedient,
Those of inland America.

Someone who is NOT **constrained** is

a. controlled
b. restricted
c. free
d. loyal

3. The mocking-bird, the American **mimic**, singing all the forenoon,
singing through the moon-lit night. . .

A bird that is a **mimic** is a(n)

a. originator
b. traitor
c. creator
d. imitator

Whitman, an American poet, wrote in a free-verse style that has influenced modern poetry.

4. Far, far at sea,
After the night's fierce drifts have strewn the shore with wrecks,
With re-appearing day as now so happy and **serene**,
The rosy and elastic dawn, the flashing sun....

A **serene** day is one that is

a. blistering
b. soothing
c. humid
d. noisy

5. ....O to be self-balanced for contingencies,
To **confront** night, storms, hunger, ridicule,
accidents, rebuffs, as the trees and animals do.

To **confront** something is to

a. ignore it
b. alert it
c. tackle it
d. support it

Snap the code, or go to **vocabularyworkshop.com**

CCSS Vocabulary: 4.d.; Reading (Literature): 4. (See pp. T14–15.)

UNIT 3

Note that not all of the 20 Unit words are used in this passage. *Bigot*, *designate*, *global*, *pacifist*, and *terrain* are not included.

*Read the following passage, taking note of the **boldface** words and their contexts. These words are among those you will be studying in Unit 3. It may help you to complete the exercises in this Unit if you refer to the way the words are used below.*

CCSS Vocabulary: 4; Reading (Informational Text): 4, 6. (See pp. T14–15.)

This Day in 1923: The *Olympic*'s the Thing!

<Archived Newspaper Article>

Before planes whisked people around the world in a day, travelers sailed to their destinations on large ocean liners. Shipping companies such as the Cunard Line and the White Star Line competed with each other to build the largest, most luxurious ships. Today the Times *archives presents a 1923 feature article about one of the most glamorous of all sea-going vessels, the* Olympic.

Tug boats push the *Olympic* out of the New York Harbour in 1912.

London, June 24, 1923—As the White Star Liner *Olympic* shoved off from New York last Monday, I stood on its giant deck and gazed at the open sea. I've traveled on big ships before, but never one quite so big. I felt small on its sprawling decks and a bit in awe of the vessel's size. I stood quietly. The **enigma** of the ocean and the equally mysterious grandeur of this gigantic boat surrounded me.

For a time the *Olympic* was the largest ocean liner in the world. She was matched once by her sister ship, the doomed *Titanic*. The *Olympic* has been plying the seas since her maiden voyage in 1910. In World War I she entered military service. She transported troops about the Atlantic. Incredibly, the *Olympic* was the only merchant vessel to sink an enemy warship during the war. She rammed a German submarine, the U-103, and sent it underwater for good. That was five years ago, in the spring of 1918.

Today on the *Olympic*, the war is ancient history. Happy passengers wander the ship. Linger in one spot, and you might be **waylaid** by a passenger who wants a partner for a game of that geat racquet sport, squash, or for shuffleboard. And the dining rooms are full of good eating. There's a great **diversity** of food, with English, French, and American cuisine on the menu. A variety of beverages is also available for guests to **slake** their summer thirsts. Open-air settings provide the **illusion** of relaxing at a Mediterranean café. At every turn, there's another surprise, another lounge, another entertainment. I've made several trips between the library and the swimming pool. And I've **vowed** to visit the gym before we get to England. I'm sure I will—just as soon as that **infuriating**

The fabulous promenade deck

Passengers enjoy the open air on deck.

fellow with the squash racquet stops irritating me and sits down for a bite to eat. Perhaps he'll trot off somewhere to **gloat** about his latest score.

The Turkish baths are a favorite stop for many guests. This area has rooms of the most fantastic decoration. They are decked out from top to bottom. The floors and walls are dressed in colorful tiles. The decoration is so fine and abundant that any more would have been gilding the lily. What **sage** was it who knew to stop at this perfection? Each day I am **motivated** to return to the baths. All cares seem to **wither** away under the **barrage** of care and attention the attendants shower upon visitors there.

If I could make it my **vocation** to wander the earth on ships like this, I'd **queue** up for the job without a moment's hesitation.

But obligation **restricts** the choices we make. My life's work lies ashore. Tomorrow we'll arrive in Southampton, England. I'll attend to my business there and look forward to the return trip to New York. Then it's back to the usual routine. For the time being, I'm happy to report, the sun is setting, the squash racquets are tucked away, and all's well on the *Olympic*.

Famous Ladies who use

The Hon. Mrs. Alfred Lyttelton

The Hon. Mrs. Alfred Lyttelton writes: "I always keep a bottle of Formamint Tablets in the house, as I think them quite excellent for Sore Throat."

The Marchioness of Sligo

"The Most Hon. the Marchioness of Sligo finds Formamint Tablets very useful for Sore Throats, and always has a bottle of it in the house."

All Chen
genuine
to A. W
of Sanat

Audio

For iWords and audio passages, snap the code, or go to **vocabularyworkshop.com**.

Note the spelling, pronunciation, part(s) of speech, and definition(s) of each of the following words. Then write the appropriate form of the word in the blank spaces in the illustrative sentence(s) following. Finally, study the lists of synonyms and antonyms.

1. barrage (bə räzh′)

(*n.*) a rapid, large-scale outpouring of something

The governor faced a **barrage** of questions about possible budget cuts.

SYNONYMS: bombardment, shelling, volley, blast

2. bigot (big′ ət)

(*n.*) an intolerant, prejudiced, or biased person

When you speak in that narrow-minded way, you sound like a **bigot**.

SYNONYM: racist

3. designate (dez′ ig nāt)

(*v.*) to indicate, point out; to appoint; (*adj.*) selected but not yet installed

Will you please tell me when the coach will **designate** a team leader?

The new student council **designate** is looking forward to making many changes to the student government.

SYNONYMS: (*v.*) name, signify, denote, nominate

4. diversity (di vər′ sə tē)

(*n.*) difference, variety; a condition of having many different types or forms

Our science teacher has a **diversity** of interests, including an appreciation of Russian literature.

SYNONYM: dissimilarity
ANTONYMS: similarity, sameness, uniformity

5. enigma (i nig′ mə)

(*n.*) someone or something that is extremely puzzling; that which cannot be understood or explained

Critics complained that the plot twists in the new mystery movie make it an **enigma**.

SYNONYMS: riddle, mystery, puzzle, conundrum

6. gloat (glōt)

(*v.*) to look at or think about with great intensity and satisfaction; to take great personal joy in

I will try not to **gloat** about winning a scholarship to music camp.

SYNONYMS: relish, revel in, crow over
ANTONYMS: regret, bemoan, mourn, feel chagrined

CCSS Vocabulary: 4.c., 4.d. (See pp. T14–15.)

7. global
(glō′ bəl)

(*adj.*) of, relating to, or involving the entire world; comprehensive

E-mail and the Internet have linked the entire world into a ____**global**____ village.

SYNONYMS: worldwide, universal, widespread
ANTONYMS: regional, provincial

8. illusion
(i lü′ zhən)

(*n.*) a false idea; something that one seems to see or to be aware of that really does not exist

Magicians use optical ____**illusions**____ to amaze their audiences.

SYNONYMS: delusion, fantasy
ANTONYMS: reality, truth, actuality

9. infuriate
(in fyu̇r′ ē āt)

(*v.*) to make very angry, enrage

It ____**infuriates**____ most parents when their children refuse to listen to them and treat them with disrespect.

SYNONYMS: provoke, incense, madden
ANTONYMS: calm, soothe, pacify, please

10. motivate
(mō′ tə vāt)

(*v.*) to provide with a reason for doing; to push on to some goal

How can we ____**motivate**____ the students to undertake more challenging work?

SYNONYMS: spur on, encourage, prompt, goad
ANTONYMS: discourage, dissuade, disincline

11. pacifist
(pas′ ə fist)

(*n.*) one who is against war or the use of violence;
(*adj.*) opposing war or violence

Martin Luther King, Jr., was a ____**pacifist**____ who influenced the civil rights movement.

____**Pacifist**____ students protested the war.

SYNONYMS: (*n.*) peacemaker, dove; ANTONYM: (*n.*) warmonger

12. queue
(kyü)

(*n.*) a line of people waiting for something (such as a bus);
(*v.*) to form such a line

A long ____**queue**____ formed at the bus stop.

Eager fans ____**queue**____ up for the best seats.

SYNONYMS: (*n.*) column, file, row, line
ANTONYM: (*n.*) disorganized crowd

13. restrict
(ri strikt′)

(*v.*) to keep within set limits; to confine

Doctors often advise patients to ____**restrict**____ their intake of fatty or salty foods.

SYNONYMS: hold back, limit; ANTONYMS: open up, enlarge, expand

14. sage (sāj)

(*adj.*) wise; (*n.*) a very wise person

My aunt always gives me **sage** advice.

Let's ask the **sage** for guidance.

SYNONYMS: (*adj.*) sagacious; (*n.*) philosopher, Solomon
ANTONYMS: (*adj.*) foolish, unwise; (*n.*) fool, dunce

15. slake (slāk)

(*v.*) to satisfy, relieve, or bring to an end

Nothing can **slake** thirst better than water.

SYNONYMS: gratify, sate, ease, assuage
ANTONYMS: increase, intensify, aggravate

16. terrain (tə rān′)

(*n.*) the landscape, especially its physical features or fitness for some use; a field of knowledge

Mountain bikes are designed to withstand even the most rugged **terrain**.

SYNONYMS: ground, topography, territory

17. vocation (vō kā′ shən)

(*n.*) any trade, profession, or occupation; a sense of fitness or special calling for one's work

After many years of searching, she found her true **vocation** as a horse trainer.

SYNONYMS: career, pursuit
ANTONYMS: hobby, pastime, avocation

18. vow (vau̇)

(*n.*) a solemn or sacred promise or pledge; (*v.*) to declare or promise in a solemn way

Prince Hamlet made a solemn **vow** to avenge his father's murder.

A bride and groom **vow** to love each other throughout their marriage.

SYNONYMS: (*n.*) word of honor; (*v.*) pledge

19. waylay (wā′ lā)

(*v.*) to lie in wait for and attack, ambush

Thugs will often choose to **waylay** weary travelers as they make their way home.

SYNONYMS: entrap, ensnare

20. wither (wiṯh′ ər)

(*v.*) to dry up, wilt, sag; to cause someone to feel ashamed, humiliated, or very small

Despite people's best efforts to remain young looking, skin will eventually **wither** with age.

SYNONYMS: shrivel, droop, shame, abash
ANTONYMS: bloom, flower, flourish, burgeon

CCSS Vocabulary: 4.c., 4.d. (See pp. T14–15.)

Choosing the Right Word

*Select the **boldface** word that better completes each sentence. You might refer to the passage on pages 32–33 to see how most of these words are used in context.*

1. Jane Addams was an outspoken (**pacifist, enigma**), yet her views about war were not embraced by everyone.

2. No matter what it may cost me to carry out, I will never break my sacred (**vow, illusion**).

3. Just how and why two people fall in love is a(n) (**queue, enigma**) that no scientist has ever been able to explain.

4. A good loser doesn't sulk over defeat; a good winner doesn't (**gloat, vow**) after victory.

5. A great teacher not only makes the material of the course understandable but also (**infuriates, motivates**) the students to want to learn more.

6. The applicants for the job will have to (**queue, slake**) up in an orderly way and wait their turns to be interviewed.

Jane Addams was a social reformer whose work earned her a Nobel Peace Prize in 1931.

7. The United States has laws that (**restrict, waylay**) the numbers and kinds of immigrants allowed to enter this country.

8. She is never bored because she has a great (**enigma, diversity**) of interests, ranging from folk dancing to mathematics.

9. Her analysis of what is wrong with our city government seems to me remarkably (**sage, global**) and helpful.

10. Because Sam is so good at stealing bases, he has become the (**slake, designated**) runner for our baseball team.

11. By the time you are old enough to enter the workforce, many (**sages, vocations**) that are important today may not even exist anymore.

12. Many view Shakespeare as the timeless (**illusion, sage**) and constantly use his words to give advice.

13. The children who are admitted free to the ball game will be allowed to sit only in certain (**motivated, designated**) parts of the stands.

14. President Jefferson sent Lewis and Clark to survey water routes, animals, plant life, and the (**terrain, waylay**) of the Louisiana Territory.

15. As the defense attorney left the courtroom, he was (**waylaid, designated**) by a group of eager reporters trying to get a statement from him.

CCSS Vocabulary: 4.d. (See pp. T14–15.)

16. Entangled in the trapper's net, the (**infuriated, withered**) lion thrashed at the ropes and roared in helpless anger.

17. With the other team ten points ahead and only a few minutes left to play, our hopes of victory began to (**gloat, wither**).

18. As you have so many prejudices of your own, you should think twice before you accuse other people of being (**enigmas, bigots**).

19. Because I am convinced that violence always creates more problems than it solves, I have become a (**pacifist, bigot**).

20. To (**slake, restrict**) our curiosity, you will have to tell us everything that happened during that strange trip.

21. Before we begin our backpacking trip, we should have a good idea of the (**terrain, vocation**) we are going to cover.

22. Has it ever occurred to you that your belief that you are a superior person and a natural leader may be no more than a(n) (**barrage, illusion**)?

23. World War II was a truly (**global, pacifist**) struggle, fought in all parts of the world by people of every race and background.

24. When the speaker asked for opinions from the audience, he was greeted with a (**terrain, barrage**) of critical remarks and angry questions.

25. Lilies are delicate and will (**wither, vow**) quickly if not protected from the hot sun.

Choose the word from this Unit that is the same or most nearly the same in meaning as the ***boldface*** *word or expression in the phrase. Write that word on the line. Use a dictionary if necessary.*

1. offering trades on the **international** market — global
2. **quench** their cravings for a refreshing drink — slake
3. a plot to **trap** unsuspecting victims — waylay
4. close-ups of the **land** of Mars — terrain
5. must **assure** to tell the truth — vow
6. ignore the ravings of **prejudiced people** — bigots
7. the magician's most unique **deception** — illusion
8. was once a **conscientious objector** — pacifist
9. trying to **irritate** the manager — infuriate
10. **choose** it as the team's new logo — designate

CCSS Vocabulary: 5. (See pp. T14–15.)

The synonyms and antonyms here do not appear on the Definitions page.

Antonyms

*Choose the word from this Unit that is most nearly opposite in meaning to the **boldface** word or expression in the phrase. Write that word on the line. Use a dictionary if necessary.*

1. wants to **withdraw** his name as candidate ______designate______
2. finding particles of pollen in the **atmosphere** ______terrain______
3. tries to be a **fair-minded person** ______bigot______
4. speeches given by a notable **hawk** ______pacifist______
5. part of a **local** charity fund ______global______

Completing the Sentence

From the words in this Unit, choose the one that best completes each of the following sentences. Write the correct word form in the space provided.

1. A person can usually tell how popular a new movie is by the length of the ______queue______ in front of the box office.
2. Even before the new president took office, he ______designated______ the men and women who were to serve in his cabinet.
3. Because the show is scheduled to end after midnight, the management will ______restrict______ admission to people over sixteen years old.
4. For better or for worse, as you become older and more experienced, you will lose many of the comforting ______illusions______ of youth.
5. Nothing ______infuriates______ my boss more than an employee who is late for work and then offers a foolish excuse for not arriving on time.
6. Our hike was not very long, but the ______terrain______ was so rocky and hilly that we were exhausted by the time we reached our goal.
7. As he greatly enjoys woodworking and also makes a living from it, his hobby and his ______vocation______ are one and the same.
8. I came to regard my grandmother as a(n) ______sage______ whose wisdom helped solve many family problems.
9. The pollution problem, far from being limited to the United States, is truly ______global______ in scope.
10. As she was sworn in, she made a(n) ______vow______ that she would never use the powers of her office for selfish or unworthy purposes.

CCSS Vocabulary: 4.a., 5. (See pp. T14–15.)

11. The police now believe that the mugger **waylaid** the victim as she entered the elevator of her apartment house.

12. No decent or kind person will **gloat** over someone else's failures or misfortunes.

13. The desire to be the world's top tennis player **motivated** the young woman to spend hours every day improving her game.

14. Is it possible to be a(n) **pacifist** in a world where so many people are using force to take unfair advantage of others?

15. The deadly **barrage** of shells from our guns pinned down the enemy troops on the narrow beach where they had landed.

16. The animals in the drought area traveled for many miles to reach a body of water where they could **slake** their thirst.

17. The rich **diversity** of plant and animal life in a tropical rain forest never ceases to amaze me.

18. How sad it is to see such beautiful flowers **wither** and die!

19. I don't understand what he is aiming at or why he behaves as he does; in fact, his whole personality is a(n) **enigma** to me.

20. Like a typical **bigot**, he believes that any customs different from his own are "wrong" and "uncivilized."

Writing: Words in Action

Answers to both prompts will vary.

1. Look back at "This Day in 1923: The *Olympic's* the Thing!" (pages 32–33). Suppose your job is to write a radio announcement that persuades people to take a cruise on the *Olympic*. Write an advertisement, using at least two details from the passage and three Unit words.

2. *"Experience, travel—these are an education in themselves."—Euripides*

   Travel not only provides people with unique and memorable experiences, but it also gives them opportunities to learn about new cultures and consider different outlooks. Think about the quotation from Euripides shown above. Do you agree with this outlook? In what ways can experience and travel be educational? Write a brief essay in which you support your opinion with specific examples, personal experience, your studies, and the reading (refer to pages 32–33). Write at least two paragraphs, and use three or more words from this Unit.

Writing prompt #2 is modeled on that of standardized tests.

CCSS Vocabulary: 6; Writing: 1.c., 2.d., 3.d., 4. (See pp. T14–15.)

Vocabulary in Context: Informational Text for Unit 3 is available online at **vocabularyworkshop.com**.

The following excerpts are from Twenty Thousand Leagues Under the Sea *by Jules Verne. Some of the words you have studied in this Unit appear in* **boldface** *type. Complete each statement below the excerpt by circling the letter of the correct answer.*

1. Commander Farragut was a good seaman, worthy of the frigate he commanded. His ship and he were one. He was its very soul. On the *cetacean* [whale] question no doubts arose in his mind, and he didn't allow the animal's existence to be disputed aboard his vessel.... The monster existed, and he had **vowed** to rid the seas of it.

If a person has **vowed**, he or she has

a. questioned
b. judged
c. promised
d. waited

2. Three seconds after reading this letter from the honorable Secretary of the Navy, I understood at last that my true **vocation**, my sole purpose in life, was to hunt down this disturbing monster and rid the world of it.

A **vocation** is a(n)

a. occupation
b. command
c. enemy
d. hobby

In Jules Verne's novel, Captain Nemo and his crew confronted many "monsters" of the sea.

3. Science has defined the **global** paths of five chief currents: one in the north Atlantic, a second in the south Atlantic, a third in the north Pacific, a fourth in the south Pacific, and a fifth in the southern Indian Ocean.

Something that is **global** is

a. limited
b. native
c. worldwide
d. confined

4. This chase dragged on for about three-quarters of an hour.... At this rate, it was obvious that we would never catch up with it.

Infuriated, Commander Farragut kept twisting the thick tuft of hair that flourished below his chin.

Someone who is **infuriated** is definitely NOT

a. furious
b. irate
c. upset
d. serene

5. I wanted to preserve a few specimens of these delicate zoophytes, but they were merely clouds, shadows, **illusions**, melting and evaporating outside their native element.

Illusions are

a. fantasies
b. studies
c. challenges
d. secrets

Snap the code, or go to **vocabularyworkshop.com**

Vocabulary for Comprehension

*Read the following passage in which some of the words you have studied in Units 1–3 appear in **boldface** type. Then answer the questions on page 43.*

This passage discusses how, from its humble beginnings, the annual winter festival in Sapporo, Japan, has become a world-class event.

(Line)

Picture a vast castle, or imagine an oversized cartoon figure. Now try to imagine each of them made of snow and ice. This is what you might see if you attend the Sapporo Snow Festival, a weeklong event held each year in northern Japan, on the island of Hokkaido.

Unlike other cities in Japan, Sapporo is fairly young. It has no ancient temples. Its streets are unusually wide and straight. The city is a popular destination for those who enjoy winter sports. In fact, the 1972 Winter Olympic Games were held in Sapporo.

The Sapporo Snow Festival draws both young and old into its wintry wonderland fantasies. Most people familiar with winter festivals **designate** the Sapporo Snow Festival as the most famous of its kind. The city plans ahead for months. It is impossible for visitors to get hotel rooms without **expressly** reserving them far in advance.

The Sapporo Snow Festival had modest beginnings. In 1950, high school students made six snow sculptures in a **serene** park in the center of town. What began as fun for creative teenagers has grown into an event that has **global** appeal. Odori Park, the location of those first snow sculptures, continues to be one of the three main festival sites.

Since the early days, much of the work to mount the festival has been done by the Self-Defense Forces. This branch of the Japanese military **dispatches** hundreds of soldiers in army trucks to haul snow from nearby mountains into the city. This peacetime work serves the public and keeps festival costs down.

Visitors to the Snow Festival today might see gigantic sculptures that **depict** prehistoric animals, Viking warriors, famous people, and even cartoon characters! Bands play music from atop huge sound stages built of snow. Daredevils can zoom down elaborate ice slides. Nightly fireworks, colored lights, and other special sound and lighting effects add extra excitement.

Make your reservations now!

CCSS Vocabulary: 4.a.; Reading (Informational Text): 2, 4, 6. (See pp. T14–15.)

1. The primary purpose of the passage is to
   a. entertain the reader with amusing anecdotes
   b. praise the Japanese Self-Defense Forces
   c. describe traditional Japanese customs
   d. persuade other cities to hold winter snow festivals
   (e.) inform the reader about the Sapporo Snow Festival

2. The meaning of **designate** (line 21) is
   (a.) name
   b. deny
   c. attend
   d. avoid
   e. photograph

3. **Expressly** (line 25) most nearly means
   a. efficiently
   (b.) explicitly
   c. tentatively
   d. accidentally
   e. quickly

4. Paragraph 3 (lines 17–26) focuses on the festival's
   a. rules
   b. history
   c. artists
   (d.) attendance
   e. main events

5. **Serene** (line 30) is best defined as
   a. pretty
   b. popular
   (c.) tranquil
   d. enormous
   e. municipal

6. The meaning of **global** (line 33) is
   (a.) widespread
   b. mysterious
   c. regional
   d. limited
   e. festive

7. How did the Sapporo Snow Festival get started in the 1950s?
   a. The Winter Olympic Games were held in Sapporo.
   b. A winter wedding was held outdoors in Odori Park.
   (c.) High school students built six snow sculptures in a park.
   d. The city held a competition for best snow sculptures.
   e. A great blizzard dumped three feet of snow on Sapporo.

8. **Dispatches** (line 41) means
   a. trains
   b. joins with
   c. recruits
   (d.) sends out
   e. rewards

9. **Depict** (line 48) is best defined as
   a. restore
   b. analyze
   c. replace
   d. surround
   (e.) represent

10. Which word best describes the author's attitude toward the subject?
    a. skeptical
    (b.) enthusiastic
    c. formal
    d. solemn
    e. critical

11. You can infer from the passage that the author is trying to
    (a.) promote attendance at the festival
    b. analyze athletic events in Japan
    c. suggest festival improvements
    d. caution visitors about dangers
    e. encourage other cities to hold festivals

12. In paragraph 6 (lines 46–56), the author makes the festival come alive by using many
    a. statistics
    (b.) sensory details
    c. exaggerations
    d. generalizations
    e. exclamation points

CCSS Vocabulary: 4.a.; Reading (Informational Text): 2, 4, 6. (See pp. T14–15.)

Two-Word Completions

Select the pair of words that best completes the meaning of each of the following sentences.

1. The demand for tickets to the play-offs was so heavy that for days the box office was ________________ like some embattled fortress by mobs of people waiting more or less impatiently in long ________________ that snaked endlessly around the whole block.

a. denounced . . . enigmas
b. besieged . . . queues
c. confronted . . . ruffles
d. encompassed . . . billows

2. As the travelers crossed the hot and ________________ wasteland known as the Sahara Desert, their eyes were deceived more than once by mirages and other optical ________________.

a. adverse . . . mimics
b. immense . . . vocations
c. groundless . . . enigmas
d. arid . . . illusions

3. Despite the ________________ of vigorous insults coming from the other gubernatorial candidate, she refused to retaliate and ________________ her competition.

a. illusion . . . libel
b. billow . . . infuriate
c. apparel . . . besiege
d. barrage . . . denounce

4. Two ruffians ________________ the weary traveler on a lonely stretch of road, but the man was able to beat off his ________________ with the help of his stout staff.

a. waylaid . . . assailants
b. dispatched . . . oafs
c. confronted . . . hypocrites
d. constrained . . . pacifists

5. It took a great deal of ________________ to keep up with the rest of the pack as they sped across the broken and hilly ________________ that separated them from the finish line in the cross-country race.

a. dispatch . . . apparel
b. misgiving . . . repast
c. stamina . . . terrain
d. diversity . . . barrage

6. Though other people have been moved to action by high ideals, Thomas Alva Edison, one of the most ________________ inventors ever to be produced by this country, seems in part to have been ________________ simply by the love of a challenge.

a. disinterested . . . manipulated
b. ingenious . . . motivated
c. inept . . . infuriated
d. immense . . . dispatched

7. Running a marathon leaves athletes feeling ________________, but months of training provide them with the incentive to reach the finish line before heading off to a satisfying ________________.

a. groundless . . . vocation
b. famished . . . repast
c. inept . . . barrage
d. adverse . . . terrain

 CCSS Vocabulary: 4.a. (See pp. T14–15.)

In the passage about the luxury liner, the *Olympic* (see pages 32–33), the narrator describes the decorations in the Turkish baths and mentions that adding more would have been "gilding the lily."

"Gilding the lily" is an idiom that means "adding extra adornments to something that is already beautiful." An **idiom** is a figure of speech or an informal expression that is not meant literally. When you say that someone is "gilding the lily," you are saying that the person is adding additional and probably unnecessary decoration to something that does not need it. You learn idioms by hearing them used in daily conversation. Idioms can be fun to use in writing and in conversations, but you should use them sparingly and in mostly informal situations.

Choosing the Right Idiom

*Read each sentence. Use context clues to figure out the meaning of each idiom in **boldface** print. Then write the letter of the definition for the idiom in the sentence.*

1. The amount of money she paid for that smartphone is **small potatoes** compared to what her fancy computer cost. ___c___
2. After yelling and cheering at last night's football game, I woke up with **a frog in my throat**. ___g___
3. We spent all afternoon praising Mom's great apple pie, so her **ears must be burning**. ___j___
4. Don't you think Mark is a little **long in the tooth** to be taking on the role of a young superhero? ___a___
5. I always have to **ride shotgun**; I get carsick when I sit in the backseat. ___i___
6. That hot chocolate sure **hit the spot** after a long hike in the snow! ___h___
7. It sure seems as if **time is flying** when we get together and play games. ___b___
8. The suspect, exhausted from the reporters' constant questioning at the courthouse, begged them to **call off the dogs**. ___d___
9. My brother always has to **put in his two cents' worth** when it comes to my choice of music. ___e___
10. Evan should stop the **monkey business** and just finish his project. ___f___

a. old

b. a certain period passes quickly

c. not very big in comparison

d. stop criticizing or harassing

e. make a comment or give an opinion

f. fooling around

g. a feeling of hoarseness in the throat

h. was refreshing and satisfying

i. sit in the front seat of a car

j. awareness that one is being talked about

CCSS Vocabulary: 5.a. (See pp. T14–15.)

WORD STUDY

Writing with Idioms

Find the meaning of each idiom. (Use a dictionary if necessary.) Then write a sentence for each idiom. **Answers will vary.**

1. one in a million
   Sample answer: Our science teacher is the best; she is one in a million.
2. put on the dog
3. crack a book
4. nose in the air
5. two shakes of a lamb's tail
6. hot off the presses
7. bat an eyelid
8. not a dry eye in the house
9. hold your horses
10. take five
11. blue blood
12. pass with flying colors

 CCSS Vocabulary: 5. (See pp. T14–15.)

Denotation and Connotation

Words have a literal meaning that you can look up in a dictionary. The literal meaning of a word is its **denotation**, which has a neutral tone.

Many words also have emotional associations beyond the literal meaning, called **connotations.** Connotations can be positive or negative.

Consider these synonyms for the verb *prompt*:

motivate *encourage* *goad* *pressure*

Goad and *pressure* have negative connotations. *Motivate* and *encourage* have positive connotations.

> **Think:** People do not want to feel that they are being goaded or pressured to do something, but they welcome being motivated or encouraged to accomplish something.

Look at these examples of words. Notice how the connotation of each word varies.

NEUTRAL	POSITIVE	NEGATIVE
recede	**ebb**	**recoil**
meet	**challenge**	**confront**
mimic	**imitate**	**impersonate**

Writers choose their words carefully in order to express a particular tone or point of view. The most precise word helps readers understand exactly what the writer is trying to say. If a writer wants the reader to view a character as a private, thoughtful person, the writer might use a word like *discreet* to describe him or her. But if the writer wants us to see the character as secretive, he or she might use words like *guarded* or *wary*.

Shades of Meaning

Write a plus sign (+) in the box if the word has a positive connotation. Write a minus sign (–) if the word has a negative connotation. Put a zero (0) if the word is neutral.

1. famished –	**2.** stamina   +	**3.** douse  –	**4.** terrain   0
5. vocation  +	**6.** assailant  –	**7.** wither  –	**8.** serene  +
9. ingenious  +	**10.** restrict  –	**11.** pacifist +	**12.** hypocrite  –
13. waylay  –	**14.** sheepish –	**15.** repast 0	**16.** gainful  +

WORD STUDY

Expressing the Connotation

Read each sentence. Select the word in parentheses that better expresses the connotation (positive, negative, or neutral) given at the beginning of the sentence.

neutral **1.** If you're shopping for sports (**duds, apparel**), I recommend the athletic supply store on Midway Drive.

positive **2.** Does anyone actually enjoy the sound of Sandra (**gloating, rejoicing**) over her tennis victories?

negative **3.** It (**infuriates, bothers**) me when I have to wait in a slow-moving line at the grocery store.

neutral **4.** In the novel, the hero vows to never (**renounce, forsake**) the girl he has loved since childhood.

negative **5.** I think it is wrong to (**constrain, imprison**) wild animals.

negative **6.** The (**inept, untrained**) gardener had trouble keeping even the hardiest plants alive.

neutral **7.** My sister always shares her opinions, but she is (**indifferent to, disinterested in**) other people's reactions to her ideas.

positive **8.** Marisa seemed to truly appreciate the (**outpouring, barrage**) of good will from her friends and neighbors after her long illness.

Challenge: Using Connotation

Choose vocabulary words from Units 1–3 to replace the highlighted words in the sentences below. Then explain how the connotation of the replacement word changes the tone of the sentence. **Answers will vary.**

immense	**dispatched**	**contemporary**
besieged	**enigma**	**mimic**

1. When we visited the state park, I was amazed at the **large** ___immense___ canyons and beautiful rock structures.
Sample response: *Immense* makes the tone of the sentence more dramatic, allowing the reader to get a better idea of how huge the canyon really is.

2. Although Hannah loves the theater, she was not impressed with this **updated** ___contemporary___ version of *Romeo and Juliet*.
Sample response: *Contemporary* is more precise and adds a more formal tone to the sentence.

3. Daniel thought he would have time during spring break to relax; instead, he was **occupied** ___besieged___ with chores.
Sample response: *Besieged* adds a more negative tone, implying that Daniel is overwhelmed by his chores and is not likely to find time to relax.

 CCSS Vocabulary: 5, 5.c. (See pp. T14–15.)

de—down; away from; completely; not

The Latin root *de* appears in **denounce** (page 14), **depict** (page 25), and **designate** (page 34). The root signifies separation or undoing. Some other words based on the same root are listed below.

debunk	**default**	**demerit**	**desperate**
decapitate	**defraud**	**depression**	**devolve**

From the list of words above, choose the one that corresponds to each of the brief definitions below. Write the word in the blank space in the illustrative sentence below the definition. Use a dictionary if necessary.

1. to cut off the head, behead

Experienced chefs know how to gut, scale, and **decapitate** a fish before cooking it.

2. an area that is sunk below its surroundings; a period of severe economic decline; a mood of dejection or sadness.

Slapstick comedy films were popular during the Great **Depression** of the 1930s.

3. to expose the falseness of unsound or exaggerated claims

New evidence allows us to **debunk** a time-honored legend.

4. a mark against, usually involving the loss of some privilege or right; a fault, defect

Bad behavior at school earned him many **demerits**.

5. to pass on (*"a duty or task"*) to someone else; to be passed on to; to be conferred on

When the mayor's powers **devolve** upon her successor, little will change at City Hall.

6. to fail to perform a task or fulfill an obligation; the failure to do something required by law or duty

Because the challenger failed to show up, the defender won the match by **default**.

7. driven to take any risk; hopeless; extreme

Lack of water led homesteaders to take **desperate** measures.

8. to cheat, take away from, or deprive of by deceit or trickery

The corrupt attorney tried to **defraud** the heirs of their rightful inheritance and fortune.

CCSS Vocabulary: 4.b. (See pp. T14–15.)

UNIT 4

Note that not all of the 20 Unit words are used in this passage. *Ingratitude*, *ovation*, *repent*, *revocation*, and *strife* are not included.

*Read the following passage, taking note of the **boldface** words and their contexts. These words are among those you will be studying in Unit 4. As you complete the exercises in this Unit, it may help to refer to the way the words are used below.*

CCSS Vocabulary: 4; Reading (Informational Text): 4, 6. (See pp. T14–15.)

The Art and Science of Traditional Healing

<Expository Essay>

Advances in science provide modern man with cures and treatments undreamed of by his prehistoric counterparts. But how did early humans deal with disease? Serious illnesses could **devastate** whole families or clans. What remedies were available? In olden times, folk medicine **generated** relief or cures. A thorough **scan** of the long history of medicine reveals some similar **strands** woven throughout the history of healing.

Plants were one source of medicine for early humans. Some vegetables or herbs were **deemed** especially effective for minor illnesses, and botanics are the source of many modern medicines. In ancient times, though, major disorders were likely to have **mortal** results. These deadly diseases needed more intensive treatment than the herbal remedies offered.

To fight these killer illnesses, early medicine men turned to magic and ritual. In many parts of the world, healers were called shamans. Although precise definitions of shamanism are **elusive**, it is likely that these shamans resembled what other societies called magicians or sorcerers. It is easy now, from a modern perspective, to dismiss them as quacks. But most shamans seem to have **acquitted** themselves honorably. Indeed, the specialized knowledge of shamans often caused society to **idolize** and revere them.

Shamans lived in different societies around the world and can still be found today. Some North American Indian nations and people in areas such as modern Siberia, Mongolia, and South America practiced shamanism. Wherever they were found, shamans revealed some common qualities. They often experienced periods of deep trance. Trances were not just **reveries** or daydreams; they were altered states of consciousness. The shaman's soul was believed to roam on journeys through the upper and lower worlds. A shaman's contact with spirits, both good and evil, was no **petty** talent. On the contrary, it was a key

A Mandan Indian medicine man during ceremonial dance

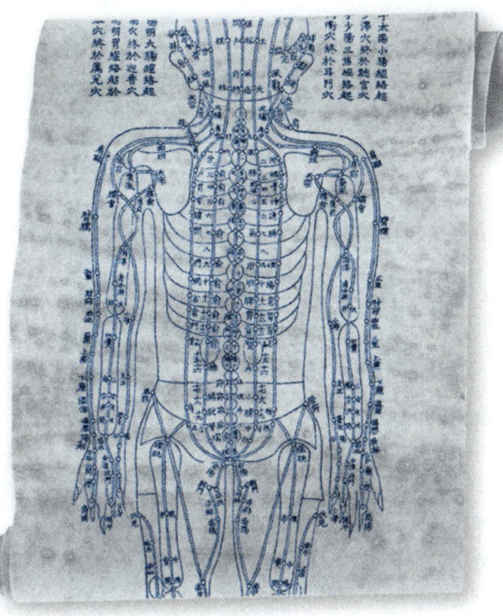

The Chinese practice of acupuncture is based on the idea that stimulating certain pressure points in the body can correct imbalances.

element in the healer's ability to rescue ailing patients from their wretched **plights**.

The early historical period had many medical traditions. In China, a typical healer's goal was to control the proportions of various elements in the body. Water therapy and acupuncture came from the Chinese tradition. Such treatments are still practiced today. In India, the classic writings on disease and treatment date back several thousand years. In both India and China, though, religious beliefs hindered efforts to learn more about anatomy. Cutting the bodies of the dead was considered a breach of the law and a source of **discredit**.

Despite their successes, early healers could not have hoped to cure all the sick. As the Arabic saying goes, "When fate arrives, the physician becomes a fool." If a healer lived in ancient Babylon, the price of failure could be steep. In the Law Code of Hammurabi around 1750 BCE, for example, doctors were warned that their hands would be cut off if a patient died from certain treatments.

In early Greek medicine, the outstanding figure was Hippocrates. Born around 460 BCE, probably on the island of Cos, he insisted that disease was a natural rather than a supernatural phenomenon. His written works began to **topple** magic from its commanding position in medicine. Perhaps his most enduring **keepsake** for the modern world is the Hippocratic Oath; this solemn promise "to do no harm" is still subscribed to by physicians today.

Hippocrates is known as the father of Western medicine.

Audio

For iWords and audio passages, snap the code, or go to **vocabularyworkshop.com**.

Note the spelling, pronunciation, part(s) of speech, and definition(s) of each of the following words. Then write the appropriate form of the word in the blank spaces in the illustrative sentence(s) following. Finally, study the lists of synonyms and antonyms.

1. acquit (ə kwit′)

(*v.*) to declare not guilty, free from blame, discharge completely; to conduct or behave oneself

Now that we have proof of their innocence, we can ____acquit____ them of all charges.

SYNONYMS: exonerate, dismiss
ANTONYMS: convict, declare guilty

2. deem (dēm)

(*v.*) to think, believe; to consider, have an opinion

Most people ____deem____ it a wise plan to set aside savings for the future.

SYNONYMS: judge, regard

3. devastate (dev′ ə stāt)

(*v.*) to destroy, lay waste, leave in ruins

Failure or harsh criticism can ____devastate____ a person who has shaky self-esteem.

SYNONYMS: wreck, desolate
ANTONYMS: develop, improve

4. discredit (dis kred′ it)

(*v.*) to throw doubt upon, cause to be distrusted; to damage in reputation; (*n.*) a loss or lack of belief, confidence, or reputation

We have gathered a considerable amount of evidence to ____discredit____ her story.

Both parents and students felt strongly that the cheating scandal was a ____discredit____ to the school.

SYNONYM: (*v.*) disparage
ANTONYMS: (*v.*) confirm, corroborate, bolster

5. elusive (ē lü′ siv)

(*adj.*) difficult to catch or to hold; hard to explain or understand

According to legend, Zorro, the heroic Mexican character, was too ____elusive____ for local police to capture.

SYNONYMS: slippery, wily, fleeting, puzzling, baffling

6. generate (jen′ ə rāt)

(*v.*) to bring into existence; to be the cause of

Solar power uses the energy of the sun to ____generate____ electricity.

SYNONYMS: create, produce, beget, cause
ANTONYMS: end, terminate, extinguish, stifle

CCSS Vocabulary: 4.c., 4.d. (See pp. T14–15.)

7. idolize (ī′ dəl īz)

(*v.*) to worship as an idol, make an idol of; to love very much

Teens who **idolize** a movie star may repeatedly see the same movie featuring that actor or actress.

SYNONYMS: adore, revere
ANTONYMS: despise, scorn, disdain, detest

8. ingratitude (in grat′ ə tüd)

(*n.*) a lack of thankfulness

Hosts who make every effort to please their guests are apt to be hurt by **ingratitude**.

SYNONYMS: thanklessness, ungratefulness
ANTONYMS: thankfulness, gratefulness, recognition

9. keepsake (kēp′ sāk)

(*n.*) something kept in memory of the giver; a souvenir

Before my grandmother died, she made me a special quilt as a **keepsake** of her love.

SYNONYMS: reminder, memento

10. mortal (môr′ təl)

(*n.*) a being that must eventually die; (*adj.*) of or relating to such a being; causing death, fatal; possible, conceivable

In the mythology of many cultures, a heavenly god can come down to Earth and act as a **mortal**.

The soldier was the only one in her battalion to suffer a **mortal** injury.

SYNONYMS: (*n.*) human; (*adj.*) fleeting, extreme
ANTONYMS: (*n.*) a god; (*adj.*) undying, everlasting, eternal, divine

11. ovation (ō vā′ shən)

(*n.*) an enthusiastic public welcome, an outburst of applause

The audience gave the dancer a standing **ovation** after his impressive performance.

SYNONYMS: bravos, hurrahs; ANTONYMS: boos, jeers

12. petty (pet′ ē)

(*adj.*) unimportant, trivial; narrow-minded; secondary in rank, minor

You say my complaint is **petty**, but to me it is an issue of great importance.

SYNONYMS: insignificant, piddling
ANTONYMS: important, major, significant, weighty

13. plight (plīt)

(*n.*) a sorry condition or state; (*v.*) to pledge, promise solemnly

The **plight** of the homeless upsets many concerned citizens.

Wedding guests watched the bride and groom **plight** their undying love.

SYNONYMS: predicament, quandary

CCSS Vocabulary: 4.c., 4.d. (See pp. T14–15.)

14. repent (ri pent′)

(*v.*) to feel sorry for what one has done or has failed to do

As people grow older and gain more maturity, some of them come to **repent** their youthful mistakes.

SYNONYM: regret; ANTONYM: rejoice over

15. reverie (rev′ ə rē)

(*n.*) a daydream; the condition of being lost in thought

My boss interrupted my pleasant **reverie** by reminding me about our deadline.

SYNONYMS: fantasy, meditation

16. revocation (rev ə kā′ shən)

(*n.*) an act or instance of calling back, an annulment, cancellation

His failure to complete the job according to schedule led to a **revocation** of his contract.

SYNONYMS: repeal, withdrawal
ANTONYMS: ratification, confirmation

17. scan (skan)

(*v.*) to examine closely; to look over quickly but thoroughly; to analyze the rhythm of a poem; (*n.*) an examination

Let's **scan** the list to see the finishing times of each marathon runner.

The doctor did a bone **scan** to discover the location of each fracture.

SYNONYMS: (*v.*) study, glance at, skim; (*v., n.*) survey

18. strand (strand)

(*n.*) a beach or shore; a string of wire, hair, etc.; (*v.*) to drive or run aground; to leave in a hopeless position

We asked the waiter to take back the soup when we discovered a **strand** of hair in it.

I don't want to be the third out in the inning and **strand** the two base runners.

SYNONYMS: (*n.*) fiber, thread; (*v.*) abandon, maroon
ANTONYMS: (*v.*) rescue, save

19. strife (strīf)

(*n.*) bitter disagreement; fighting, struggle

The experienced senator from South Carolina was a veteran of political **strife**.

SYNONYMS: conflict, discord, turmoil
ANTONYMS: peace, calm, agreement

20. topple (täp′ əl)

(*v.*) to fall forward; to overturn, bring about the downfall of

The trains that rumble past our apartment often cause books to **topple** from the shelves.

SYNONYMS: unseat, upset, tumble
ANTONYMS: remain upright, establish, set up

CCSS Vocabulary: 4.c., 4.d. (See pp. T14–15.)

*Select the **boldface** word that better completes each sentence. You might refer to the passage on pages 50–51 to see how most of these words are used in context.*

The great Greek hero Heracles had to accomplish twelve labors, or difficult tasks, to atone for the deaths of his sons. One task was to wrestle and subdue the powerful Cretan bull.

1. During several of Heracles's labors, Athena noticed the (**ovation, plight**) the hero was in and offered her assistance.

2. Our supervisor (**topples, scans**) the newspaper each morning for items that may serve as leads for the sales force.

3. Once order had been restored, the leaders of the opposition called for the (**revocation, keepsake**) of martial law.

4. By reelecting him to Congress, the court of public opinion has forever (**generated, acquitted**) him of the charges of neglecting his duties.

5. In Shakespeare's *A Midsummer Night's Dream*, which character speaks the line, "Lord, what fools these (**mortals, keepsakes**) be"?

6. Imagine his (**plight, ingratitude**)—penniless, unemployed, and with a large family to support!

7. A team of filmmakers spent a year in the rain forests of South America, searching for the (**elusive, toppled**) harpy eagle.

8. Since you are the only one of us who has had experience with this kind of problem, we shall do whatever you (**deem, scan**) necessary.

9. The children stood on the southern (**reverie, strand**) and waved at the boats sailing into the harbor.

10. Are we going to allow (**elusive, petty**) quarrels to destroy a friendship that has endured for so many years?

11. While the actors were busy rehearsing, the manager ran away with all the money and left them (**stranded, plighted**) in a strange town.

12. After so many years of (**strife, ovation**)—in business, politics, and the family—he wants only to retire to the peace and quiet of his ranch.

13. A special edition of poems by the noted writer was presented as a (**reverie, keepsake**) to all who attended her eightieth birthday party.

14. In my composition, I tried to give a definition of "humor," but I found the idea too (**petty, elusive**) to pin down.

15. At times we all enjoy a(n) (**ovation, reverie**) about "what might have been," but before long we must return to "the way things are."

16. It was upsetting to see that his best friend was trying to (**discredit, scan**) his record as the best receiver on the team.

17. I knew that she was wrapped up in herself, but I never dreamed that even she could be guilty of such (**revocation, ingratitude**).

18. Many diseases that have disappeared in the United States continue to (**devastate, idolize**) countries in other parts of the world.

19. At times it is quite natural to feel afraid, and it is certainly no (**discredit, mortal**) to anyone to admit it.

20. We will never allow such vicious, unfounded rumors to (**deem, generate**) discord and conflict in our school!

21. What a(n) (**ovation, reverie**) he received when he trotted back to the bench after scoring the winning touchdown!

22. Our business is barely managing to pay its bills; one bad break will be enough to (**acquit, topple**) it into bankruptcy.

23. Our father often says that he has never stopped (**repenting, devastating**) the decision he made many years ago to give up the study of medicine.

24. We should respect our national leaders, but we should not (**idolize, discredit**) them and assume that they can do no wrong.

25. Katie purchased a (**revocation, keepsake**) box to store letters and photographs.

*Choose the word from this Unit that is the same or most nearly the same in meaning as the **boldface** word or expression in the phrase. Write that word on the line. Use a dictionary if necessary.*

1. asked for a **retraction** of the news column	revocation
2. pitied her for the **difficult situation** she was in	plight
3. too much **friction** to remain partners	strife
4. to **desert** them on a dangerous island	strand
5. may never **apologize for** his wrongdoing	repent
6. power to **demolish** an entire community	devastate
7. waved his cap to acknowledge the **cheers**	ovation
8. **search** the night sky for shooting stars	scan
9. immersed in **contemplation**	reverie
10. a **lack of appreciation** that was uncalled for	ingratitude

CCSS Vocabulary: 5. (See pp. T14–15.)

The synonyms and antonyms here do not appear on the Definitions page.

Antonyms

*Choose the word from this Unit that is most nearly opposite in meaning to the **boldface** word or expression in the phrase. Write that word on the line. Use a dictionary if necessary.*

1. **heckling** that was not appreciated ____ovation____
2. to **boast** about a crime ____repent____
3. show our **appreciation** for your kindness ____ingratitude____
4. cooperation that produces **harmony** ____strife____
5. giving the nominee our **approval** ____revocation____

Completing the Sentence

From the words in this Unit, choose the one that best completes each of the following sentences. Write the correct word form in the space provided.

1. Why argue about such ____petty____ matters when there are so many important problems to deal with?
2. The sudden racket produced by a noisy car radio jolted me out of my deep and peaceful ____reverie____.
3. Tom is not a very fast runner, but he is so ____elusive____ that he is extremely hard to tackle on the football field.
4. Though that actress's name and face are all but forgotten today, she used to be ____idolized____ by adoring fans all over the world.
5. I don't have the time to read every word of that long newspaper article, but I'll ____scan____ it quickly to get the main idea.
6. Instead of telling us how much you ____repent____ your outrageous conduct, why don't you sincerely try to reform?
7. We learned that even unfavorable reviews of a new book may help to ____generate____ a certain amount of public interest in it.
8. Regardless of what you might think proper, I do not ____deem____ it necessary for someone of your age to wear an evening gown to the dance.
9. The famous Leaning Tower of Pisa looks as though it might ____topple____ over any minute.
10. The evidence against the accused man proved to be so weak that the jury had no choice but to ____acquit____ him.

11. As it is clear that his only interest is to make money for himself, his plan for building a new highway has been completely **discredited**.

12. Because the members of my family disagree on so many matters, the dinner table is often the scene of much verbal **strife**.

13. The wound at first did not appear to be too serious, but to our great grief it proved to be **mortal**.

14. The TV program made us keenly aware of the **plight** of retired people trying to live solely on Social Security payments.

15. The defendant was warned that another speeding ticket would result in the **revocation** of her driver's license.

16. The rope is made of many **strands** of fiber woven together.

17. The hurricane so **devastated** a large section of the coast that the president declared it a disaster area.

18. As I sincerely appreciate all my parents have done for me, how can you accuse me of **ingratitude**?

19. She richly deserved the audience's **ovation** for her brilliant performance of Lady Macbeth.

20. I plan to save this old notebook as a(n) **keepsake** of one of the best and most enjoyable classes I have ever had.

Writing: Words in Action

Answers to both prompts will vary.

1. Look back at "The Art and Science of Traditional Healing" (pages 50–51). How is the traditional approach to disease and healing similar to or different from contemporary approaches? Write a brief essay comparing traditional healing to modern-day healing. Support your comparison using at least two details from the passage and three Unit words.

2. Modern medicine has made tremendous scientific advances. Yet today, many physicians and patients embrace holistic approaches. Holistic, or alternative, medicine considers the emotional and spiritual as well as the physical aspects of illness. Holistic approaches may include the use of herbs, massage, acupuncture, and practices such as yoga and meditation. Do you think a holistic approach to medicine makes sense in today's world? Write a brief essay in which you support your opinion with specific examples, personal experience, your studies, and the reading (refer to pages 50–51). Write at least three paragraphs, and use three or more words from this Unit.

Writing prompt #2 is modeled on that of standardized tests.

CCSS Vocabulary: 6; Writing: 1.c., 2.d., 3.d., 4. (See pp. T14–15.)

Vocabulary in Context: Informational Text for Unit 4 is available online at **vocabularyworkshop.com**.

The following excerpts are from A Princess of Mars *by Edgar Rice Burroughs. Some of the words you have studied in this Unit appear in* **boldface** *type. Complete each statement below the excerpt by circling the letter of the correct answer.*

1. I have never told this story, nor shall **mortal** man see this manuscript until after I have passed over for eternity. I know that the average human mind will not believe what it cannot grasp, and so I do not purpose being pilloried by the public, the pulpit, and the press, and held up as a colossal liar when I am but telling the simple truths which some day science will substantiate.

One who is **mortal**

a. will live forever
b. has a strong sense of duty
c. will die one day
d. has trouble believing the truth

2. "Cannot the war be ended at once?" spoke Sab Than. "It requires but the word of Than Kosis to bring peace. Say it, my father, say the word that will hasten my happiness, and end this unpopular **strife**."

Strife is a(n)

a. reign
b. war
c. peace
d. conversation

3. When Woola had finished his meal I again took up my weary and seemingly endless wandering in quest of the **elusive** waterway.

A waterway that is **elusive** is

a. very large
b. hard to find
c. difficult to navigate
d. rough and choppy

Edgar Rice Burroughs set many of his adventure stories on the planet Mars, but he became famous for his tales of Tarzan.

4. On the seventh day following the battle with the air craft we again took up the march toward Thark, all probability of another attack being **deemed** remote by Lorquas Ptomel.

Something that is **deemed** is

a. ignored
b. described
c. approved
d. considered

5. "Good-bye, my princess," I whispered, "we may meet in Helium yet. I have escaped from worse **plights** than this," and I tried to smile as I lied.

"What," she cried, "are you not coming with us?"

A **plight** is NOT a(n)

a. great difficulty
b. easy circumstance
c. dangerous situation
d. serious vow

Snap the code, or go to **vocabularyworkshop.com**

UNIT 5

Note that not all of the 20 Unit words are used in this passage. *Bungle*, *remorse*, *smug*, and *tarry* are not included.

Read the following passage, taking note of the ***boldface*** *words and their contexts. These words are among those you will be studying in Unit 5. As you complete the exercises in this Unit, it may help to refer to the way the words are used below.*

CCSS Vocabulary: 4; Reading (Informational Text): 4, 6. (See pp. T14–15.)

Continue Space Exploration, Now!

<Persuasive Speech>

The United States should continue to support an active program of space exploration. Opponents of such a policy have **blustered** that space exploration is a waste of resources. Why spend money on rockets, they argue, when desperate needs here on Earth are so **acute**? Billions of the planet's **inhabitants** struggle from day to day. The **numbing** curses of war, famine, and poverty cry out for attention and relief.

For all but the most stubborn and **headstrong**, however, this argument can be convincingly **refuted**. For the entire **duration** of the space program's existence—a little more than half a century—the budget of the National Aeronautics and Space Administration (NASA) has averaged under one percent of total federal annual expenditures. One must keep these numbers in perspective. In a country where appetites are often **ravenous**, Americans spend nearly twenty times more money at restaurants every year than the government spends on NASA! Even a brief **synopsis** of costs and budgets shows that space exploration does not account for major outlays.

Apollo 15 astronaut on the moon, 1971

But how about astronaut safety? Opponents in the **fray** over space policy point to the risks of human spaceflight. They argue that these risks justify an end to space exploration. It is true that the space shuttle disasters of 1986 and 2003 marked major **setbacks** for NASA. In over 50 years, however, only 18 people worldwide have died in spaceflights. This one **facet** of the debate over future policy certainly elicits strong emotions. Yet the vast majority of astronauts undergo rigorous training. To **pacify** the critics, some have suggested that spaceflights should depend on robotics, which are less costly and risky than manned flights. It may well be cheaper and safer to organize unmanned missions into space. Human intelligence and flexibility, though, will still be invaluable for many purposes. Astronauts, moreover, have served as powerful role models for generations of young people.

Sputnik 1, orbit

Fidelity to balance and fairness demands an evaluation of the numerous benefits derived from the space program so far. These include many advances in technology. What are some of these breakthroughs? Among them are satellites, microchips, and fuel cells. Take just one example. Satellites have vastly improved global communications. Better weather forecasts from satellites save lives. More accurate data make research on climate change possible. The demands and challenges of space exploration have meant that scientists and inventors can't risk being complacent. Ever bolder objectives in space require ever more ingenious responses.

Finally, the most important reason to press on in space is psychological, not material. The writer and inventor Arthur C. Clarke won fame for his achievements in science and science fiction. In one essay, Clarke offered this insightful **commentary** on human nature. He said that civilization cannot exist without new frontiers and that people have a physical and spiritual need for them. Clarke was right. The fascination with the *Apollo 11* moon landing of July 1969 swept the world. Humanity should continue to press forward in space. This effort is not so much to explore space's **eerie** depths but rather to explore the soul and timeless aspirations of humans themselves.

Space Shuttle *Discovery* launch, Kennedy Space Center, September 9, 1994

Note the spelling, pronunciation, part(s) of speech, and definition(s) of each of the following words. Then write the appropriate form of the word in the blank spaces in the illustrative sentence(s) following. Finally, study the lists of synonyms and antonyms.

1. acute (ə kyüt′)

(*adj.*) with a sharp point; keen and alert; sharp and severe; rising quickly to a high point and lasting for a short time

One who is an **acute** observer of human nature may notice subtle changes in people's behavior.

SYNONYMS: clever, penetrating
ANTONYMS: blunted, mild, stupid, obtuse

2. bluster (bləs′ tər)

(*v.*) to talk or act in a noisy and threatening way; to blow in stormy gusts; (*n.*) speech that is loud and threatening

When we saw harsh winds **bluster** around our tent, we decided to change our plans for the weekend.

Dad's manner is all **bluster**, but beneath it all, he's really a kind-hearted man.

SYNONYMS: (*v.*) spout, rant, brag, swagger; (*n.*) bravado

3. bungle (bəŋ′ gəl)

(*v.*) to act or work clumsily and awkwardly; to ruin something through clumsiness

If we **bungle** this project, we may never get another chance to prove ourselves as a worthy team.

SYNONYMS: blunder, mess up

4. commentary (käm′ ən ter ē)

(*n.*) a series of notes clarifying or explaining something; an expression of opinion

Our spiritual leader gave us a **commentary** on the true meaning of charity.

SYNONYMS: explanation, narration, description, account, review, analysis

5. duration (dů rā′ shən)

(*n.*) the length of time that something continues or lasts

Even though the story was hard to follow, my friends decided to stay for the **duration** of the opera.

6. eerie (ē′ rē)

(*adj.*) causing fear because of strangeness; weird, mysterious

It is a lot of fun to tell **eerie** ghost stories around a campfire.

SYNONYMS: frightening, spooky, creepy

CCSS Vocabulary: 4.c., 4.d. (See pp. T14–15.)

7. facet (fas′ ət)

(*n.*) one aspect or side of a subject or problem; one of the cut surfaces of a gem

One important ______facet______ of problem solving is to recognize when a solution makes no sense.

SYNONYMS: angle, characteristic, factor, element

8. fidelity (fi del′ ə tē)

(*n.*) the state of being faithful; accuracy in details, exactness

The ______fidelity______ of scratchy old records can't match the clarity of CDs.

SYNONYMS: loyalty, faithfulness; ANTONYMS: disloyalty, treachery

9. fray (frā)

(*n.*) a brawl, a noisy quarrel; (*v.*) to wear away by rubbing; make ragged or worn; to strain, irritate

After the two loudest students began arguing, the whole class jumped into the ______fray______.

A faucet that drips continuously can ______fray______ anyone's nerves.

SYNONYMS: (*n.*) scuffle; (*v.*) unravel

10. headstrong (hed′ strôŋ)

(*adj.*) willful, stubborn

Even the most patient caregiver may feel challenged when faced with a ______headstrong______ child.

SYNONYMS: obstinate, mulish, unruly
ANTONYMS: obedient, docile, submissive

11. inhabitant (in hab′ ə tənt)

(*n.*) one living permanently in a given place

Although she enjoys traveling to exotic places, she's a lifelong ______inhabitant______ of this small town.

SYNONYMS: resident, native, tenant
ANTONYMS: stranger, outsider, visitor

12. numb (nəm)

(*adj.*) having lost the power of feeling or movement; (*v.*) to dull the feelings of; to cause to lose feeling

Bitter cold may leave your toes ______numb______.

This injection will ______numb______ the area so that the doctor can stitch the cut painlessly.

SYNONYMS: (*adj.*) unfeeling, insensible; (*v.*) deaden
ANTONYMS: (*adj.*) sensitive, alert

13. pacify (pas′ ə fī)

(*v.*) to make peaceful or calm; to soothe

The factory owners hope to ______pacify______ the angry protesters with promises of higher wages.

SYNONYMS: mollify, placate
ANTONYMS: anger, arouse, stir up, foment, ignite

CCSS Vocabulary: 4.c., 4.d. (See pp. T14–15.)

14. ravenous
(rav′ ə nəs)

(*adj.*) greedy; very hungry; eager for satisfaction

Exercising vigorously for several hours gives me a ___**ravenous**___ appetite.

SYNONYMS: starved, voracious, wolfish
ANTONYMS: not hungry, well-fed, satisfied

15. refute
(ri fyüt′)

(*v.*) to prove incorrect

After analyzing the situation, I now know a foolproof way to ___**refute**___ the original claim.

SYNONYMS: disprove, rebut
ANTONYMS: prove, confirm, corroborate

16. remorse
(ri mors′)

(*n.*) deep and painful regret for one's past misdeeds; pangs of conscience

When the driver realized what a terrible accident he had caused, he was overcome with ___**remorse**___.

SYNONYM: guilt
ANTONYMS: clear conscience, guiltlessness

17. setback
(set′ bak)

(*n.*) something that interferes with progress; a disappointment, unexpected loss or defeat; a step-like recession in a wall

A broken toe can be a major ___**setback**___ for a skater who hopes to qualify for the Olympics.

SYNONYMS: failure, reversal
ANTONYMS: advance, gain, progress, triumph

18. smug
(sməg)

(*adj.*) overly self-satisfied, self-righteous

Just because he got the lead in the school play doesn't justify his irritating air of ___**smug**___ superiority.

SYNONYMS: conceited, complacent
ANTONYMS: discontented, disgruntled

19. synopsis
(si näp′ sis)

(*n.*) a brief statement giving a general view of some subject, book, etc.; a summary

The teacher's guide gives a ___**synopsis**___ of the plot of each story in the collection.

SYNONYMS: outline, digest, abstract

20. tarry
(tar′ ē)

(*v.*) to delay leaving; to linger, wait; to remain or stay for a while

He will be tempted to ___**tarry**___ longer if he thinks that this might be their last visit together.

SYNONYMS: dawdle, dally
ANTONYMS: rush, hasten, leave, depart

CCSS Vocabulary: 4.c., 4.d. (See pp. T14–15.)

Choosing the Right Word

*Select the **boldface** word that better completes each sentence. You might refer to the passage on pages 60–61 to see how most of these words are used in context.*

1. The character Scrooge in Charles Dickens's *A Christmas Carol* starts out as a(n) (**acute, ravenous**) miser, but he undergoes a great change of heart.

2. The bloodhound's (**numb, acute**) sense of smell led the trackers to the bank robber's hideout in record time.

3. When I realized how deeply I had hurt my dear friend with my careless insult, I suffered a terrible pang of (**remorse, duration**).

4. With a winter storm (**blustering, bungling**) outside, what could be more welcome than a warm room, a good meal, and my favorite TV program?

5. Since it had seemed that winter would (**tarry, pacify**) forever, we were all heartily glad when it finally quit dragging its heels and departed.

Ebenezer Scrooge, the holiday-hating miser, is one of the most famous characters in fiction.

6. His (**headstrong, acute**) analysis of the housing problem in our town gave us a clear idea of what we would have to overcome.

7. Although I don't agree with all her ideas, I must admire her unshakable (**fidelity, synopsis**) to them.

8. We cannot assume that all the people one sees on the streets of a large city are actually (**facets, inhabitants**) of the place.

9. When the plane encountered turbulence, we had to remain seated with our seat belts fastened for the (**duration, synopsis**) of the flight.

10. The idea that most people usually behave in a calm and reasonable way is (**refuted, numbed**) by all the facts of history.

11. On the camping trip out West, some of the children were frightened when they first heard the (**smug, eerie**) howls of coyotes at night.

12. The victims of the disaster were so (**numbed, tarried**) by the scope of the tragedy that they scarcely showed any emotion at all.

13. I keep telling you things for your own good, but you're just too (**eerie, headstrong**) to listen.

14. Have you ever wondered if there is life on other planets and, if so, what the (**frays, inhabitants**) might look like?

15. We know that we are going through a period of economic instability, but there is no way of telling what its (**duration, remorse**) will be.

CCSS Vocabulary: 4.d. (See pp. T14–15.)

16. Maria's illness, after she had been chosen for the leading role in the class show, was a serious (**setback, commentary**) to our plans.

17. The lost hikers, having endured several days in the blistering sun, became discouraged after sighting (**headstrong, ravenous**) vultures circling overhead.

18. If you read no more than a(n) (**inhabitant, synopsis**) of the plot of any one of Shakespeare's plays, you will get very little idea of what it is all about.

19. "It's your job to help (**pacify, fray**) the conquered area," the general said, "not to add fuel to an already explosive situation."

20. There is so much wear and tear on the ropes in this pulley system that they become (**frayed, refuted**) in only a few days.

21. The fact that so many people are still living in poverty is indeed a sad (**fidelity, commentary**) on our civilization.

22. Each time she answered a question correctly, she rewarded herself with a (**smug, ravenous**) little smile of self-congratulation.

23. The strength of this book lies in the author's ability to describe and explain different (**setbacks, facets**) of human experience.

24. After the way you (**bungled, blustered**) the job of arranging the class trip, I can never again trust you with anything important.

25. My lawyer prepared to (**bungle, refute**) the outrageous accusations against me.

Choose the word from this Unit that is the same or most nearly the same in meaning as the ***boldface*** *word or expression in the phrase. Write that word on the line. Use a dictionary if necessary.*

1. reflected off the **cuts** of the diamond — facets
2. shock that left them **dazed** and speechless — numb
3. lip-smacking sounds of the **famished** eaters — ravenous
4. to expect yet another **holdup** — setback
5. should not **loiter** in the hall — tarry
6. after they **botched** the paint job — bungled
7. offer a brief **summation** of the movie — synopsis
8. flashing that **haughty** grin of hers — smug
9. tried to **contradict** her argument — refute
10. no sense of **shame** for what happened — remorse

 CCSS Vocabulary: 5. (See pp. T14–15.)

Antonyms

*Choose the word from this Unit that is most nearly opposite in meaning to the **boldface** word or expression in the phrase. Write that word on the line. Use a dictionary if necessary.*

1. needs to **hurry** to get ready — tarry
2. could never **support** their opinion — refute
3. presenting a **modest** outlook — smug
4. hopes to **succeed** at her job — bungle
5. maintains **peace of mind** despite his actions — remorse

Completing the Sentence

From the words in this Unit, choose the one that best completes each of the following sentences. Write the correct word form in the space provided.

1. I had a(n) ______eerie______ feeling that we were being followed and that something bad might happen.
2. Although the rain was heavy, it was of such short ______duration______ that it didn't interfere with our plans.
3. Because I ______tarried______ at the book fair, I was ten minutes late for my piano lesson.
4. Warmth and understanding are two outstanding ______facets______ of her memorable personality.
5. His ______smug______ expression showed how highly he valued his own opinions and scorned the views of others.
6. The program contained a(n) ______synopsis______ of the opera, so we were able to follow the action even though the singing was in Italian.
7. Is it true that the ______inhabitants______ of Maine are often called "Mainiacs"?
8. No one can question her complete ______fidelity______ to basic American ideas and ideals.
9. After the dentist gave me an injection of novocaine, the whole side of my jaw and face turned ______numb______.
10. Some children are as docile as sheep; others are as ______headstrong______ as mules.

CCSS Vocabulary: 4.a., 5. (See pp. T14–15.)

11. By **blustering** in a loud, confident voice, he tried to convince us that he had nothing to do with the accident.

12. Our team suffered a tough **setback** when our best player was hurt in the first few minutes of play.

13. Anyone who has never had a sprained ankle will find it hard to imagine how **acute** the pain is.

14. Because of our inexperience and haste, we **bungled** the little repair job so badly that it became necessary to replace the entire motor.

15. We had eaten only a light breakfast before hiking for hours in the crisp mountain air, so you can imagine how **ravenous** we were by lunchtime.

16. The newscaster on my favorite TV program not only tells the facts of the news but also offers a(n) **commentary** that helps us to understand it.

17. Do you think it is a good idea to try to **pacify** the weeping child by giving her a lollipop?

18. When my two sisters began their bitter quarrel, only Mother had enough nerve to enter the **fray** and tell them to stop.

19. Since the convicted felon had shown no **remorse** for his crimes, the judge sentenced him to the maximum prison term allowed.

20. The accused person must be given every chance to **refute** the charges against him or her.

Writing: Words in Action

Answers to both prompts will vary.

1. Look back at "Continue Space Exploration, Now!" (pages 60–61). What is your position on funding space exploration? Should the United States continue to spend federal money to support NASA? Write an editorial persuading your audience either to support or oppose funding space travel. Clearly state your position and use at least two details from the passage and three Unit words to support your claim.

2. A current argument states that privately held aerospace businesses, and not government agencies like NASA, should invest in and develop the spacecraft and new technologies that will transport people into space. What are the pros and cons of leaving space program development in the hands of private entrepreneurs and non-government-affiliated aerospace companies? Consider issues such as inspecting for safety, training, sharing of knowledge, and profit. Write a brief essay in which you support your opinion with specific examples, your studies, and the reading (refer to pages 60–61). Write at least three paragraphs, and use three or more words from this Unit.

Writing prompt #2 is modeled on that of standardized tests.

CCSS Vocabulary: 6; Writing: 1.c., 2.d., 3.d., 4. (See pp. T14–15.)

Vocabulary in Context: Informational Text for Unit 5 is available online at **vocabularyworkshop.com**.

The following excerpts are from The First Men in the Moon *by H.G. Wells. Some of the words you have studied in this Unit appear in* **boldface** *type. Complete each statement below the excerpt by circling the letter of the correct answer.*

1. There were several amazing forms, with heads reduced to microscopic proportions and blobby bodies . . . And oddest of all, as it seemed to me for the moment, two or three of these weird **inhabitants** of a subterranean world, a world sheltered by innumerable miles of rock from sun or rain, *carried umbrellas* in their tentaculate hands—real terrestrial-looking umbrellas!

Inhabitants are best described as

a. invaders **c.** exiles
b. creatures **d.** dwellers

2. He reminded me of mountain sickness, and of the bleeding that often afflicts aeronauts who have ascended too swiftly, and he spent some time in the preparation of a sickly tasting drink which he insisted on my sharing. It made me feel a little **numb**, but otherwise had no effect on me.

If someone's senses are **numb**, they are

a. deadened **c.** delicate
b. heightened **d.** clear

3. We ate and presently drank like tramps in a soup kitchen. Never before nor since have I been hungry to the **ravenous** pitch, and save that I have had this very experience I could never have believed that . . . it would be possible for me to eat in utter forgetfulness of all these things.

A person who is **ravenous** is definitely NOT

a. famished **c.** satiated
b. eager **d.** alert

In the movie based on the H.G. Wells novel, astronauts discover they are not the first to land on the moon!

4. One imagines him about the moon with the **remorse** of this fatal indiscretion growing in his mind. During a certain time I am inclined to guess the Grand Lunar was deliberating the new situation.

To have **remorse** is to feel

a. demands **c.** enthusiasm
b. regrets **d.** irresponsibility

5. The outline of things had gained in character, had grown **acute** and varied; save for a shadowed space of white substance here and there . . . the arctic appearance had gone altogether.

Something that appears **acute** is

a. dull **c.** sharp
b. peaceful **d.** unruly

Snap the code, or go to **vocabularyworkshop.com**

CCSS Vocabulary: 4.d.; Reading (Literature): 4. (See pp. T14–15.)

UNIT 6

Note that not all of the 20 Unit words are used in this passage. *Amiable*, *blight*, *limber*, *oracle*, and *vagabond* are not included.

*Read the following passage, taking note of the **boldface** words and their contexts. These words are among those you will be studying in Unit 6. As you complete the exercises in this Unit, it may help to refer to the way the words are used below.*

CCSS Vocabulary: 4; Reading (Informational Text): 4, 6. (See pp. T14–15.)

The Fine Art of War: WWI Propaganda Images

<Textbook Entry>

The Great War Begins

Austrian Archduke Franz Ferdinand was assassinated in Sarajevo, Bosnia, in 1914 by a Serbian **partisan**. This event was the spark that ignited the tinderbox. Long-simmering international resentments and a complex and **befuddling maze** of military alliances erupted into the world's first global conflict: World War I (1914–1918).

The United States was neutral for the first three years. President Woodrow Wilson tried to play peacemaker. But by 1917, events like the torpedoing of passenger ships by German U-boats (submarines), which took a **gross** toll of civilian lives, convinced Wilson to declare war. Now the United States was one of the Allies (along with France, Great Britain, Russia, Italy, and Japan).

U-boat attacks spurred the U.S. into WWI. The public was urged to help defeat the U-boat.

The War at Home

When World War I began, propaganda campaigns were waged on all sides. Propaganda aimed to win the hearts and minds of citizens and discourage the enemy. The United States entered the war in 1917. Its publicity machine went into overdrive to **induce** public support. In a speech to the nation, President Wilson said, "The world must be made safe for democracy." With that **clarity** of vision, Wilson **debuted** the new Committee on Public Information (CPI), which, along with other government agencies such as the U.S. Food Administration, mobilized support for the war effort. Journalist George Creel, a **boisterous** supporter of America's entry into the war, led the CPI.

Creel hired 150,000 writers, actors, artists, and others to help drum up American support for the war. CPI planned a clear **agenda**. It had plenty of freedom and **leeway** in its efforts. It presented pro-war speeches, articles, pamphlets, books, and films.

Division of Pictorial Publicity

The CPI writers, directors, actors, and speechmakers were successful in getting the message out. But there were still Americans out of reach. So Creel created the Division of Pictorial Publicity within the CPI. It is said that a bad cause requires many words. Creel needed few words for

Flagg's iconic 1917 poster of Uncle Sam is still familiar.

his mission. He hired well-known artists, illustrators, and cartoonists to create posters, banners, and advertisements for the war effort.

Newspapers and magazines were full of powerful images that packed a punch. Roadside billboards urged citizens to join the army or navy, buy bonds, knit socks for soldiers, **conserve** scarce food, and guard against the danger of spies.

Images as a Recruiting Tool

James Montgomery Flagg created some of the most memorable posters. His famous "I Want You" image of Uncle Sam compelled young men to enlist. (Uncle Sam was a fictional grey-haired man used to represent the U.S. government.) Another famous example is a poster for the Treasury Department's Liberty Bonds. It shows an image of a German soldier with a bloody sword. Below him were the words "Beat Back the Hun with Liberty Bonds." ("Hun" was a insulting term for the Germans used by the Allies.) These patriotic messages worked. Soon, war fever swept the country.

The War to End All Wars Ends

In 1918, the **gory** war came to an end. It left 8.5 million dead and 20 million wounded. Germany signed a peace treaty that required it to **vacate** occupied countries and **reimburse** money to war victims. The harsh penalties forced the defeated nation to be **compliant**. With the end of the war came the end of the Committee on Public Information. CPI's U.S.-based work ended on November 11, 1918. Its overseas operations ended eight months later. Its images are still used and still powerful today.

Posters informed those at home how they could directly help the war effort.

Note the spelling, pronunciation, part(s) of speech, and definition(s) of each of the following words. Then write the appropriate form of the word in the blank spaces in the illustrative sentence(s) following. Finally, study the lists of synonyms and antonyms.

1. agenda (ə jen′ də)

(*n.*) the program for a meeting; a list, outline, or plan of things to be considered or done

The ____**agenda**____ for today's assembly includes a plan for recycling in the classroom.

SYNONYMS: schedule, docket

2. amiable (ā′ mē ə bəl)

(*adj.*) friendly, good-natured

Marty, whose sense of humor and good spirits never fail, is an ____**amiable**____ companion.

SYNONYMS: pleasant, agreeable
ANTONYMS: unfriendly, ill-humored, hostile

3. befuddle (bi fəd′ əl)

(*v.*) to confuse, make stupid

A difficult scientific experiment with many steps is likely to ____**befuddle**____ most beginners.

SYNONYMS: bewilder, boggle, stupefy
ANTONYMS: enlighten, set straight

4. blight (blīt)

(*n.*) a disease that causes plants to wither and die; a condition of disease or ruin; (*v.*) to destroy, ruin

Dutch elm disease was a ____**blight**____ that forever changed the look of my neighborhood.

Though she received several letters of rejection, she determined not to let them ____**blight**____ her hopes of going to college.

SYNONYMS: (*n.*) eyesore; (*v.*) spoil, nip
ANTONYMS: (*v.*) foster, promote, nourish, encourage

5. boisterous (boi′ strəs)

(*adj.*) rough and noisy in a cheerful way; high-spirited

The ____**boisterous**____ schoolchildren made it clear to their teacher how much they enjoyed the class trip.

SYNONYMS: loud, unruly, disorderly
ANTONYMS: quiet, calm, peaceful, well-behaved

6. clarity (klar′ ə tē)

(*n.*) clearness, accuracy

The vet explained with great ____**clarity**____ how best to housebreak our new puppy.

SYNONYMS: lucidity, precision
ANTONYMS: confusion, murkiness, ambiguity

CCSS Vocabulary: 4.c., 4.d. (See pp. T14–15.)

7. compliant (kəm plī′ ənt)

(*adj.*) willing to do what someone else wants; obedient

A ___**compliant**___ child is easy to discipline, even when in an unfamiliar environment.

SYNONYMS: meek, docile, submissive
ANTONYMS: disobedient, obstinate, rebellious, perverse

8. conserve (kən sərv′)

(*v.*) to preserve; to keep from being damaged, lost, or wasted; to save

Responsible citizens try to ___**conserve**___ our precious natural resources.

SYNONYMS: guard, care for; ANTONYMS: waste, squander, dissipate

9. debut (dā′ byü)

(*n.*) a first public appearance; a formal entrance into society; (*v.*) to make a first appearance

The talented flute player in the marching band finally made her ___**debut**___ as a soloist today.

Many theaters will ___**debut**___ the film tonight.

SYNONYM: (*n.*) coming-out; ANTONYMS: (*n.*) retirement, departure

10. gory (gôr′ ē)

(*adj.*) marked by bloodshed, slaughter, or violence

The Civil War battle of Antietam is, to this day, the most ___**gory**___ one-day fight in our history.

SYNONYMS: bloody, gruesome; ANTONYM: bloodless

11. gross (grōs)

(*adj.*) coarse, vulgar; very noticeable; total; overweight; (*n.*) an overall total (without deductions); twelve dozen; (*v.*) to earn

They responded to the ___**gross**___ injustice in an unsatisfactory manner.

A ___**gross**___ of pencils lasts all year.

She expects to ___**gross**___ $3,000 in tips.

SYNONYMS: (*adj.*) sheer, utter, flagrant, fat
ANTONYMS: (*adj.*) delicate, fine, partial, slender, thin; (*n.*, *v.*) net

12. induce (in düs′)

(*v.*) to cause, bring about; to persuade

Can drinking warm milk ___**induce**___ sleep?

SYNONYMS: prevail upon, influence
ANTONYMS: prevent, deter, hinder

13. leeway (lē′ wā)

(*n.*) extra space for moving along a certain route; allowance for mistakes or inaccuracies; margin of error

Experienced planners allow ___**leeway**___ of a week or so in case a project runs into snags or delays.

SYNONYMS: latitude, elbow room

CCSS Vocabulary: 4.c., 4.d. (See pp. T14–15.)

14. limber (lim′ bər)

(*adj.*) flexible; (*v.*) to cause to become flexible

Serious dancers develop ___limber___ bodies.

Runners ___limber___ up before a race.

SYNONYMS: (*adj.*) supple, pliable; (*v.*) stretch
ANTONYMS: (*adj.*) stiff, wooden; (*v.*) stiffen

15. maze (māz)

(*n.*) a network of paths through which it is hard to find one's way; something very mixed-up and confusing

Ancient Rome was a ___maze___ of narrow streets and winding alleys.

SYNONYMS: labyrinth, puzzle, tangle

16. oracle (ôr′ ə kəl)

(*n.*) someone or something that can predict the future; someone who gives astute answers or advice that seems authoritative

According to Greek legend, people sought prophecy at the great ___Oracle___ at Delphi.

SYNONYMS: prophet, seer, sibyl

17. partisan (pärt′ ə zən)

(*n.*) a strong supporter of a person, party, or cause; one whose support is unreasoning; a resistance fighter, guerrilla; (*adj.*) strongly supporting one side only

That candidate is a ___partisan___ of term limits.

___Partisan___ hometown fans can be hostile to those from out of town.

SYNONYMS: (*n.*) fan, booster; (*adj.*) partial, biased
ANTONYMS: (*n.*) critic, foe; (*adj.*) impartial, neutral

18. reimburse (rē im bərs′)

(*v.*) to pay back; to give payment for

When you go on business trips, the company will ___reimburse___ all your traveling expenses.

SYNONYMS: repay, refund, compensate

19. vacate (vā′ kāt)

(*v.*) to go away from, leave empty; to make empty; to void, annul

We have a lot of cleaning up to do before we ___vacate___ the apartment for good.

SYNONYMS: depart, abandon; ANTONYMS: occupy, keep, hold

20. vagabond (vag′ ə bänd)

(*n.*) an idle wanderer; a tramp; (*adj.*) wandering; irresponsible

The ___vagabond___ carried his few belongings in a shabby cardboard suitcase.

The ___vagabond___ life interests some people, but it doesn't appeal to me.

SYNONYMS: (*n.*) vagrant; (*adj.*) unsettled, footloose
ANTONYMS: (*n.*) homebody, resident; (*adj.*) settled

CCSS Vocabulary: 4.c., 4.d. (See pp. T14–15.)

Choosing the Right Word

*Select the **boldface** word that better completes each sentence. You might refer to the passage on pages 70–71 to see how most of these words are used in context.*

Victor Hugo, the French Romantic author, wrote plays, poems, and novels.

1. My sister made her (**agenda, debut**) in the Broadway production of *Les Misérables*, a musical based on Victor Hugo's novel.

2. Over the years, so many of the columnist's predictions have come true that he is now looked on as something of a(n) (**debut, oracle**).

3. One of the biggest problems facing the United States today is how to stop the (**blight, agenda**) that is creeping over large parts of our great cities.

4. Until we were in (**compliance, conservation**) with the neighborhood regulations, we could not build a tree house.

5. An experienced backpacker can give you many useful suggestions for (**befuddling, conserving**) energy on a long, tough hike.

6. After all the deductions had been made from my (**gross, limber**) salary, the sum that remained seemed pitifully small.

7. Students must take many required courses, but they also have a little (**oracle, leeway**) to choose courses that they find especially interesting.

8. What I thought was going to be a(n) (**amiable, vagabond**) little chat with my boss soon turned into a real argument.

9. Don't let the (**clarity, leeway**) of the water fool you into supposing that it's safe for drinking.

10. To become a good all-around athlete, you not only need a strong and (**induce, limber**) body, but also a quick, disciplined mind.

11. Because she is usually so (**compliant, partisan**), we were all surprised when she said that she didn't like our plans and wouldn't accept them.

12. Poland was at the top of Adolf Hitler's (**maze, agenda**) of military conquests in the fall of 1939.

13. If you want to get a clear picture of just what went wrong, you must not (**befuddle, induce**) your mind with all kinds of wild rumors.

14. As we moved higher up the mountain, I was overcome by dizziness and fatigue (**induced, grossed**) by the thin air.

15. This video game is not appropriate for children or minors due to its violent and (**amiable, gory**) content.

CCSS Vocabulary: 4.d. (See pp. T14–15.)

16. Because he is an expert gymnast and works out every day, his body has remained as (**limber**, **gory**) as that of a boy.

17. Many a student dreams about spending a (**vagabond**, **partisan**) year idly hiking through Europe.

18. In her graphic description of the most gruesome scenes in the horror film, Maria left out none of the (**amiable**, **gory**) details.

19. At the end of the long series of discussions and arguments, we felt that we were trapped in a (**maze**, **blight**) of conflicting ideas and plans.

20. The landlord ordered all tenants to (**vacate**, **reimburse**) the premises by noon.

21. This matter is so important to all the people of the community that we must forget (**boisterous**, **partisan**) politics and work together.

22. I will feel fully (**reimbursed**, **conserved**) for all that I have done for her if I can see her in good health again.

23. The disc jockey promised to (**vacate**, **debut**) the band's long-awaited new song as soon as it was released by the recording company.

24. Mr. Roth, our school librarian, may seem mild and easygoing, but he cracks down hard on (**compliant**, **boisterous**) students.

25. One of the items on the council's (**agenda**, **partisan**) is the proposal of a curfew.

*Choose the word from this Unit that is the same or most nearly the same in meaning as the **boldface** word or expression in the phrase. Write that word on the line. Use a dictionary if necessary.*

1. acrobats who are quite **agile** — limber
2. **encourage** them to speak softly — induce
3. an **affliction** hidden from society's view — blight
4. when he saw the **horrific** spectacle — gory
5. can't rely on their **one-sided** viewpoint — partisan
6. had never consulted the **visionary** before — oracle
7. seemed like a **delightful** fellow — amiable
8. enough **breathing space** for a beginner to succeed — leeway
9. no choice but to **desert** the cabin — vacate
10. a **hobo** who hopped freight trains — vagabond

CCSS Vocabulary: 5. (See pp. T14–15.)

The synonyms and antonyms here do not appear on the Definitions page.

Antonyms

*Choose the word from this Unit that is most nearly opposite in meaning to the **boldface** word or expression in the phrase. Write that word on the line. Use a dictionary if necessary.*

1. rains that will **restore** the vegetation — **blight**
2. a long-term **occupant** of this apartment — **vagabond**
3. the guitar player's **rigid** fingers — **limber**
4. try to avoid an **uninformed fool** — **oracle**
5. socializing with our **gruff** neighbors — **amiable**

Completing the Sentence

From the words in this Unit, choose the one that best completes each of the following sentences. Write the correct word form in the space provided.

1. Before the game starts, the players **limber** up by doing a few deep knee bends, sit-ups, and other exercises.

2. How can a mind **befuddled** by alcohol make the type of snap decisions needed to drive safely in heavy traffic?

3. We cannot allow the lives of millions of people to be **blighted** by poverty.

4. You certainly have a right to cheer for your team, but try not to become too **boisterous** and unruly.

5. Because of her outgoing and **amiable** personality, she is liked by nearly everyone at school.

6. The crowd is so **partisan** that the umpire is booed every time he makes a decision against the home team.

7. The high standard of excellence that the woman had set for herself left her no **leeway** for mistakes.

8. For years, his restless spirit led him to wander the highways and byways of this great land like any other footloose **vagabond**.

9. Because you are working with older and more experienced people, you should be **compliant** with their requests and advice.

10. None of us could possibly overlook the **gross** error that the waiter had made in adding up our check.

CCSS Vocabulary: 4.a., 5. (See pp. T14–15.)

11. If you would be kind enough to buy a loose-leaf notebook for me while you are in the stationery store, I'll ____**reimburse**____ you immediately.

12. If the Superintendent of Schools should ____**vacate**____ his position by resigning, the Mayor has the right to name someone else to the job.

13. Trying to untangle a badly snarled fishing line is like trying to find one's way through a(n) ____**maze**____.

14. Ms. Fillmer explained with such ____**clarity**____ how to go about changing a tire that I felt that even someone as clumsy as I could do it.

15. Because our energy resources are limited, the American people must try to do everything possible to ____**conserve**____ fuel.

16. No matter what you may say, you cannot ____**induce**____ me to do something that I know is wrong.

17. The high point of the social season was the formal ____**debut**____ of young ladies at the annual Society Ball.

18. Each of the items on the ____**agenda**____ for our meeting today will probably require a good deal of discussion.

19. I was not prepared for the ____**gory**____ sight that met my eyes at the scene of that horrible massacre.

20. Why do you always ask me what's going to happen? I'm no ____**oracle**____!

Writing: Words in Action

Answers to both prompts will vary.

1. Look back at "The Fine Art of War: WWI Propaganda Images" (pages 70–71). Study the posters that became popular during World War I. Using the passage and posters, write a short essay that explains why these images were so effective in persuading Americans to support the war effort. Use at least two details from the passage and three Unit words to support your claim.

2. Advertisements are all around us, from billboards and television commercials to newspaper ads and pop-ups on the Internet. The messages and images of a clever advertising campaign can be powerful and persuasive. Would it ever be appropriate today for the government to use slick advertising tactics to get the American public to support a particular cause, such as a war? At some point might such "advertising" become propaganda—one-sided and even false support of a cause? Write a brief essay in which you support your opinion with specific examples, your studies, and the reading (refer to pages 70–71). Write at least three paragraphs, and use three or more words from this Unit.

Writing prompt #2 is modeled on that of standardized tests.

CCSS Vocabulary: 6; Writing: 1.c., 2.d., 3.d., 4. (See pp. T14–15.)

Vocabulary in Context: Informational Text for Unit 6 is available online at **vocabularyworkshop.com**.

The following excerpts are from the novel The Prince and The Pauper *and the short story "The Celebrated Jumping Frog of Calaveras County," both by Mark Twain. Some of the words you have studied in this Unit appear in* **boldface** *type. Complete each statement below the excerpt by circling the letter of the correct answer.*

1. The houseless prince, the homeless heir to the throne of England, still moved on, drifting deeper into the **maze** of squalid alleys where the swarming hives of poverty and misery were massed together. (*The Prince and the Pauper*)

Alleys that are like a **maze** are

a. intertwined **c.** dirty
b. amazing **d.** orderly

2. With **boisterous** mirth they dropped upon their knees in a body and did mock homage to their prey. The prince spurned the nearest boy with his foot, and said fiercely—

"Take thou that, till the morrow come and I build thee a gibbet!" (*The Prince and the Pauper*)

Something that is **boisterous** is NOT

a. rowdy and noisy **c.** calm and controlled
b. silly and pointless **d.** windy and wild

In one film adaptation of *The Prince and the Pauper*, twins Billy and Bobby Mauch played the roles of Tom and the Prince.

3. He was in a fine fury when he found himself described as a "sturdy **vagabond**" and sentenced to sit two hours in the stocks for bearing that character. . . . (*The Prince and the Pauper*)

A **vagabond** is someone who is a(n)

a. student **c.** witness
b. drifter **d.** official

4. In **compliance** with the request of a friend of mine, who wrote me from the East, I called on good-natured, garrulous old Simon Wheeler, and inquired after my friend's friend. . . . ("The Celebrated Jumping Frog of Calaveras County")

People who are in **compliance** are

a. curious **c.** stubborn
b. demanding **d.** accommodating

5. They used to give [the horse] two or three hundred yards start . . . but always at the [end] of the race she'd get excited and desperate-like, and come cavorting and straddling up, and scattering her legs around **limber**, sometimes in the air, and sometimes out to one side amongst the fences. . . . ("The Celebrated Jumping Frog of Calaveras County")

A **limber** horse is one that is

a. hostile **c.** stocky
b. mature **d.** nimble

Vocabulary for Comprehension

*Read the following passage in which some of the words you have studied in Units 4–6 appear in **boldface** type. Then answer the questions on page 81.*

This passage discusses Oseola McCarty (1908–1999), a woman who led a simple life but managed to amass a fortune and make an amazing contribution to others.

(Line)

Oseola McCarty left school after sixth grade to help care for ailing relatives. She was sorry not to be able to continue her education, but her family needed her. Pursuing an education was an **elusive** dream to this lifelong **inhabitant** of Mississippi. She eked out a living washing and ironing other people's clothing. She lived most of her life in a small house her uncle had once owned.

For seventy-five years, Oseola McCarty served her customers. She walked wherever she had to go. She earned little money yet managed to put aside a small amount almost every week. She knew it was wise to plan for the future.

Oseola McCarty never felt right about taking money out of her bank account. The money she put into the bank earned interest. What must have seemed like **petty** deposits of nickels and dimes eventually grew into a fortune. By the time McCarty was 87, she had nearly $300,000! McCarty's dreams of education had never faded. She knew she was too old to attend college but felt no **remorse** about her life. Instead she thought of an **agenda** to help others attend college. She gave $150,000 of her life's savings to the University of Southern Mississippi. Suddenly an elderly laundry woman was a local hero! Oseola McCarty's generosity touched people. Many were moved to make their own contributions to increase the Oseola McCarty Scholarship Fund.

Although she was finally rich, McCarty remained a straightforward, honest, and humble person. Her **commentaries** on life were right to the point. "If you want to feel proud of yourself," she once said, "you've got to do things you can be proud of." When McCarty died at the age of 91, people throughout the United States remembered her with pride and admiration.

CCSS Vocabulary: 4.a.; Reading (Informational Text): 2, 4, 6. (See pp. T14–15.)

1. The primary purpose of the passage is to
   a. tell an inspirational true story
   b. tell an inspirational fictional story
   c. persuade the reader to help others
   d. persuade the reader to save money
   e. persuade the reader to stay in school

2. The meaning of **elusive** (line 6) is
   a. steady
   b. magical
   c. fleeting
   d. passionate
   e. cherished

3. **Inhabitant** (line 7) most nearly means
   a. fan
   b. visitor
   c. student
   d. worker
   e. resident

4. From paragraph 2 (lines 13–19), we can infer that Oseola McCarty was all of the following EXCEPT
   a. humble
   b. nervous
   c. frugal
   d. hard-working
   e. independent

5. **Petty** (line 24) is best defined as
   a. major
   b. regular
   c. sensible
   d. insignificant
   e. narrow-minded

6. The meaning of **remorse** (line 31) is
   a. regret
   b. responsibility
   c. sympathy
   d. confusion
   e. failure

7. **Agenda** (line 32) most nearly means
   a. way
   b. plan
   c. dream
   d. contest
   e. scheme

8. Which saying best describes how McCarty amassed her wealth?
   a. Out of sight, out of mind.
   b. Live only in the here and now.
   c. Here today, gone tomorrow.
   d. Slow and steady wins the race.
   e. Eat, drink, and be merry, for tomorrow we may die.

9. Who started the Oseola McCarty Scholarship Fund?
   a. Oseola's students
   b. Oseola's relatives
   c. Oseola's employers
   d. Oseola McCarty
   e. Oseola's neighbors

10. **Commentaries** (line 45) is best defined as
    a. keepsakes
    b. writings
    c. ideas
    d. anecdotes
    e. remarks

11. Which word best describes the author's attitude toward the subject?
    a. pitying
    b. respectful
    c. critical
    d. disbelieving
    e. amused

12. With which generalization would the author most likely agree?
    a. One person can make a big difference in the lives of others.
    b. The most important thing in life is a college education.
    c. Live as if today were your last day on Earth.
    d. Without an education, a person is permanently handicapped.
    e. If you do not save money for a rainy day, someone will always help you.

CCSS Vocabulary: 4.a.; Reading (Informational Text): 2, 4, 6. (See pp. T14–15.)

Two-Word Completions

Select the pair of words that best completes the meaning of each of the following sentences.

1. When the new government came to power, its first order of business was to ____________ a country that had been torn by ____________ and revolution for over ten years.

a. pacify . . . strife
b. topple . . . ingratitude
c. strand . . . fidelity
d. conserve . . . remorse

2. The TV special not only brought in huge sums of money to help relieve the ____________ of millions of Africans suffering from the effects of a severe famine but also ____________ a great deal of sympathy for them.

a. setback . . . induced
b. plight . . . generated
c. duration . . . deemed
d. strife . . . conserved

3. In the third century, bands of savage barbarians repeatedly broke through the frontier defenses of the Roman province of Gaul, ____________ the countryside with fire and sword, and either slew or carried off the ____________.

a. scanned . . . partisans
b. pacified . . . vagabonds
c. devastated . . . inhabitants
d. blighted . . . oracles

4. "I want to maintain ____________ to the book in bringing this story to the screen," the director instructed the scriptwriter. "However, I recognize that one has to have a little ____________ when translating print into film."

a. clarity . . . synopsis
b. fidelity . . . leeway
c. strife . . . facet
d. partisan . . . commentary

5. After the speech in which Thomas Paine ____________ against unfair taxes, it became obvious to all colonists that his ____________ was to promote freedom.

a. vacated . . . keepsake
b. repented . . . revocation
c. blustered . . . agenda
d. idolized . . . ingratitude

6. The defense was able to ____________ the prosecution's case so convincingly that the members of the jury ____________ the defendant after only five minutes of deliberation.

a. devastate . . . befuddled
b. refute . . . acquitted
c. topple . . . discredited
d. bungle . . . reimbursed

7. "The Scholar Gypsy" tells the tale of a poor student who left school to join a band of ____________. He and his companions roamed the countryside endlessly, never ____________ in one place for long.

a. inhabitants . . . deeming
b. bunglers . . . vacating
c. partisans . . . generating
d. vagabonds . . . tarrying

 CCSS Vocabulary: 4.a. (See pp. T14–15.)

In the passage "Continue Space Exploration, Now!" (see pages 60–61), the narrator says that space program funds do not "account for" all the over-spending of the federal government.

"Account for" is an idiom that means "explain" or "to be the determining factor." An **idiom** is an informal phrase or expression whose words should not be interpreted literally. We learn idioms from everyday usage, and they become so ingrained in our daily speech that we often forget we are using them.

Choosing the Right Idiom

*Read each sentence. Use context clues to figure out the meaning of each idiom in **boldface** print. Then write the letter of the definition for the idiom in the sentence.*

1. Jared was **up a creek** when he arrived at class without his books. d
2. I really wish Jamie would quit **bugging me** about going to the football game. h
3. Our class did not win first place at the tournament, but **that's the way the cookie crumbles**. f
4. How will Tonya react when she **gets wind of** the news that Leanne can run faster than she can? j
5. The mayor refused to **back down** on her position about the new hike and bike trail. a
6. If you're having a party, one of the best ways to **break the ice** is to play a name game. b
7. After a long day at school, Megan **lets off steam** by playing with her dog. i
8. Greg, tired of doing all the work on the class project, asked his partner to **pull his own weight**. e
9. It was difficult for the excited child to **sit tight** and wait his turn. g
10. My brother tried to **butter me up**, hoping I would agree to wash the dishes. c

a. retreat or give in

b. start conversations; get people to relax

c. flatter someone in order to gain something

d. in a bad situation

e. take responsibility; do one's fair share

f. that's how things turn out differently than planned

g. be patient

h. annoying or pestering

i. releases energy or stress

j. hears about

CCSS Vocabulary: 5.a. (See pp. T14–15.)

Writing with Idioms

Find the meaning of each idiom. (Use a dictionary if necessary.) Then write a sentence for each idiom. **Answers will vary.**

1. face the music **Sample response: It's time for Chloe to face the music and tell her parents that she broke their favorite vase.**
2. hang on
3. a full plate
4. take the cake
5. run across
6. to coin a phrase
7. in mint condition
8. a raw deal
9. down to earth
10. the last resort
11. the middle of nowhere
12. against the clock

 CCSS Vocabulary: 5. (See pp. T14–15.)

Denotation and Connotation

When you look up a word in a dictionary, you find its definition, or its **denotation**. A word's denotation is its literal meaning, and it conveys a neutral tone.

Many words have additional shades of meaning called connotations. **Connotations** are the emotional associations we have with words. A word might have several synonyms, or words that have related meanings, but each synonym will have a particular connotation that sets it apart from the others. Connotations can be positive, negative, or neutral.

Consider these synonyms for the neutral word *remembrance*.

memento *souvenir* *keepsake* *relic*

Memento, souvenir, and *keepsake* have positive connotations, whereas *relic* has a more negative one, suggesting something old and outdated.

> **Think:** Travelers like to collect mementos, souvenirs, and keepsakes during trips; these objects inspire happy memories. But relics are objects that are old and worthless.

Look at these examples of words that have similar denotations but very different connotations.

NEUTRAL	POSITIVE	NEGATIVE
pacify	**soothe**	**placate**
pleased	**proud**	**smug**
agenda	**proposal**	**conspiracy**

Writers know the emotional power of words. If a writer wants to elicit emotional response from readers, he or she will choose powerful words. Think about how advertisers use words. Would you rather be the *proud owner* of a new car or a *smug purchaser*?

Shades of Meaning

Write a plus sign (+) in the box if the word has a positive connotation. Write a minus sign (–) if the word has a negative connotation. Put a zero (0) if the word is neutral.

1. amiable [+]	**2.** eerie [–]	**3.** commentary [0]	**4.** plight [–]
5. duration [0]	**6.** strife [–]	**7.** ovation [+]	**8.** maze [–]
9. reimburse [+]	**10.** clarity [+]	**11.** scan [0]	**12.** bungle [–]
13. devastate [–]	**14.** gory [–]	**15.** limber [+]	**16.** inhabitants [0]

CCSS Vocabulary: 5.c. (See pp. T14–15.)

Expressing the Connotation

Read each sentence. Select the word in parentheses that better expresses the connotation (positive, negative, or neutral) given at the beginning of the sentence.

neutral 1. Our cat is quite (**elusive, mystifying**) and seldom makes an appearance when we have company.

negative 2. The criticism he made was (**minor, petty**), but I don't think anyone in the class took offense.

positive 3. Ruby is a (**determined, headstrong**) child, and she prefers getting dressed on her own.

neutral 4. You should be (**compliant, submissive**) when addressing a police officer if he stops your car.

negative 5. The coffee shop owner does not want people to (**loiter, tarry**) in front of her place of business.

neutral 6. Some people (**idolize, admire**) the idea of physical beauty, but I think personality is more important.

positive 7. When they heard that their troop had sold the most cookies, the scouts responded with (**unruly, boisterous**) shouts and applause.

negative 8. One member banged his shoe on the desk, prompting a (**fray, disagreement**) among the politicians.

Challenge: Using Connotation

Choose vocabulary words from Units 4–6 to replace the highlighted words in the sentences below. Then explain how the connotation of the replacement word changes the tone of the sentence. **Answers will vary.**

conserve	**ingratitude**	**ravenous**
remorse	**gross**	**induce**

1. Even when the judge pointed out Daniel's misdeeds, Daniel felt no **guilt** **remorse**.
Sample response: *Remorse* makes the tone of the sentence more negative, suggesting that Daniel has no conscience.

2. It is important that we **safeguard** **conserve** our natural resources so that future generations can enjoy them.
Sample response: *Conserve* adds a more formal, diplomatic tone to the sentence. It sounds less one-sided than *safeguard*.

3. The movie featured a **hungry** **ravenous** shark that attacked a large ship and its entire crew.
Sample response: *Ravenous* adds a more negative tone, suggesting a more dangerous and voracious shark.

 CCSS Vocabulary: 5, 5.c. (See pp. T14–15.)

re—back; again

The Latin root *re* appears in **repent** (page 54), **revocation** (page 54), **refute** (page 64), **remorse** (page 64), and **reimburse** (page 74). Some other words based on the same root are listed below.

rebuke	**refrain**	**renege**	**retract**
redeem	**relic**	**restraint**	**revive**

From the list of words above, choose the one that corresponds to each of the brief definitions below. Write the word in the blank space in the illustrative sentence below the definition. Use a dictionary if necessary.

1. to scold, express sharp disapproval; a scolding

The babysitter had to ______**rebuke**______ the children for misbehaving after dinner.

2. to go back on a promise

They were surprised when the buyer suddenly decided to ______**renege**______ on the deal.

3. to buy back; to make up for; to fulfill a pledge

Consumers who ______**redeem**______ discount coupons they clip from magazines and newspapers can lower their weekly grocery bills.

4. something that has survived the passage of time

We marveled at the delicate artistry in the Indian ______**relics**______ we saw at the museum.

5. to take back something that has been said, offered, or published

The angry candidate demanded that the newspaper ______**retract**______ the scandalous story.

6. to give new life to; to restore

Lively cheers from a hopeful crowd may ______**revive**______ a team's dampened spirits.

7. a device that restricts or confines; control over the expression of one's feelings or behavior

The police officers placed ______**restraints**______ on the violent prisoner.

8. to hold oneself back; a repeated verse, chorus

On Thanksgiving, it is always hard for me to ______**refrain**______ from eating too much delicious food.

CCSS Vocabulary: 4.b. (See pp. T14–15.)

UNIT 7

Note that not all of the 20 Unit words are used in this passage. *Fatality*, *illicit*, *inflammatory*, *memorandum*, and *writhe* are not included.

*Read the following passage, taking note of the **boldface** words and their contexts. These words are among those you will be studying in Unit 7. As you complete the exercises in this Unit, it may help to refer to the way the words are used below.*

CCSS Vocabulary: 4; Reading (Informational Text): 4, 6. (See pp. T14–15.)

Made for the Shade

<Informational Essay>

Most people who wear sunglasses might say they wear shades to protect their eyes from the sun's harmful ultraviolet rays or to ward off glare. They aren't **prevaricating**. Those *are* the most popular reasons people wear sunglasses. But the "coolness factor" is another reason. With so many shapes, sizes, and colors to choose from, just about everyone can pick shades that look stylish. But modern sunglasses are a far cry from earlier models.

People today might not **relish** wearing the "sunglasses" of the ancient Inuit. The Inuit wore sun goggles made from bone, ivory, and wood. These were fashioned into eye coverings with slits so the wearer could see. These goggles were functional, but not exactly a fashion statement.

Roman emperors used a more glamorous way of protecting their eyes. Supposedly, the emperor Nero shielded his eyes with pieces of emerald. But lowly citizens were not **authorized** to do the same, even if they could afford the gems.

In the twelfth century, Chinese judges hid their eyes behind planes of smoky quartz crystals to appear detached or impartial. The judges could **immerse** themselves in the trial without betraying their thoughts about the alleged **culprit** or witnesses. This gesture **quashed** any suspicion that they were taking sides.

Centuries later, sunglasses similar to modern shades were developed. Around 1750, British optician, designer, and inventor James Ayscough experimented with tinted lenses. He **dissected** and remade existing spectacles to create shaded ones. He was trying to correct specific eye ailments. While he might have felt his early efforts **pathetic**, he **persevered**. Although Ayscough was not designing the glasses for sun protection, he is still known as the father of modern sunglasses.

Snow goggles helped protect the Inuit from snow blindness.

Advancements in the manufacture of sunglasses followed over the years. In 1929, entrepreneur Sam Foster started selling his own inexpensive shades in Atlantic City, New Jersey. That is when sunglasses really became both fashionable and functional. Foster founded Foster Grant—still a successful company today.

Foster could not have picked a better time to start his company. As the film industry took off in the twentieth century, sunglasses became popular among movie stars. Silent-film stars wore shades to disguise red eyes caused by lamps used while shooting films. Even after this problem was fixed, stars continued to wear shades—probably for the glamour factor. Or perhaps celebrities who want to remain incognito believe that the public is **gullible** enough not to recognize a star wearing shades.

Audrey Hepburn in *Breakfast at Tiffany's*

Although celebrities and the general public alike wear them to be fashionable, sunglasses have become a staple in various professions. In 1936, photography pioneer Edwin H. Land developed polarized sunglasses using his patented Polaroid filter. These fast became popular with fishermen. The polarized lenses reduced glare and allowed fishermen to see into the water. There are also special shades for athletes, airline pilots, and astronauts. Astronauts need sunglasses for inside the spacecraft as well as out. Sunlight is much stronger in space.

Nowadays, sunglasses are more popular than ever. It is a **testimonial** to their staying power. Some people **expend** time carefully **scouring** websites for the odd or unusual pair of shades. A person might look at vintage shades and **reminisce** about the past. But **dawdling** fondly over old memories and the "good old days" might be a case of looking at the world through rose-colored glasses. If only those who yearn for vintage shades could see the primitive methods of blocking the sun's rays, they might not see sunglasses in such a romantic light.

Astronauts require eye protection from the sun outside and inside their spacecraft.

Audio

For iWords and audio passages, snap the code, or go to **vocabularyworkshop.com**.

Note the spelling, pronunciation, part(s) of speech, and definition(s) of each of the following words. Then write the appropriate form of the word in the blank spaces in the illustrative sentence(s) following. Finally, study the lists of synonyms and antonyms.

1. authorize (ô′ thə rīz)

(*v.*) to approve or permit; to give power or authority to

I wonder if Congress will someday **authorize** U.S. citizens to cast official votes over the Internet.

SYNONYMS: order, entitle, empower
ANTONYMS: forbid, ban, prohibit

2. culprit (kəl′ prit)

(*n.*) a person who has committed a crime or is guilty of some misconduct; an offender

Thanks to their efficient tracking methods, the police were able to catch the **culprit** red-handed.

SYNONYMS: lawbreaker, wrongdoer

3. dawdle (dôd′ əl)

(*v.*) to waste time; to be idle; to spend more time in doing something than is necessary

It's relaxing to **dawdle** in the shower, but it wastes water.

SYNONYMS: delay, loiter, dillydally
ANTONYMS: hurry, hasten, speed up, bustle

4. dissect (di sekt′)

(*v.*) to cut apart in preparation for scientific study; to analyze with great care

I can't wait to **dissect** a frog in biology class next week.

SYNONYM: examine
ANTONYMS: sew together, fuse, weld

5. expend (ek spend′)

(*v.*) to pay out, spend; to use up

The most experienced long-distance runners learn not to **expend** their energy too soon.

SYNONYMS: utilize, consume, disburse
ANTONYMS: save, hoard

6. fatality (fā tal′ ə tē)

(*n.*) an event resulting in death; an accidental death

The driver slammed on the brakes, but it was too late to prevent the traffic **fatality**.

SYNONYMS: casualty, mortality
ANTONYM: injury

CCSS Vocabulary: 4.c., 4.d. (See pp. T14–15.)

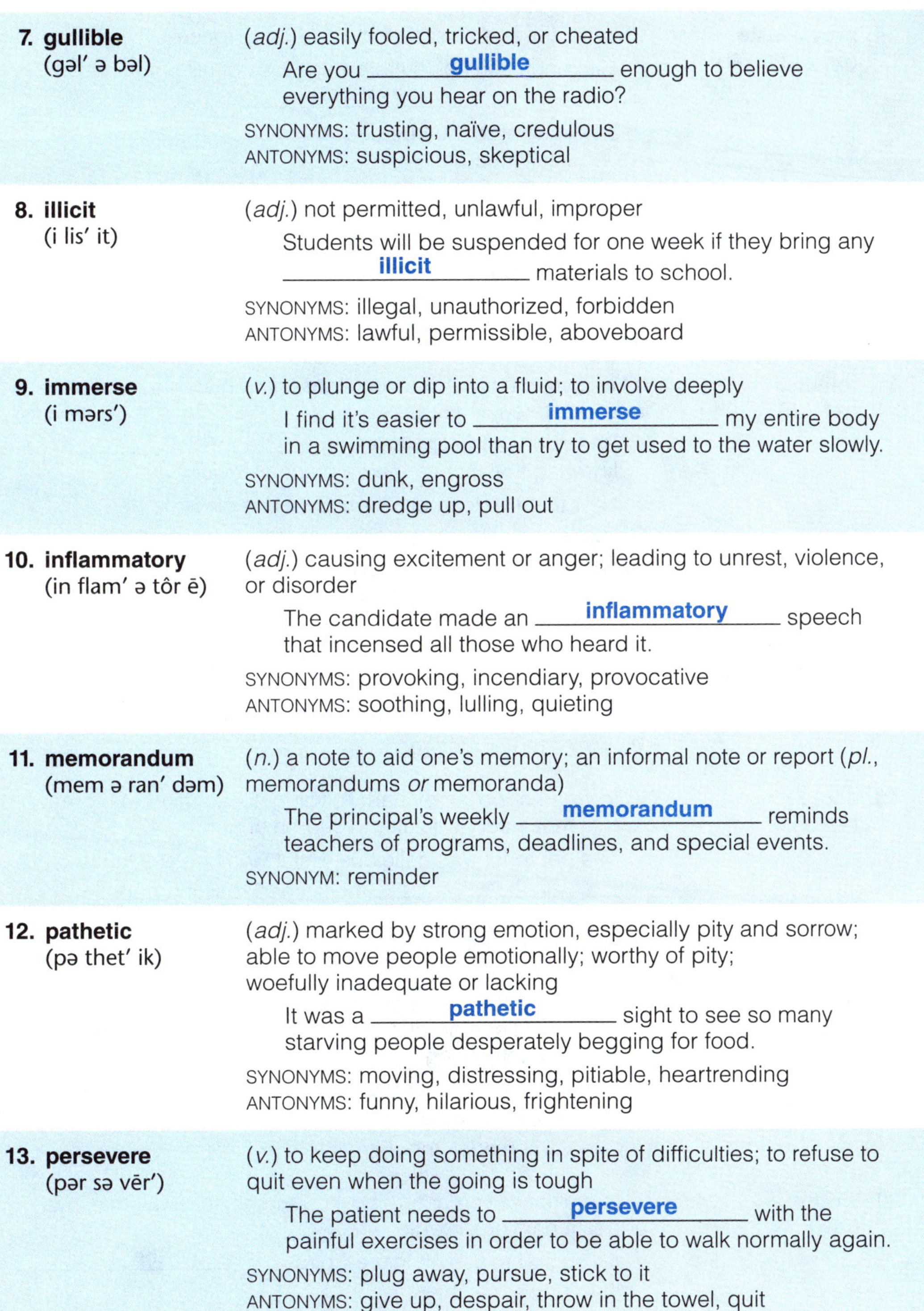

7. gullible (gəl′ ə bəl)

(*adj.*) easily fooled, tricked, or cheated

Are you **gullible** enough to believe everything you hear on the radio?

SYNONYMS: trusting, naïve, credulous
ANTONYMS: suspicious, skeptical

8. illicit (i lis′ it)

(*adj.*) not permitted, unlawful, improper

Students will be suspended for one week if they bring any **illicit** materials to school.

SYNONYMS: illegal, unauthorized, forbidden
ANTONYMS: lawful, permissible, aboveboard

9. immerse (i mərs′)

(*v.*) to plunge or dip into a fluid; to involve deeply

I find it's easier to **immerse** my entire body in a swimming pool than try to get used to the water slowly.

SYNONYMS: dunk, engross
ANTONYMS: dredge up, pull out

10. inflammatory (in flam′ ə tôr ē)

(*adj.*) causing excitement or anger; leading to unrest, violence, or disorder

The candidate made an **inflammatory** speech that incensed all those who heard it.

SYNONYMS: provoking, incendiary, provocative
ANTONYMS: soothing, lulling, quieting

11. memorandum (mem ə ran′ dəm)

(*n.*) a note to aid one's memory; an informal note or report (*pl.*, memorandums *or* memoranda)

The principal's weekly **memorandum** reminds teachers of programs, deadlines, and special events.

SYNONYM: reminder

12. pathetic (pə thet′ ik)

(*adj.*) marked by strong emotion, especially pity and sorrow; able to move people emotionally; worthy of pity; woefully inadequate or lacking

It was a **pathetic** sight to see so many starving people desperately begging for food.

SYNONYMS: moving, distressing, pitiable, heartrending
ANTONYMS: funny, hilarious, frightening

13. persevere (pər sə vēr′)

(*v.*) to keep doing something in spite of difficulties; to refuse to quit even when the going is tough

The patient needs to **persevere** with the painful exercises in order to be able to walk normally again.

SYNONYMS: plug away, pursue, stick to it
ANTONYMS: give up, despair, throw in the towel, quit

CCSS Vocabulary: 4.c., 4.d. (See pp. T14–15.)

14. prevaricate
(pri var′ ə kāt)

(*v.*) to lie, tell an untruth; to mislead on purpose

His reputation has suffered because of his unfortunate tendency to **prevaricate**.

SYNONYMS: stretch the truth, equivocate
ANTONYM: tell the truth

15. quash
(kwäsh)

(*v.*) to crush, put down completely

Swift military action was required to **quash** the revolt before anyone was injured.

SYNONYM: suppress
ANTONYMS: start, kindle, ignite, encourage

16. relish
(rel′ ish)

(*n.*) enjoyment or satisfaction; something that adds a pleasing flavor; (*v.*) to enjoy greatly

She opened the tiny box with **relish**, knowing that it contained a piece of jewelry.

Now that I've learned about Japan in class, I **relish** the chance to travel there.

SYNONYMS: (*n.*) pleasure, gusto; (*v.*) take delight in
ANTONYMS: (*v.*) loathe, hate, despise

17. reminisce
(rem ə nis′)

(*v.*) to recall one's past thoughts, feelings, or experiences

At the family reunion, we got to hear 94-year-old Tía Luzia **reminisce** about life in old Havana.

SYNONYMS: remember, recollect

18. scour
(skaủr)

(*v.*) to clean or polish by hard rubbing; to examine with great care; to move about quickly in search of

The pot roast was delicious, but it won't be any fun to **scour** the burned roasting pan.

SYNONYMS: scrub, search, comb
ANTONYMS: dirty, soil

19. testimonial
(tes′ tə mō′ nē əl)

(*n.*) a statement that speaks to a person's character or to the benefits of a product; expressing the value and worth of someone or something

The famous athlete's **testimonial** about the thirst-quenching drink made an impression on TV viewers.

SYNONYMS: memorial, tribute, evidence, statement

20. writhe
(rīth)

(*v.*) to make twisting or turning movements in a way that suggests pain or struggle

It's so sad to see an injured bird **writhe** in pain.

SYNONYMS: twist, squirm, thrash

CCSS Vocabulary: 4.c., 4.d. (See pp. T14–15.)

Choosing the Right Word

*Select the **boldface** word that better completes each sentence. You might refer to the passage on pages 88–89 to see how most of these words are used in context.*

Though plagued by illness, family difficulties, and the loss of his hearing, Ludwig van Beethoven created some of the world's greatest musical compositions.

1. Though he was losing his hearing, Beethoven (**authorized, immersed**) himself in his music.

2. We were impressed with Ella's (**testimonial, culprit**), as she described how a new shampoo made her hair grow faster.

3. The charges against the suspected mugger will probably not hold up in court, so the district attorney has decided to (**authorize, quash**) them.

4. Despite several rejection letters from publishers, the young writer (**prevaricated, persevered**) and continued to write stories.

5. In spite of all your talk about how hard it is to get into medical school, I intend to (**persevere, relish**) in my plans to become a doctor.

6. Is there any sight more (**pathetic, illicit**) than a kitten stranded in a tree?

7. When the class comedian imitated my way of speaking, it was all I could do not to (**writhe, reminisce**) with embarrassment.

8. What good does it do for the president of the Student Council to issue (**fatalities, memorandums**) if no one takes the trouble to read them?

9. We learned in our social studies class that the Constitution (**dissects, authorizes**) the president to arrange treaties with foreign countries.

10. She is so worried about appearing (**inflammatory, gullible**) that she sometimes refuses to believe things that are well supported by facts.

11. The more he tried to protect himself by (**scouring, prevaricating**), the more he became entrapped in his own web of lies.

12. Whenever my Aunt Joan hears a hit from the 1990s on the radio, she starts to (**reminisce, expend**) about her days in high school.

13. His sticky fingers and the crumbs around his mouth convinced us that he was the (**culprit, relish**) in the Case of the Empty Cookie Jar.

14. Although our coach can spend hours (**writhing, reminiscing**) about his victories, he doesn't have an equally good memory for his defeats.

15. She (**expends, dawdles**) so much time and energy on small matters that she can't prepare properly for the things that are really important.

CCSS Vocabulary: 4.d. (See pp. T14–15.)

16. Dictators like Hitler and Mussolini used (**pathetic, inflammatory**) language to stir up the emotions of the crowds they addressed.

17. Because my sister is so (**gullible, inflammatory**), I have to avoid reading scary stories to her before her bedtime.

18. When it became known that four explorers were lost in the jungle, special search parties were sent out to (**quash, scour**) the area for them.

19. I am afraid that our ambitious plan to modernize the gym has become a (**fatality, memorandum**) of the School Board's economy drive.

20. She was so deeply (**immersed, expended**) in the book she was reading that she did not even hear us enter the room.

21. It was plain from the way that he (**dawdled, persevered**) over breakfast that he was in no hurry to visit the dentist.

22. With the skill of a trained debater, she (**prevaricated, dissected**) her opponent's arguments one by one to reveal their basic weaknesses.

23. His scheme to make money by preparing term papers for other students is not only completely (**gullible, illicit**) but immoral as well.

24. No one (**relishes, immerses**) being reminded of his or her mistakes, but if you are wise you will try to learn from such criticism.

25. I spent three hours (**authorizing, scouring**) my room, looking for my homework.

*Choose the word from this Unit that is the same or most nearly the same in meaning as the **boldface** word or expression in the phrase. Write that word on the line. Use a dictionary if necessary.*

1. upsetting to learn the **heartbreaking** details ____pathetic____
2. targeted the most **innocent** people ____gullible____
3. a monthly **notice** to all her patients ____memorandum____
4. destroying the **banned** books ____illicit____
5. **carry on** despite many setbacks ____persevere____
6. miracle that we suffered only one **loss of life** ____fatality____
7. is certainly no time to **fib** ____prevaricate____
8. promoting **confrontational** ideas to start a riot ____inflammatory____
9. desperate to **wriggle** free from the ropes ____writhe____
10. **submerge** the vegetables in cold water ____immerse____

 CCSS Vocabulary: 5. (See pp. T14–15.)

Antonyms

*Choose the word from this Unit that is most nearly opposite in meaning to the **boldface** word or expression in the phrase. Write that word on the line. Use a dictionary if necessary.*

1. a snake that **lies still** ___writhes___
2. suffering only a **minor wound** ___fatality___
3. made **calming** gestures to the group ___inflammatory___
4. sent a **long formal report** to the Board of Directors ___memorandum___
5. participating in **legal** activities ___illicit___

Completing the Sentence

From the words in this Unit, choose the one that best completes each of the following sentences. Write the correct word form in the space provided.

1. You may not ___relish___ being told that your carelessness was responsible for the accident, even though it happens to be true.
2. Many people were injured in the explosion, but luckily there was not a single ___fatality___.
3. The story of the homeless child was so ___pathetic___ that it moved us all to tears.
4. Before you ___immerse___ yourself in the bath, be sure to test the temperature of the water.
5. We tried to hold Tom steady, but he ___writhed___ with pain as the doctor put splints on his broken leg.
6. Is it wise to ___expend___ so much of your hard-earned money on things that you don't really want or need?
7. The dictator ordered his secret police to ___quash___ any attempt to organize a protest rally.
8. Our supervisor prepared a(n) ___memorandum___ that reminded the salespeople of the procedures to be followed during the holiday season.
9. "Only a bigot would dare to make such a rude and ___inflammatory___ remark, even in jest," I replied.
10. The children won't ___dawdle___ over their homework if they know they'll be getting cheese and crackers as soon as they finish.

11. Because he was seen near the scene of the crime at the time the deed was committed, he was suspected of being the ___**culprit**___.

12. I love to listen to my grandfather ___**reminisce**___ about his boyhood adventures in Coney Island.

13. The new library that will bear Ann Parker's name is a ___**testimonial**___ to her commitment to teaching children how to read.

14. Do you really think that I am ___**gullible**___ enough to believe his foolish story about being a member of the Olympic team?

15. This pass ___**authorizes**___ you to visit certain rooms in this museum that are not open to the general public.

16. You may be tempted to ___**prevaricate**___, but in the long run it will be to your advantage to own up to the truth about your unfortunate error.

17. We had to ___**scour**___ the walls for hours to get rid of the dirt and grease with which they were encrusted.

18. Cracking down on ___**illicit**___ drug traffic is one of the biggest problems facing law-enforcement agencies in the United States.

19. No matter how talented you may be, you will never be successful unless you learn to ___**persevere**___ in what you undertake.

20. After we had ___**dissected**___ the animal, we had to point to each of its important organs and explain its main function.

Writing: Words in Action

Answers to both prompts will vary.

1. Look back at "Made for the Shade" (pages 88–89). Suppose you have been put in charge of an advertising campaign for a company that manufactures sunglasses. Your job is to write a television commercial that introduces a new line of shades and persuades viewers to purchase them. Use at least two details from the passage and three Unit words to support your ad.

2. People are often very vulnerable to the claims of advertising and feel that they must have certain brand-name items: designer sunglasses, a specific manufacturer's running shoes, or an article of clothing that carries a particular logo. Write a position paper in which you state your opinion about some of the effects of advertising on people your age. What is harmful about advertising? How does it affect your daily life? What should young people know about advertising techniques? Support your opinion with your observations, specific examples, the reading (refer to pages 88–89), or your personal experience. Write at least three paragraphs, and use three or more words from this Unit.

Writing prompt #2 is modeled on that of standardized tests.

 CCSS Vocabulary: 6; Writing: 1.c., 2.d., 3.d., 4. (See pp. T14–15.)

Vocabulary in Context: Informational Text for Unit 7 is available online at **vocabularyworkshop.com**.

The following excerpts are from Oliver Twist *by Charles Dickens. Some of the words you have studied in this Unit appear in* **boldface** *type. Complete each statement below the excerpt by circling the letter of the correct answer.*

1. The man shook his fist, as he uttered these words incoherently. He advanced towards Oliver, as if with the intention of aiming a blow at him, but fell violently on the ground: **writhing** and foaming, in a fit.

A person who is **writhing** is

a. talking　　**c.** yelling
b. praying　　**d.** thrashing

2. The dogs, who, in common with their masters, seemed to have no particular **relish** for the sport in which they were engaged, readily answered to the command.

People who do NOT **relish** a sport

a. enjoy it　　**c.** excel in it
b. dislike it　　**d.** fail at it

3. It was not until the two boys had **scoured**, with great rapidity, through a most intricate maze of narrow streets and courts, that they ventured to halt beneath a low and dark archway. Having remained silent here, just long enough to recover breath to speak, [Bates] uttered an exclamation of amusement and delight.

Someone who has **scoured** through a place has moved

a. joylessly　　**c.** intently
b. happily　　**d.** cautiously

Oliver Twist is about a young orphan who joins a group of boys trained to steal.

4. The snow lay on the ground, frozen into a hard thick crust, so that only the heaps that had drifted into byways and corners were affected by the sharp wind that howled abroad: which, as if **expending** increased fury on such prey as it found, caught it savagely up in clouds, and, whirling it into a thousand misty eddies, scattered it in air.

The act of **expending** involves

a. using up　　**c.** choosing
b. saving for　　**d.** approving

5. "I hope the gentleman will understand that it isn't my fault, sir?" said Mrs. Mann, whimpering **pathetically**.

A person who sobs **pathetically** does so in a(n)

a. miserable manner　　**c.** respectable manner
b. impartial manner　　**d.** playful manner

Snap the code, or go to **vocabularyworkshop.com**

UNIT 8

Note that not all of the 20 Unit words are used in this passage. *Cascade*, *immobile*, *impassable*, *martial*, and *perishable* are not included.

Read the following passage, taking note of the ***boldface*** *words and their contexts. These words are among those you will be studying in Unit 8. As you complete the exercises in this Unit, it may help to refer to the way the words are used below.*

CCSS Vocabulary: 4; Reading (Informational Text): 4, 6. (See pp. T14–15.)

From Big Dream to Big Top

<Interview>

This month, Teen Talk Magazine *interviews Mike Quintus Bessy, an aerialist with the Empire Circus. Mike tells TT about the history of the circus, his job, and circus life.*

Editor's Note: Englishman Philip Astley (1742–1814) is one of the most important figures in circus history. He was a skilled equestrian who opened a popular riding school and performing arena, and then became a circus impresario when he built Astley's Amphitheatre in London in 1770. Astley worked hard, took risks, gained money and **affluence**, and was living proof that there is no luck except when there is discipline.

TT: Mike, many circus performers are born into a family of performers, but your parents are dentists. What made you want to join the circus?

Mike Q. Bessy: When I was quite young, I read a book about Philip Astley. I was fascinated and started taking tumbling classes. Astley is known as the father of the modern circus because his circus is the **template** for the circuses we see today.

TT: How did Astley go about founding a circus?

MQB: From the **onset**, Astley had a passion for horses. He enlisted in a cavalry regiment and then took up performing. One of his specialties was to **retrieve** a handkerchief from the ground while his horse cantered. He could maintain his balance better if his horse traveled in circles, so that's why he had a ring for his circus. Back then, animals and trick riders were the stars, and Astley's circus supposedly featured a horse that could perform card tricks and a pig that could solve math problems. I would pay to see that!

Philip Astley was one of the great showmen of his time.

TT: What was a typical show like back in Astley's time?

MQB: Astley staged massive spectacles featuring a **minimum** of 100 horses and riders. There would also be fireworks, music, magicians, tightrope walkers, clowns, performing dogs...you name it! Well, except for wild-animal acts—that **innovation** came later. There was a stage, a circular pit, and audience galleries. There was no **partition** between the stage and the arena, so the shows were held

Astley's Amphitheatre was home to the first true modern circus.

simultaneously. The amphitheatre was rebuilt a number of times after fires, and it was eventually demolished in the 1890s because bad decisions and bad luck left the owner in **arrears**. Meanwhile, Astley retired from performing when he was still in his 30s, but he was often the ringmaster, dressed in his customary military costume.

TT: **The story goes that although Astley was charming, he also had a quick temper. I guess even circus folk aren't always happy-go-lucky.**

MQB: It's a mistake to assume that circus performers are happy and **jovial** 100 percent of the time. We're all **crotchety** sometimes—even clowns!

TT: **Besides a taste for adventure, what makes a good aerialist?**

MQB: You have to have a strong, **taut** body, and you must be alert, quick, and **nimble** to fly through the air and catch your partners.

TT: **Do you feel as if the circus is your home?**

MQB: I do, although I know some people don't care for circuses. They think the atmosphere is a little creepy and **sinister**, or they're uncomfortable with crowds, or they harbor an image of elephants in **manacles** and chains. It makes me **cringe** to hear that animals are abused. I believe most circuses treat their animals with kindness and respect, the same way Philip Astley cared for his beloved horses.

Note the spelling, pronunciation, part(s) of speech, and definition(s) of each of the following words. Then write the appropriate form of the word in the blank spaces in the illustrative sentence(s) following. Finally, study the lists of synonyms and antonyms.

1. affluence (af′ lü əns)
(*n.*) wealth, riches, prosperity; great abundance, plenty

Education, hard work, and a very strong desire to succeed can raise a person from poverty to **affluence**.

SYNONYM: opulence; ANTONYMS: poverty, want, destitution, scarcity

2. arrears (ə rērz′)
(*n., pl.*) unpaid or overdue debts; an unfinished duty

Bad spending habits and unexpected expenses left my aunt in **arrears**.

SYNONYMS: in default, in the red, late, overdue

3. cascade (kas kād′)
(*n.*) a steep, narrow waterfall; something falling or rushing forth in quantity; (*v.*) to flow downward (like a waterfall)

We were thrilled when we hit the jackpot, which produced a **cascade** of loudly jangling coins.

I watched the clear, sparkling water **cascade** down the mountainside.

SYNONYMS: (*v.*) plunge, rush, tumble
ANTONYMS: (*n.*) dribble, drop; (*v.*) trickle, ooze

4. cringe (krinj)
(*v.*) to shrink back or hide in fear or submissiveness

My father told me to be brave and not to **cringe** when the doctor vaccinated me.

SYNONYMS: flinch, duck, fawn; ANTONYMS: strut, swagger

5. crotchety (kräch′ ə tē)
(*adj.*) cranky, ill-tempered; full of odd whims

It is unfortunate that the teacher asked me to work with the most **crotchety** partner in the class.

SYNONYMS: grumpy, grouchy, crabby, disagreeable
ANTONYMS: sociable, friendly, agreeable, amiable

6. immobile (i mō′ bəl)
(*adj.*) not movable; not moving

Models must remain **immobile** for a long time in order for an artist to draw or paint them accurately.

SYNONYMS: fixed, unmoving; ANTONYMS: movable, nimble, agile

7. impassable (im pas′ ə bəl)
(*adj.*) blocked so that nothing can go through

Fallen trees formed an **impassable** barrier across the highway after the storm.

SYNONYMS: closed, impenetrable; ANTONYMS: unblocked, clear

CCSS Vocabulary: 4.c., 4.d. (See pp. T14–15.)

8. innovation (i nō vā′ shən)

(*n.*) something new, a change; the act of introducing a new method, idea, device, etc.

Our furnace has an energy-saving **innovation** that turns the heat on and off at certain intervals.

SYNONYMS: novelty, modernization, new wrinkle

9. jovial (jō′ vē əl)

(*adj.*) good-humored, in high spirits; merry

My **jovial** friend is very entertaining and is always the life of the party.

SYNONYMS: jolly, cheerful, festive
ANTONYMS: gloomy, morose, melancholy, cheerless

10. manacle (man′ ə kəl)

(*n., usually pl.*) a handcuff, anything that chains or confines; (*v.*) to chain or restrain (as with handcuffs)

The kidnappers clamped **manacles** on their frightened hostages.

The guards **manacled** the uncooperative prisoner to the chair.

SYNONYMS: (*v.*) put in chains, fetter
ANTONYMS: (*v.*) unchain, set free, emancipate, release

11. martial (mär′ shəl)

(*adj.*) warlike, fond of fighting; relating to war, the army, or military life

The army band plays **martial** music as the troops formally march past the visiting general.

SYNONYMS: hostile, bellicose
ANTONYMS: peace-loving, pacific, unwarlike

12. minimum (min′ ə məm)

(*n.*) the smallest possible amount; (*adj.*) the lowest permissible or possible

I need to sleep a **minimum** of seven hours every night.

The **minimum** age to get a driver's license in this state is sixteen.

SYNONYM: (*adj.*) least
ANTONYMS: (*n.*) maximum; (*adj.*) highest, most

13. nimble (nim′ bəl)

(*adj.*) quick and skillful in movement, agile; clever

As the **nimble** climber scaled Mount Everest, it looked as if she was barely exerting any energy at all.

SYNONYMS: lively, keen, flexible
ANTONYMS: awkward, clumsy, stiff, inflexible

14. onset (än′ set)

(*n.*) the beginning, start (especially of something violent and destructive); an attack, assault

At the **onset** of the heavy storm, frightened people ran to find shelter.

SYNONYMS: outset, commencement
ANTONYMS: conclusion, close, end

15. partition (pär tish′ ən)

(*n.*) something that divides (such as a wall); the act of dividing something into parts or sections; (*v.*) to divide or subdivide into parts or shares

A cloth **partition** in the study gave each of us some privacy.

If you like, we can easily **partition** the backyard into four separate play areas.

SYNONYMS: (*n.*) divider, separation
ANTONYMS: (*v.*) join, combine, consolidate, merge

16. perishable (per′ ə shə bəl)

(*adj.*) likely to spoil or decay

You must keep **perishable** foods chilled, or they will spoil.

SYNONYMS: short-lived, fleeting
ANTONYMS: long-lasting, undying, permanent

17. retrieve (ri trēv′)

(*v.*) to find and bring back, get back; to put right, make good

I don't relish having to **retrieve** the tennis balls every time you hit them over the fence!

SYNONYMS: regain, fetch, remedy, rectify

18. sinister (sin′ ə stər)

(*adj.*) appearing evil or dangerous; threatening evil or harm

A **sinister** message left on our voicemail made us suspect the caller had the wrong number.

SYNONYMS: frightening, ominous
ANTONYMS: cheering, encouraging, reassuring, benign

19. taut (tôt)

(*adj.*) tightly drawn, tense; neat, in good order

A **taut** chain kept the curious dog away from the swimming pool.

SYNONYMS: tight, strained, orderly, shipshape
ANTONYMS: loose, slack, drooping, messy, sloppy

20. template (tem′ plit)

(*n.*) a pattern, typically in the form of metal, wood, or plastic; something that is used as a model to imitate

The carpenter created a wooden **template** for a stair step so that he could easily construct the staircase.

SYNONYMS: mock-up, stencil, guide, shape, mold

CCSS Vocabulary: 4.c., 4.d. (See pp. T14–15.)

Choosing the Right Word

*Select the **boldface** word that better completes each sentence. You might refer to the passage on pages 98–99 to see how most of these words are used in context.*

Howard Pyle, an American illustrator and writer, arranged all the Robin Hood tales into a unified story.

1. Robin Hood's faithful merry men were not only (**crotchety, jovial**) companions, but brave and clever fighters as well.

2. Some hikers are surprised when they get a poison ivy rash, as its (**cringe, onset**) can sometimes be several days after the encounter with the vine.

3. Although we all recognize that there must be changes, it is a mistake to think that every (**arrears, innovation**) is necessarily an improvement.

4. Instead of acting as though you were permanently (**manacled, retrieved**) to your small circle of friends, you should try to meet new people.

5. More than once, our skillful running backs managed to find a way through our opponents' supposedly (**impassable, affluent**) line.

6. Normally, I'm very even tempered, but I can become a little (**martial, crotchety**) when I'm tired or hungry.

7. We learned in our history class that the ancient Romans were very fine soldiers and excelled in all the (**martial, perishable**) arts.

8. Everyone in the auditorium (**retrieved, cringed**) when the singer hit a sour note while performing his most famous song.

9. I felt that there was something thoroughly (**sinister, immobile**) about the way he kept trying to duck questions on that subject.

10. With the (**affluence, onset**) of the heat wave, vast numbers of city dwellers began to stream toward the beaches and mountains.

11. Of all the different types of writing, humor may be the most (**perishable, jovial**), since each generation has its own idea of what is funny.

12. To keep a (**nimble, sinister**) mind, doctors advise working on crossword puzzles or learning a foreign language.

13. In the moment of danger, my nerves were so (**taut, sinister**) that I would have screamed if someone had touched me.

14. Although we are proud of our high standard of living, we should not forget that there are those who do not share in this (**affluence, minimum**).

15. Her blond hair fell upon her shoulders like a shimmering (**onset, cascade**) of gold.

CCSS Vocabulary: 4.d. (See pp. T14–15.)

16. Thanks to my brother's (**templates, innovations**) to a classic recipe, we won first prize at the fair for best hot sauce.

17. Her mind is so (**impassable, nimble**) that she always seems to be one step ahead of us in any matter under discussion.

18. The self-styled "tough guy" (**cringed, manacled**) in terror and begged the police not to shoot.

19. The first thing the bankrupt firm must do with its funds is pay the (**arrears, templates**) due on the employees' wages.

20. A high school student looking for a vacation job usually can't expect to earn more than the (**perishable, minimum**) wage.

21. Despite all his efforts, he was never able to (**retrieve, partition**) the fine reputation he had lost by that crooked deal.

22. In the eighteenth century, Russia, Prussia, and Austria made a series of deals to (**partition, cringe**) and annex Poland right out of existence.

23. The speed with which the boxer darted about the ring made his lumbering opponent seem utterly (**nimble, immobile**) by comparison.

24. Did you know that most computer software provides several different (**templates, onsets**) for letter writing?

25. This facial cream claims that it will help keep your skin (**taut, jovial**) and youthful.

Choose the word from this Unit that is the same or most nearly the same in meaning as the ***boldface*** *word or expression in the phrase. Write that word on the line. Use a dictionary if necessary.*

1. **recover** data from my computer — retrieve
2. in the **clogged** section of the pipe — impassable
3. under strict **military** law — martial
4. a **menacing** look in his eyes — sinister
5. installed to make it remain **stationary** — immobile
6. begged not to be **shackled** — manacled
7. to **cower** when the storm approaches — cringe
8. avoid eating food that can become **rotten** — perishable
9. as confetti **spilled** onto the stage — cascaded
10. resisting the latest **improvement** — innovation

CCSS Vocabulary: 5. (See pp. T14–15.)

The synonyms and antonyms here do not appear on the Definitions page.

Antonyms

*Choose the word from this Unit that is most nearly opposite in meaning to the **boldface** word or expression in the phrase. Write that word on the line. Use a dictionary if necessary.*

1. using a **transportable** device ____immobile____
2. materials that are strong and **durable** ____perishable____
3. water **dripping** from the spout ____cascading____
4. living among **peaceable** people ____martial____
5. looking for an **open** lane ____impassable____

Completing the Sentence

From the words in this Unit, choose the one that best completes each of the following sentences. Write the correct word form in the space provided.

1. The ____jovial____ mood of our cheerful little gathering changed abruptly to sorrow when news of the tragedy came over the radio.
2. It's a pleasure to watch the expert typist's ____nimble____ fingers move swiftly over the keyboard.
3. The patients will have a much better chance to recover quickly if they receive treatment at the ____onset____ of the fever.
4. Sherlock Holmes detected in the wicked scheme the ____sinister____ hand of the evil Professor Moriarty.
5. Can you explain why there is not only a maximum speed limit but also a(n) ____minimum____ speed limit on many modern highways?
6. We plan to update the ____template____ of our school brochure to make it more attractive and readable.
7. I know that my payments on the car are in ____arrears____, but I will catch up as soon as I get my next paycheck.
8. Today ____perishable____ foods are transported in refrigerated trucks to prevent spoilage.
9. Unless you pull the ropes ____taut____, the tennis net will sag.
10. Although we are sure that the prisoners will make no attempt to escape, the law requires us to place ____manacles____ on them.

CCSS Vocabulary: 4.a., 5. (See pp. T14–15.)

11. Frank Lloyd Wright was a great American architect who was responsible for many ___innovations___ in the design of buildings.

12. The sunlight caught the waters of the stream as they ___cascaded___ over the steep cliff and formed a brilliant rainbow.

13. I was able to ___retrieve___ my baggage promptly after leaving the plane.

14. The more we tried to humor the ___crotchety___ crossing guard, the more irritable and demanding he seemed to become.

15. His back injury was so severe that he has been placed in a cast and will have to remain ___immobile___ for months.

16. I don't expect you to be a hero, but do you have to ___cringe___ in that cowardly fashion whenever anyone so much as disagrees with you?

17. During the war years, the government tried all kinds of propaganda to arouse the ___martial___ spirit of the people.

18. All roads throughout the area became ___impassable___ as a result of the record-breaking snowstorm.

19. The feeling of ___affluence___ I had when I was paid lasted only until I had finished taking care of my bills.

20. We made use of a(n) ___partition___ to break up the floor space into a large number of small offices.

Writing: Words in Action

Answers to both prompts will vary.

1. Look back at "From Big Dream to Big Top" (pages 98–99). Suppose that you are a circus performer, and you want others to consider a career with the circus. Write a letter to young people to persuade them that the circus offers challenging and interesting career paths. Use at least two details from the passage and three Unit words.

2. Some people feel that animals should not be trained to perform in circuses. Others feel that circuses are educational, allowing people to see how intelligent animals are and marvel at the amazing feats they can perform. Write a brief essay in which you state your position on this topic. Support your opinion with your observations, specific examples, the reading (refer to pages 98–99), or personal experience. Write at least three paragraphs, and use three or more words from this Unit.

Writing prompt #2 is modeled on that of standardized tests.

CCSS Vocabulary: 6; Writing: 1.c., 2.d., 3.d., 4. (See pp. T14–15.)

Vocabulary in Context: Informational Text for Unit 8 is available online at **vocabularyworkshop.com**.

The following excerpts are from The Adventures of Sherlock Holmes *by Sir Arthur Conan Doyle. Some of the words you have studied in this Unit appear in* **boldface** *type. Complete each statement below the excerpt by circling the letter of the correct answer.*

1. "Get back into your chair!" said Holmes sternly. "It is very well to **cringe** and crawl now, but you thought little enough of this poor Horner in the dock for a crime of which he knew nothing." ("The Adventure of the Blue Carbuncle")

To **cringe** is to

a. change
b. escape
c. cower
d. mumble

2. The trees and wayside hedges were just throwing out their first green shoots, and the air was full of the pleasant smell of the moist earth. To me at least there was a strange contrast between the sweet promise of the spring and this **sinister** quest upon which we were engaged. ("The Adventure of the Speckled Band")

Something that is **sinister** is definitely NOT

a. terrifying
b. comforting
c. startling
d. chilling

3. . . .I met Mr. Rucastle coming out through this door, his keys in his hand, and a look on his face which made him a very different person to the round, **jovial** man to whom I was accustomed. His cheeks were red, his brow was all crinkled with anger, and the veins stood out at his temples with passion. ("The Adventure of the Copper Beeches")

A person who is **jovial** is

a. joyful
b. thoughtful
c. crabby
d. dangerous

Basil Rathbone played Sherlock Holmes in this 1939 film adaptation of *The Adventures of Sherlock Holmes.*

4. "Yet if the lady is correct in saying that the flooring and walls are sound, and that the door, window, and chimney are **impassable**, then her sister must have been undoubtedly alone when she met her mysterious end." ("The Adventure of the Speckled Band")

If something is **impassable**, it is

a. stubborn
b. old-fashioned
c. stiff
d. blocked

5. . . .[W]ith a cry, she sprang at a small deal box which lay upon the table and tore the lid from it. Out there fell a **cascade** of children's bricks. ("The Man with the Twisted Lip")

A **cascade** is something that

a. fails
b. streams
c. crumbles
d. cries

Snap the code, or go to **vocabularyworkshop.com**

UNIT 9

Note that not all of the 20 Unit words are used in this passage. *Discretion*, *misrepresent*, *optional*, *rendezvous*, and *rotund* are not included.

*Read the following passage, taking note of the **boldface** words and their contexts. These words are among those you will be studying in Unit 9. As you complete the exercises in this Unit, it may help to refer to the way the words are used below.*

CCSS Vocabulary: 4; Reading (Informational Text): 4, 6. (See pp. T14–15.)

From Fire Arrows to Space Flight: A History of Rockets

<Informational Essay>

As early as 400 BCE, **logical** and observant inventors in Greece used steam to propel simple devices. A man named Archytas used steam to send a wooden pigeon gliding along high wires. These early steam-propelled devices were of little practical use. They were mainly used for entertainment. Over a thousand years later and thousands of miles away from Greece, Chinese alchemists learned to make gunpowder. By around 1100 CE, the Chinese were using gunpowder to make fireworks, which were used for celebrations. Simple grenade-like bombs were used in war. Before long, the Chinese learned to use gunpowder to propel "fire arrows" through the air. The same basic principle of propulsion was at work in Archytas's **giddy** pigeon and in Chinese fire arrows. But the special properties of gunpowder made the fire arrows useful tools of war.

In 1232, Chinese soldiers used fire arrows to defeat Mongol invaders at the Battle of Kai-Keng. This is the first known use of rockets in the history of warfare. To make these simple rockets, the Chinese filled a short bamboo tube with gunpowder. They capped one end of the tube. Then they attached it to an arrow. Then the gunpowder was ignited. It produced fire, smoke, and gas that escaped through the open end of the tube. This force propelled the rocket through the air. The arrow helped to keep the rocket steady during flight, though its course remained quite **variable**. These earliest rockets may not always have done much damage on **impact**. But a **deluge** of many fire arrows could cause **outright** fear in the enemy. Gaining something in defeat, the Mongols learned to make similar rockets. The new technology spread rapidly across Asia and Europe. But improvements in the basic design proceeded slowly at a **sluggish** pace until more modern days.

Early Chinese fire arrow rockets, c. 1000

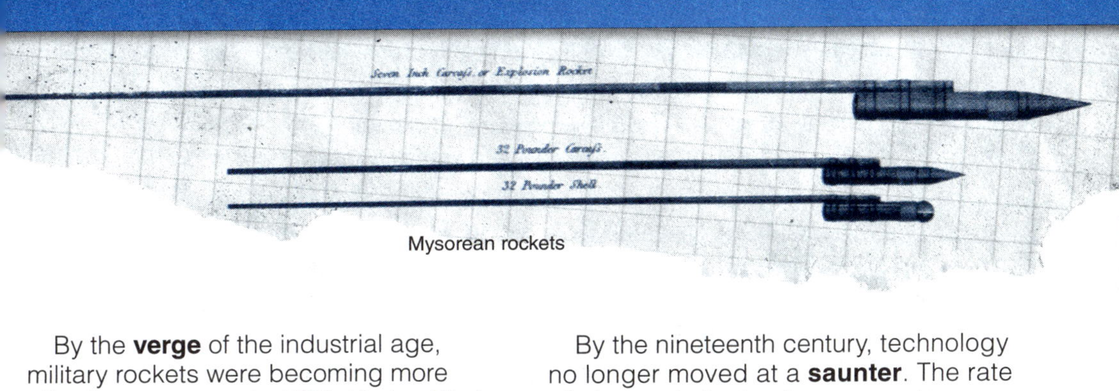

Mysorean rockets

By the **verge** of the industrial age, military rockets were becoming more effective weapons. In 1780, Hyder Ali of Mysore, a kingdom in India, used heavy, iron-cased rockets to defeat British forces. His son, Tipu Sultan, used the same rockets against the British with similar success. Mysorean rockets were not used merely to scare and **intimidate** the enemy. They were deadly weapons that cut down troops in their path. They were also used to set fire to ammunition and supplies. Determined to **avenge** themselves, British forces finally defeated Tipu Sultan's army in 1799. The Kingdom of Mysore **ceded** territory to the British Empire and became **subordinate** to its authority. The British soon developed their own weapons. The British based their rockets on the Mysorean rockets. A model described by William Congreve in 1807 set the standard for the Congreve rocket.

The British used the Congreve rocket against the United States during the War of 1812. The "rockets' red glare" remembered in the "Star-Spangled Banner" refers to the fiery **tint** of Congreve rockets in action.

By the nineteenth century, technology no longer moved at a **saunter**. The rate of change in tools of peace and war was accelerating as never before. Advances in artillery made rockets obsolete for several decades. But by the twentieth century, engineers were designing sophisticated rockets for use as spacecraft and as devastating missile systems. Rockets returned to the forefront of military technology. They also helped **liberate** humanity from Earth's gravity to explore outer space. And while rocket science has come a long way since its beginnings, it's likely to wind up light years ahead of its present state, in time.

Saturn V launch

Audio

For iWords and audio passages, snap the code, or go to **vocabularyworkshop.com**.

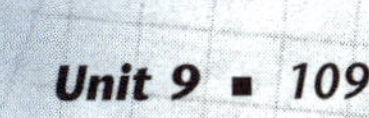

Definitions

Note the spelling, pronunciation, part(s) of speech, and definition(s) of each of the following words. Then write the appropriate form of the word in the blank spaces in the illustrative sentence(s) following. Finally, study the lists of synonyms and antonyms.

1. avenge (ə venj′)

(*v.*) to get revenge for, get even for, settle a score; to punish someone or get satisfaction for a wrong or injury

In Shakespeare's *Hamlet*, the title character vows to **avenge** his father's death.

SYNONYM: retaliate

2. cede (sēd)

(*v.*) to give up, surrender; to hand over to another

Spain **ceded** territory to France.

SYNONYMS: deliver up, transfer

3. deluge (del′ yüj)

(*n.*) a great flood; a heavy fall of rain; anything that comes in a vast quantity (like a flood); (*v.*) to flood

Owners are hoping this summer will bring a **deluge** of visitors to their new theme park in Minneapolis.

A torrential downpour **deluged** the entire town.

SYNONYMS: (*v.*) swamp, inundate
ANTONYMS: (*n.*) trickle, dribble

4. discretion (dis kresh′ ən)

(*n.*) good judgment; care in speech and action; freedom to judge or choose

My teacher suggested I use **discretion** in dealing with my difficult classmate.

SYNONYMS: prudence, tact, discrimination

5. giddy (gid′ ē)

(*adj.*) dizzy; light-headed; lacking seriousness

After the long and grueling race, the marathoner felt **giddy** and exhausted.

SYNONYMS: faint, frivolous, flighty
ANTONYMS: levelheaded, serious, earnest, sober

6. impact (*n.*, im′ pakt; *v.*, im pakt′)

(*n.*) the striking of one object against another; the shock caused by a collision; (*v.*) to affect, especially forcefully

The **impact** of the car crash destroyed both vehicles, but miraculously no one was hurt.

Budget cuts will **impact** the number of hours the public library can stay open.

SYNONYMS: (*n.*) collision, blow, effect

CCSS Vocabulary: 4.c., 4.d. (See pp. T14–15.)

7. intimidate (in tim′ ə dāt)

(*v.*) to make timid or frighten by threats; to use fear to get someone to do (or not to do) something

Bullies may try to **intimidate** us, but if we act brave and stand tall, we can diminish their threats.

SYNONYMS: browbeat, hector

8. liberate (lib′ ə rāt)

(*v.*) to free from bondage or domination; to release

The police **liberated** the anxious hostages after sixteen hours of confinement.

SYNONYMS: untie, unshackle
ANTONYMS: imprison, fetter, shackle, bind

9. logical (läj′ ə kəl)

(*adj.*) reasonable; making use of reason and good sense

Our parents are constantly encouraging us to look for **logical** solutions to our problems.

SYNONYMS: rational, sensible
ANTONYMS: absurd, ridiculous, unsound, preposterous

10. misrepresent (mis rep ri zent′)

(*v.*) to give a false or untrue idea

If witnesses **misrepresent** the facts, the defense attorney has proof to support our story.

SYNONYMS: falsify, twist, exaggerate

11. optional (äp′ shə nəl)

(*adj.*) left to one's own choice; not required

The hotel will charge us for breakfast and dinner, but lunch is **optional**.

SYNONYMS: voluntary, discretionary
ANTONYMS: required, mandatory, compulsory

12. outright (au̇t′rīt)

(*adj.*) complete; instantaneous; without reservation, thoroughgoing; (*adv.*) completely, instantaneously

When the teacher asked her why she didn't do her homework, she told an **outright** lie.

Even though they had already heard it several times, the hilarious joke made them laugh **outright**.

SYNONYMS: (*adj.*) total, out-and-out; (*adv.*) utterly, instantly
ANTONYMS: (*adj.*) partial, incomplete; (*adv.*) by degrees

13. rendezvous (rän′ dā vü)

(*v.*) to meet in accordance with a plan; (*n.*) a meeting by agreement; a meeting place

Let's all agree to **rendezvous** by the fountain on Saturday afternoon.

They kept their **rendezvous** a secret.

SYNONYMS: (*n.*) date, assignation

CCSS Vocabulary: 4.c., 4.d. (See pp. T14–15.)

14. rotund (rō tənd′)

(*adj.*) rounded and plump; full or rich in sound

My friends like to display the largest and most **rotund** pumpkin outside their front door.

SYNONYMS: portly, sonorous; ANTONYMS: angular, lanky, gaunt

15. saunter (sôn′ tər)

(*v.*) to stroll; walk in an easy, leisurely way; (*n.*) a stroll

The star **sauntered** past his adoring fans.

It's such a beautiful day to take a **saunter**.

SYNONYMS: (*v.*) ramble, amble; (*n.*) promenade
ANTONYMS: (*v.*) speed, race, hurry, dash, scurry, rush

16. sluggish (sləg′ ish)

(*adj.*) lazy; slow-moving; not active, dull

After a big lunch, I feel **sluggish**.

SYNONYMS: unhurried, lethargic; ANTONYMS: energetic, brisk

17. subordinate (*adj., n.,* sə bôr′ də nət; *v.,* sə bôr′ də nāt)

(*adj.*) lower in rank or position, secondary; (*n.*) one who is in a lower position or under the orders of someone else; (*v.*) to put in a lower or secondary position

A corporal is **subordinate** to a sergeant.

Let's ask a **subordinate** to help us file.

Parents often **subordinate** their own wishes for the sake of their children's needs.

SYNONYMS: (*n.*) assistant, helper
ANTONYMS: (*adj.*) superior, higher; (*n.*) chief, supervisor

18. tint (tint)

(*n.*) a delicate color or hue; a slight trace of something; (*v.*) to give color to something; to dye

He's painting his room a **tint** of blue.

I want to **tint** my sunglass lenses pink.

SYNONYMS: (*n.*) tone; (*v.*) color, stain; ANTONYM: (*v.*) bleach

19. variable (vâr′ ē ə bəl)

(*adj.*) likely to undergo change; changeable; (*n.*) a value or quantity that varies; a symbol for such

Spring weather can be extremely **variable**.

In math, the letter *x* can stand for a **variable**.

SYNONYMS: (*adj.*) fluctuating, shifting, inconstant
ANTONYMS: (*adj.*) constant, unchanging, steady

20. verge (vərj)

(*n.*) the point at which something begins or happens; a border; (*v.*) to incline, tend toward, approach; to be in the process of becoming something else

I was on the **verge** of tears today.

That chatter **verges** on baby talk.

SYNONYMS: (*n.*) threshold, edge

CCSS Vocabulary: 4.c., 4.d. (See pp. T14–15.)

*Select the **boldface** word that better completes each sentence. You might refer to the passage on pages 108–109 to see how most of these words are used in context.*

1. In times of crisis, we may be called on to (**deluge, subordinate**) our personal interests to the needs of the nation as a whole.

2. I look forward to the time when my parents will agree that I have reached the "age of (**discretion, misrepresentation**)."

3. Modern household appliances have done much to (**liberate, deluge**) homemakers from tedious and time-consuming chores.

4. Many Western films include a character who is out to (**intimidate, avenge**) a wrong done to a close friend or relative.

5. Wasn't it annoying to see Michael (**verge, saunter**) into the party as though he were the coolest person ever to walk the face of the earth?

President Kennedy, in his famous Inaugural Address, said: "Ask not what your country can do for you—ask what you can do for your country."

6. He soon learned that the moods of a youngster—happy one moment, miserable the next—can be as (**variable, sluggish**) as the winds.

7. If you know that you are late for school, why do you (**saunter, rendezvous**) along as though you had all the time in the world?

8. A fastball pitcher will often try to (**liberate, intimidate**) an opposing batter by "shaving" him with an inside pitch.

9. At the State Fair, we separated to visit different exhibits, but we agreed to (**saunter, rendezvous**) at the refreshment stand at five o'clock.

10. This biased editorial has deliberately (**misrepresented, avenged**) the stand of our candidate on the important issues of the election.

11. Though once her peer, I became Caitlin's (**variable, subordinate**) when she was promoted to company president.

12. We held a meeting to discuss why the sale of tickets to the class dance has been so (**sluggish, rotund**) and what we can do about it.

13. Only the (**optional, outright**) repeal of this unfair nuisance tax will satisfy the voters.

14. I knew my dog was not feeling well when he suddenly became (**deluged, sluggish**) and refused to get up.

15. The aged millionaire, wishing to spend his last years in peace and quiet, (**ceded, impacted**) all his business interests to his sons.

16. It is good for you to "stand up for your rights," but you should not do so in a way that (**verges, subordinates**) on discourtesy.

17. It is up to the teacher's (**discretion, impact**) what topics can be chosen for our research papers.

18. It is shocking to see how, in just a few years, the lean young athlete has allowed himself to become flabby and (**giddy, rotund**).

19. Many people, unhappy with what nature has given them, seek to improve their appearance by (**tinting, ceding**) their hair.

20. There are times in life when you should be guided more by your feelings, without trying to be strictly (**outright, logical**) about everything.

21. The invitation to the party said that formal wear was (**optional, variable**).

22. Letters of protest (**deluged, tinted**) the Mayor's office when he proposed an increase in the sales tax.

23. We had regarded her as a rather (**logical, giddy**) young girl, but in this tough situation she showed that she had courage and good sense.

24. I plan to write a term paper that will discuss the different ways in which commercial television has had a major (**impact, verge**) on American life for more than sixty years.

25. The people rejoiced after being (**liberated, intimidated**) from oppression.

*Choose the word from this Unit that is the same or most nearly the same in meaning as the **boldface** word or expression in the phrase. Write that word on the line. Use a dictionary if necessary.*

1. taking an **elective** class	optional
2. an **aide** to the principal	subordinate
3. on the **brink** of a new beginning	verge
4. according to the judge's **ruling**	discretion
5. could **bully** us into giving in	intimidate
6. kissed the baby's **chubby** cheek	rotund
7. the jarring sound of the **crash**	impact
8. as if they made an **appointment** with danger	rendezvous
9. had to **yield** that point in the debate	cede
10. not to **distort** the facts of the case	misrepresent

CCSS Vocabulary: 5. (See pp. T14–15.)

*Choose the word from this Unit that is most nearly opposite in meaning to the **boldface** word or expression in the phrase. Write that word on the line. Use a dictionary if necessary.*

1. eating right in order to stay **lean** — rotund
2. your attendance is **obligatory** — optional
3. expected to **tell the truth** — misrepresent
4. to **part** without saying goodbye — rendezvous
5. apologizing for their **tactlessness** — discretion

Completing the Sentence

From the words in this Unit, choose the one that best completes each of the following sentences. Write the correct word form in the space provided.

1. Many older residents of Paris can still recall the day in 1944 when Allied troops ___liberated___ the city from German occupation.

2. After the heavy meal, we felt so ___sluggish___ that we just sat in the living room and watched whatever was on television.

3. Next year, when we have a stronger, more experienced team, we hope to ___avenge___ the crushing defeat we have just suffered.

4. By not ordering ___optional___ features, we can hold down the cost of the new car we want to buy.

5. By late September, the leaves on the trees in the woods have begun to take on their normal autumn ___tint___.

6. After being defeated in a war that lasted from 1846 to 1848, Mexico was forced to ___cede___ vast territories to the United States.

7. Her argument was so ___logical___ that she convinced us that her solution to the math problem was the correct one.

8. Our "truth in advertising" laws are designed to discourage manufacturers from ___misrepresenting___ the virtues of their products.

9. We believe that the world is now on the ___verge___ of new and exciting developments that may dramatically change the way we live.

10. Because of the lawyer's long experience in legal matters, we left it to his ___discretion___ how to proceed with the case.

11. When they realized that sweet talk and flattery were getting them nowhere, they tried to **intimidate** me into doing what they wanted.

12. Every eye was on us as we **sauntered** down Main Street in our new outfits.

13. The force of the head-on collision was so severe that the drivers of both vehicles were killed **outright**.

14. You may like to live where the sun shines all the time, but I prefer a more **variable** climate.

15. Uncle Eddie, with his **rotund** figure, is often called on to play Santa Claus.

16. According to the eyewitness, the great **deluge** that arrived after the hurricane caused more damage than the winds.

17. Even fans sitting high in the stands could hear the **impact** when the big fullback crashed into the line.

18. As a young and inexperienced employee, you cannot expect to hold more than a(n) **subordinate** job in that big company.

19. Many people say that they become quite **giddy** when they look down from the top of a tall building.

20. The two groups of hikers, setting out from different points, have planned a(n) **rendezvous** at four o'clock at Eagle Rock.

Writing: Words in Action

Answers to both prompts will vary.

1. Look back at "From Fire Arrows to Space Flight: A History of Rockets" (pages 108–109). Think about how Archytas's wooden pigeon led to the invention of rockets. Write a letter to Archytas in which you tell him some of the effects, or consequences, of his invention over the centuries. Incorporate at least two details from the passage and three Unit words in your writing.

2. Imagination is what motivates people to invent. Write an editorial for your local newspaper stating what you think can be done to encourage creativity and technological innovations in your own community. Support your opinion with your observations, specific examples, the reading (refer to pages 108–109), or personal experience. Write at least three paragraphs, and use three or more words from this Unit.

Writing prompt #2 is modeled on that of standardized tests.

 CCSS Vocabulary: 6; Writing: 1.c., 2.d., 3.d., 4. (See pp. T14–15.)

Vocabulary in Context: Informational Text for Unit 9 is available online at **vocabularyworkshop.com**.

The following excerpts are from Anne of the Island *by L.M. Montgomery. Some of the words you have studied in this Unit appear in* ***boldface*** *type. Complete each statement below the excerpt by circling the letter of the correct answer.*

1. Gilbert and Anne, happily unconscious that their future was thus being settled by Mrs. Rachel, were **sauntering** through the shadows of the Haunted Wood.

The act of **sauntering** involves

a. hiding
b. tumbling
c. running
d. wandering

2. "But this morning I was quite well, so it couldn't have been the fever. I suppose if I did catch it last night it couldn't have developed so soon. I can remember that in daytime, but at three o'clock at night I never can be **logical**."

Someone who is **logical** is definitely NOT

a. confused
b. lucid
c. elderly
d. coherent

The 1934 film version of *Anne of Green Gables* focuses on the developing romance between Anne Shirley and Gilbert Blythe.

3. "This has been Patty's Place ever since my brother Aaron left it to me in his will, and Patty's Place it shall remain until I die and Maria dies. After that happens the next possessor can call it any fool name he likes," concluded Miss Patty, much as she might have said, "After that—the **deluge**."

A **deluge** is a(n)

a. agenda
b. flood
c. proposal
d. residence

4. To their right lay the harbor, taking on **tints** of rose and copper as it stretched out into the sunset. Before them the water shimmered, satin smooth and silver gray, and beyond, clean-shaven William's Island loomed out of the mist, guarding the town like a sturdy bulldog.

Tints of colors are

a. noble
b. loud
c. delicate
d. measurable

5. But Joseph [the cat] rashly sat up and yawned. [The other cat] Rusty, burning to **avenge** his disgrace, swooped down upon him. Joseph, pacific by nature, could fight upon occasion and fight well. The result was a series of drawn battles.

An animal who wants to **avenge** an action

a. gets even
b. ignores it
c. falls back
d. acts aloof

Snap the code, or go to **vocabularyworkshop.com**

Vocabulary for Comprehension

*Read the following passage in which some of the words you have studied in Units 7–9 appear in **boldface** type. Then answer the questions on page 119.*

This passage discusses a strange-looking bird called the dodo, which once lived on an island in the Indian Ocean, and what became of it.

(Line)

Alas, the dodo bird is no more. None of these funny-looking relatives of pigeons and doves exist today. In fact, dodos have been extinct for over three centuries.

The **pathetic** dodo never got much respect in its time. People said it was "disgusting." The clumsy-looking bird looked a bit like a deformed pigeon, but larger. Others thought it might be a kind of **rotund** turkey. Its hooked bill led still others to think it might be a flightless cockatoo. Had the dodo understood what people said about it, it probably wouldn't have **cringed** a bit. That's because of its strangely docile, gentle nature.

The dodo was slow-moving and unusually trusting. Little would **intimidate** the easygoing bird. Its natural home was Mauritius, a small island in the Indian Ocean. Dutch and Portuguese sailors who visited Mauritius in their travels were fascinated by the dodo. Its odd looks made it seem fantastic and otherworldly, appealing to artists, naturalists, and writers.

But the dodo's trusting nature left it vulnerable. Several categories of **culprits** contributed to the extinction of the dodo. Enterprising sailors began to steal dodos from Mauritius. They sold them to eager collectors, who would pay handsomely for the homely birds. Also, the dodo was dinner for the colonists of and visitors to the island and for the animals that they brought with them. By 1681, no more dodos lived on Mauritius or anywhere else. The ones that had been held in captivity were never bred. As a result, they left no descendants.

Lack of scientific evidence led nineteenth-century naturalists to ask whether the dodo ever existed at all. With no bodies to **dissect** and few bones to examine, skeptics came to denounce the dodo as a fraud. Later research proved that the dodo had indeed existed but that its lack of natural enemies and overly trusting nature probably cost it a lasting place in the animal world.

CCSS Vocabulary: 4.a.; Reading (Informational Text): 2, 4, 6. (See pp. T14–15.)

1. The primary purpose of the passage is to identify several
a. animals that have become extinct
(b.) causes of the dodo's extinction
c. effects of the dodo's extinction
d. characteristics of the dodo's nature
e. characteristics of the island of Mauritius

2. The meaning of **pathetic** (line 6) is
a. shy
b. repulsive
(c.) pitiable
d. aggressive
e. gullible

3. **Rotund** (line 11) most nearly means
a. tall
b. huge
c. skinny
d. flighty
(e.) plump

4. **Cringed** (line 16) is best defined as
a. wept
b. argued
c. minded
(d.) flinched
e. strutted

5. Paragraph 2 focuses on the dodo bird's
a. history
b. extinction
(c.) appearance
d. environment
e. temperament

6. The meaning of **intimidate** (line 21) is
(a.) bully
b. anger
c. pursue
d. tease
e. imprison

7. You can tell from paragraphs 1 and 2 that the passage's tone will be
a. very critical
b. rather skeptical
c. totally objective
d. purely scientific
(e.) somewhat humorous

8. All of the following describe the dodo EXCEPT
a. docile
b. trusting
(c.) imaginary
d. easygoing
e. strange-looking

9. **Culprits** (line 32) most nearly means
a. thieves
b. causes
c. merchants
(d.) wrongdoers
e. people

10. **Dissect** (line 49) is best defined as
a. compare
(b.) analyze
c. dig up
d. weigh
e. bury

11. You can infer that the "later research" mentioned in lines 51–56 involved
a. stories and songs about the dodo
b. eyewitness testimony about the dodo
(c.) skeletal or fossil remains of the dodo
d. paintings and drawings of the dodo
e. photographs of the last dodos in captivity

12. With which of the following generalizations would the author agree?
(a.) The only enemy of the dodo bird was human beings.
b. If the dodo had been more trusting, it might still exist today.
c. The dodo had many natural enemies.
d. The dodo bird was intelligent.
e. The dodo bird was beautiful.

CCSS Vocabulary: 4.a.; Reading (Informational Text): 2, 4, 6. (See pp. T14–15.)

Two-Word Completions

Select the pair of words that best completes the meaning of each of the following sentences.

1. Joan of Arc spent most of her brief career as the "warrior maiden of France," attempting to ____________ lands that the French had been forced to ____________ to England as a result of English victories in the initial stages of the Hundred Years' War.

a. partition . . . expend
b. avenge . . . authorize
c. liberate . . . misrepresent
d. retrieve . . . cede

2. After Grandpa ____________ a large investment in an obviously crooked scheme and lost most of his savings as a result, I said that he could no longer be so ____________ when it came to taking the advice of financial "wizards."

a. reminisced . . . jovial
b. intimidated . . . taut
c. deluged . . . giddy
d. authorized . . . gullible

3. The Emancipation Proclamation ____________ enslaved people in the South once and for all from the ____________ that bound them to a life of servitude and humiliation.

a. immersed . . . arrears
b. liberated . . . manacles
c. subordinated . . . memoranda
d. retrieved . . . discretion

4. The bully down the block is so big and so ____________ that I find myself unconsciously ____________ in fear every time he looks in my direction.

a. intimidating . . . cringing
b. rotund . . . prevaricating
c. sinister . . . dawdling
d. martial . . . sauntering

5. During "Operation Dragnet," the police ____________ the city in search of the two ____________ who had pulled off the daring bank robbery.

a. immersed . . . fatalities
b. quashed . . . innovators
c. scoured . . . culprits
d. deluged . . . subordinates

6. The ____________ of their sudden collision left one of the players ____________ on the ice in agony, while the other was hurled five feet into the air.

a. testimonial . . . cringing
b. impact . . . writhing
c. fatality . . . verging
d. onset . . . scouring

7. The spy was a double agent, a person of great ____________, who, though tormented by enemies and allies alike, proceeded to carry out secretive and sometimes ____________ deeds.

a. culprit . . . optional
b. innovation . . . pathetic
c. arrears . . . crotchety
d. discretion . . . sinister

 CCSS Vocabulary: 4.a. (See pp. T14–15.)

Adages

In the passage "Made for the Shade" (see pages 88–89), the writer remarks that people seeking out vintage sunglasses might be "looking at the world through rose-colored glasses." What the writer means is that these consumers are optimistic or overly cheerful.

"Looking at the world through rose-colored glasses" is an adage. **Adages** are wise and clever traditional or "folksy" sayings that have been passed down from generation to generation. Adages can be serious or humorous, but they are always colorful. It is easy to see why they are often sprinkled throughout daily speech and informal writing.

Choosing the Right Adage

Read each sentence. Use context clues to figure out the meaning of each adage in ***boldface*** *print. Then write the letter of the definition for the adage in the sentence.*

1. Instead of trying to find a new partner for your group, **dance with the one that brought you**. j
2. You should think twice about hanging out with those troublemakers; **people are known by the company they keep**. g
3. Don't worry about how you'll juggle coursework, team sports, and a job when you're in college; **cross that bridge when you come to it.** c
4. Our neighbor never says hello to us, which is rather sad, since **courtesy costs nothing**. b
5. Yes, I guess it was dangerous to try and break up the fight, but **fools rush in where angels fear to tread**. h
6. It's not surprising that the organist's daughter is also a musician. After all, **the apple doesn't fall far from the tree**. d
7. Our cat has gained so much weight that we've stopped giving him the snacks he likes. Sometimes **you have to be cruel to be kind**. i
8. You shouldn't take Ryan's tough-guy talk very seriously, because **barking dogs seldom bite**. a
9. If you want to be on the team, you need to build some muscle, because **a chain is only as strong as its weakest link**. e
10. Every time I enjoy a walk or observe nature, I realize that **the best things in life are free**. f

a. People who do a lot of tough talking seldom act on their words.

b. It's always a good idea to be polite.

c. Deal with problems when you have to; don't worry about them in advance.

d. Children often take after their parents.

e. Team members need to pull their own weight.

f. True happiness comes not from money but from simple things.

g. The people you associate with will affect your reputation.

h. Inexperienced people often don't know where danger lurks.

i. You sometimes have to be strict in order to help another.

j. Stay loyal to those who look after you.

CCSS Vocabulary: 5.a. (See pp. T14–15.)

Writing with Adages

Find the meaning of each adage. (Use a dictionary if necessary.) Then write a sentence for each adage. **Answers will vary.**

1. Make haste slowly. **Sample response: If you want to get your report done on time *and* get a good grade, make haste slowly.**

2. All good things must come to an end.

3. Silence is golden.

4. If you don't have anything good to say, don't say anything at all.

5. Don't put the cart before the horse.

6. Strike while the iron is hot.

7. Talk is cheap.

8. Health is better than wealth.

9. A sound mind lives in a sound body.

10. The fat is in the fire.

11. Nothing will come of nothing.

12. Truth is stranger than fiction.

 CCSS Vocabulary: 5. (See pp. T14–15.)

The literal meaning of a word, which you can find in a dictionary, is its **denotation**. The emotional association connected to a word is its **connotation**. The connotation can be either positive or negative.

A connotation is an implied, or suggested, meaning. Several words may share the same basic denotation, but that doesn't mean the words are interchangeable. You can end up conveying an unintended meaning if you don't carefully consider the implied meanings of the words you use. Consider these synonyms for the neutral word *walk*.

saunter *stroll* *trudge* *plod*

Saunter and *stroll* have positive connotations, suggesting leisure and ease, whereas *trudge* and *plod* have negative connotations, suggesting effort and exertion.

Think: If you saunter or stroll, you're walking easily and with little effort. If you trudge or plod, your walk is a struggle!

Look at these examples of words that have similar denotations. Notice how the connotation of each word varies.

NEUTRAL	POSITIVE	NEGATIVE
cancel	**overturn**	**quash**
continue	**persevere**	**persist**
tint	**highlight**	**stain**

Writers choose their words carefully, knowing that readers are aware of connotations and draw on those emotional associations as they read. For example, a writer knows that describing the star of an action movie as "burly" will have a very different effect from describing him as "hefty." Good writers keep in mind how a word's connotation might affect their audience.

Shades of Meaning

Write a plus sign (+) in the box if the word has a positive connotation.
Write a minus sign (–) if the word has a negative connotation.
Put a zero (0) if the word is neutral.

1. fatality  –
2. onset  –
3. sluggish  –
4. pathetic  –

5. affluence  +
6. partition 0
7. template 0
8. innovation +

9. illicit –
10. nimble  +
11. jovial   +
12. testimonial 0

13. cringe  –
14. dawdle  –
15. optional 0
16. crotchety  –

WORD STUDY

Expressing the Connotation

Read each sentence. Select the word in parentheses that expresses the connotation (positive, negative, or neutral) given at the beginning of the sentence.

positive **1.** The day was so enjoyable that we wanted to (**dawdle, linger**) on the beach for a few more hours.

negative **2.** The (**gullible, trusting**) man entrusted his entire life savings to a swindler.

neutral **3.** Melinda is the only employee at the bank who can (**sanction, authorize**) a cashier's check.

negative **4.** The gang members hung out on the street corner, hoping to (**deter, intimidate**) passers-by.

positive **5.** I spent hours (**polishing, scouring**) the silverware for the New Year's Eve party.

positive **6.** It was fun to (**reminisce, chat**) about our previous summers at the camp.

negative **7.** No one was laughing when Henry accidentally (**immersed, dunked**) his motorcycle in the lake.

neutral **8.** Years of irresponsibility with money left my cousin in (**debt, arrears**).

Challenge: Using Connotation

Choose vocabulary words from Units 7–9 to replace the highlighted words in the sentences below. Then explain how the connotation of the replacement word changes the tone of the sentence. **Answers will vary.**

rendezvous	**giddy**	**retrieve**
sinister	**logical**	**culprit**

1. Not used to staying up late, Chuck began acting **odd** ____ giddy ____ in the hours after midnight.

Sample response: *Giddy* makes the tone of the sentence more playful and less serious by suggesting that a sleepy Chuck was silly and punchy.

2. My brother tried to drag me to that **spooky** ____ sinister ____ haunted house, but I told him I wouldn't go within a mile of the place.

Sample response: *Sinister* creates a more negative tone, suggesting that the haunted house is not just creepy but somehow dangerous and threatening.

3. The police chief was pleased to announce that his officers had caught the **wrongdoer** ____ culprit ____ after a lengthy sting operation.

Sample response: *Culprit* makes the tone more serious by suggesting that the person who was caught is indeed guilty of a crime.

 CCSS Vocabulary: 5, 5.c. (See pp. T14–15.)

Classical Roots

log, logue—speech, word, discourse

The Greek root *log* appears in **logical** (page 111). The word means "capable of reasoning," and reasoning is expressed through speech and discourse. Some other words about speech or speaking are based on the same root. They are listed below.

apology	**dialogue**	**eulogy**	**neologism**
decalogue	**epilogue**	**monologue**	**prologue**

From the list of words above, choose the one that corresponds to each of the brief definitions below. Write the word in the blank space in the illustrative sentence below the definition. Use a dictionary if necessary.

1. an introductory statement, act, or event; a preface; opening remarks

   The novel's ____**prologue**____ offers background on the main character.

2. words of regret to express remorse and ask pardon for an accident, fault, failure, or offense; an explanation, defense, or excuse

   "If you'd like me to accept your ____**apology**____," he explained, "I need to believe that you know what you did wrong and that you will strive to do better."

3. a concluding section at the end of a play or literary work, intended to provide further comment, interpretation, or information; an afterword

   After the curtain fell, a narrator gave a brief ____**epilogue**____ to tie up loose ends.

4. a speech or written tribute composed to honor someone who has died

   Lincoln's Gettysburg Address was delivered on November 19, 1863 as a(n) ____**eulogy**____ to those who died at the Battle of Gettysburg.

5. a conversation between two or more people or characters; the lines in a script that are to be spoken; an airing of ideas or views

   Abbott and Costello's wacky routine, "Who's on First?," is one of the funniest baseball ____**dialogues**____ in American comedy.

6. a newly invented word, expression, or usage; new meaning for an old word

   Evolving technology has led to many ____**neologisms**____, such as *smartphone* and *blog*, that have become part of our everyday language.

7. a set of ten authoritative rules or laws; (*usu. cap.*) the Ten Commandments (*in the Bible*)

   The stained-glass window shows Moses holding the ____**Decalogue**____.

8. a long speech made by one person; a speech that monopolizes conversation; a series of jokes or comedic stories delivered by one comedian

   The opening ____**monologue**____ given by talk-show hosts, consisting of light banter and political humor, has become a staple of late-night television.

CCSS Vocabulary: 4.b. (See pp. T14–15.)

UNIT 10

Note that not all of the 20 Unit words are used in this passage. *Engulf*, *null and void*, *refurbish*, and *unerring* are not included.

Read the following passage, taking note of the ***boldface*** *words and their contexts. These words are among those you will be studying in Unit 10. As you complete the exercises in this Unit, it may help to refer to the way the words are used below.*

CCSS Vocabulary: 4; Reading (Informational Text): 4, 6. (See pp. T14–15.)

Farewell, Blue Yodeler

<Obituary>

June 1, 1933
Asheville Evening Post
by Floyd O. Merryll

With the passing last week of Jimmie Rodgers, the country lost a great performer. But it's a testament to the kind of man he was that many of his fans will take the loss personally, as if that Blue Yodeler, as we like to call him and will remember him, was a friend of ours. Thankfully, we've got his records to keep with us as **mementos**.

James Charles Rodgers was born in Meridian, Mississippi, in 1897. His mama died when he was just a kid, and Jimmie was raised by relatives in Mississippi and Alabama. When he was a little older, he returned to Meridian to live with his father, Aaron, who was a maintenance foreman on the Mobile and Ohio Railroad.

Jimmie had no **rigorous** musical training, but he learned to sing and play guitar. Still a boy, Jimmie proved to be a **nonconformist**. He secretly organized a traveling show. When Aaron Rodgers found out, he had the good sense to **foil** his son's plans—he tracked Jimmie down, and dragged him home. But the stunt was more than the **bumbling** behavior of an unruly kid. Jimmie showed the same **initiative** again, **formulating** a second plan to get out on the road and sing. He charged a pricey canvas tent in his father's name and hit the road to make music. His father might have understood Jimmie's love of music, but he probably didn't want the boy to **delude** himself about a musician's life. He set out again to **pry** his son from the road. Soon Aaron got Jimmie a job as a waterboy with the railroad. Within a few years, Jimmie was a brakeman on the New Orleans and Northeastern Railroad. Now Jimmie was a steady working man. But he never lost his love of music.

Jimmie came down with the deadly respiratory disease called tuberculosis in 1924, when he was 27 years old. As a **consequence** of that **abominable** disease, he had to quit his railroad job. Ever **resourceful**, Jimmie organized a traveling show and played across the Southeast. He worked as a brakeman again and later as a switchman but couldn't keep those jobs because of his tuberculosis. But his travels gave him a look at the whole **panorama** of Southern music. In 1927, Jimmie went to Asheville, North Carolina, where the city's first radio station had just hit the airwaves, and he played on the radio and earned himself a weekly slot. The exposure served him well in **subsequent** months. He recorded songs for a record company. One of them, "Blue Yodel," sold like hotcakes and made Jimmie Rodgers a star.

Propelled by fame, the Blue Yodeler traveled the country for the next few years. It was hard times for the nation. But while so many people were on the **dole** and looking for work, Jimmie was living his dream. He was making music, touring, and starring in a movie short called "The Singing Brakeman." Eventually, his illness caught up with him. During a recording session in New York City last week, he couldn't get through all of his songs. He took the day off to recover, but Jimmie was in a race against time. So before he'd sung his last song, Jimmie Rodgers was gone. But in a few years as a recording artist and a few more as a performer who rambled around the country, he made such a mark for **posterity** that we'll never forget him. Jimmie leaves behind his wife, Carrie, and daughter, Carrie Anita, and a legion of fans and recordings.

Farewell, Blue Yodeler.

Left: Promotional photo for The Singing Brakeman

Inset: Jimmie posing with his sweet Model T Ford, in 1930

Note the spelling, pronunciation, part(s) of speech, and definition(s) of each of the following words. Then write the appropriate form of the word in the blank spaces in the illustrative sentence(s) following. Finally, study the lists of synonyms and antonyms.

1. abominable (ə bäm′ ə nə bəl)

(*adj.*) arousing hatred; disgusting, detestable

Unfortunately, there are many **abominable** ideas circulating on the Internet.

SYNONYMS: hateful, despicable, loathsome
ANTONYMS: praiseworthy, delightful, charming

2. bumbling (bəm′ bliŋ)

(*adj.*) blundering and awkward; (*n.*) clumsiness

The **bumbling** burglars were so inept that they actually left some of their own money at the home they were planning to rob!

The old cartoon character Mr. Magoo was well known for his **bumbling**.

SYNONYMS: (*adj.*) clumsy, stumbling
ANTONYMS: (*adj.*) forceful, effective, skillful, adroit

3. consequence (kän′ sə kwens)

(*n.*) a result, effect; importance

Does he truly comprehend the **consequences** of his actions?

SYNONYMS: outcome, significance
ANTONYMS: cause, source

4. delude (di lüd′)

(*v.*) to fool, deceive; to mislead utterly

Don't **delude** yourself into thinking that you will become a famous concert pianist just because you played one song at the school's talent show.

SYNONYMS: trick, hoodwink

5. dole (dōl)

(*v.*) to give out in small amounts; (*n.*) money, food, or other necessities given as charity; a small portion

Let's **dole** out scraps of food to the hungry dogs.

The people at the homeless shelter lined up to receive their weekly **dole**.

SYNONYMS: (*v.*) ration, allot, distribute; (*n.*) handout

6. engulf (en gəlf′)

(*v.*) to swallow up, overwhelm, consume

The truck was **engulfed** in flames after its fuel tank exploded.

SYNONYMS: encompass, immerse

CCSS Vocabulary: 4.c., 4.d. (See pp. T14–15.)

7. foil (foil) — (*v.*) to defeat; to keep from gaining some end; (*n.*) a thin sheet of metal; a light fencing sword; a person or thing serving as a contrast to another

The police will ____**foil**____ the criminals' plot.

Glum characters make a good ____**foil**____ for the upbeat star of that new comedy.

SYNONYMS: (*v.*) frustrate, thwart, counter; (*n.*) rapier
ANTONYMS: (*v.*) aid, abet, assist, advance, promote

8. formulate (fôr′ myə lāt) — (*v.*) to express definitely or systematically; to devise, invent; to state as a formula

The town board will ____**formulate**____ a tax policy.

SYNONYMS: define, articulate, frame, specify

9. initiative (i nish′ ə tiv) — (*n.*) the taking of the first step or move; the ability to act without being directed or urged from the outside

Dad is proud of my ____**initiative**____ with chores.

SYNONYMS: leadership, enterprise
ANTONYMS: laziness, sloth, shiftlessness

10. memento (mə men′ tō) — (*n.*) something that serves as a reminder

This cap is a ____**memento**____ of our recent trip.

SYNONYMS: remembrance, souvenir, token

11. nonconformist (nän kən fôr′ mist) — (*n.*) a person who refuses to follow established ideas or ways of doing things; (*adj.*) of or relating to the unconventional

Jake, a ____**nonconformist**____, is not swayed by opinion.

Her ____**nonconformist**____ poetry appears in several small literary magazines.

SYNONYMS: (*n.*) maverick, individualist, bohemian
ANTONYMS: (*n.*, *adj.*) traditionalist, conventionalist; (*adj.*) traditional, conventional, conservative

12. null and void (nəl and void) — (*adj.*) without legal force or effect; no longer binding

This contract becomes ____**null and void**____ at noon.

SYNONYMS: canceled, repealed, abolished
ANTONYMS: in effect, binding

13. panorama (pan ə ram′ ə) — (*n.*) a wide, unobstructed view of an area; a complete survey of a subject; a continuously passing or changing scene; a range or spectrum

Displays of old picture postcards present an entertaining ____**panorama**____ of twentieth-century life.

SYNONYM: overview

14. posterity (pä ster′ ət ē)

(*n.*) all of a person's offspring, descendants; all future generations

Let's keep the photo album for **posterity**.

ANTONYMS: ancestry, ancestors, forebears, the past

15. pry (prī)

(*v.*) to pull loose by force; to look at closely or inquisitively; to be nosy about something

We can use this tool to **pry** the lid off a can of paint.

SYNONYMS: snoop, meddle

16. refurbish (ri fər′ bish)

(*v.*) to brighten, freshen, or polish; to restore or improve

Every five years, the hotel **refurbishes** the décor of its elegant lobby.

SYNONYMS: remodel, renew
ANTONYMS: dilapidate, run down

17. resourceful (ri sôrs′ fəl)

(*adj.*) able to deal promptly and effectively with all sorts of problems; clever in finding ways and means of getting along

A **resourceful** guide will know how to handle any questions or surprises that come up on the tour.

SYNONYMS: inventive, ingenious, skillful
ANTONYMS: uninventive, incompetent, dull-witted

18. rigorous (rig′ ər əs)

(*adj.*) severe, harsh, strict; thoroughly logical

"Boot camp" is the nickname for the place where new soldiers receive **rigorous** basic training.

SYNONYMS: tough, trying, challenging, rousing
ANTONYMS: easy, lax, indulgent, tiresome

19. subsequent (səb′ sə kwent)

(*adj.*) coming after; following in time, place, or order

The country enjoyed peace and prosperity in the years **subsequent** to the war.

SYNONYMS: later, following, ensuing
ANTONYMS: previous, prior, preceding

20. unerring (ən er′ iŋ)

(*adj.*) making no mistakes, faultless, completely accurate

Even a pilot with **unerring** judgment can be surprised by sudden changes in the weather.

SYNONYMS: sure, certain, unfailing
ANTONYMS: faulty, fallible, unreliable

CCSS Vocabulary: 4.c., 4.d. (See pp. T14–15.)

Choosing the Right Word

*Select the **boldface** word that better completes each sentence. You might refer to the passage on pages 126–127 to see how most of these words are used in context.*

1. In devising the Constitution, the Founding Fathers sought to "secure the blessings of liberty to ourselves and our (**posterity, foils**)."

2. Our foreign policy embraces a vast (**consequence, panorama**) of aims and objectives, problems and concerns.

3. Here I am on my first vacation in years, and I have to put up with this (**abominable, bumbling**) weather day after day!

4. All these things in the attic may seem like a lot of junk to you, but to me they are priceless (**mementos, nonconformists**) of childhood.

Among the fifty-five framers of the U.S. Constitution were George Washington and Benjamin Franklin.

5. Sasha was pleasantly surprised with all the perks, such as free tickets, that the producers (**doled, foiled**) out to the actors.

6. She hopes to win the election by convincing voters that the city's troubles result from the (**unerring, bumbling**) policies of the present mayor.

7. With his serious face and his dignified way of speaking, he is an excellent (**foil, memento**) for the clownish comedian.

8. It is too late to attempt to (**formulate, refurbish**) the old city charter; we must have a completely new plan for our city government.

9. Since you have failed to carry out your promises, I must tell you that the agreement between us is now (**resourceful, null and void**).

10. By coaxing and questioning hour after hour, Tom finally managed to (**pry, delude**) the big secret from his sister.

11. When we reached the top of the volcano, the (**panoramic, resourceful**) view was well worth the five-hour hike.

12. The war that began with Germany's invasion of Poland in 1939 spread until it had (**refurbished, engulfed**) almost the entire world.

13. Brad is the kind of (**rigorous, resourceful**) quarterback who can always come up with something new when it is a matter of victory or defeat.

14. My father, an electrical engineer, is an expert at computing (**rigorous, abominable**) math problems.

15. We worked several hours shoveling dirt and removing roots, hoping to (**engulf, pry**) the tree stump loose from the ground.

16. Why is it that such hardworking, self-reliant people now have to depend on a (**posterity, dole**) of food and other necessities from charitable agencies?

17. We all know that it is a long time since the speeding laws in our community have been (**rigorously, subsequently**) enforced.

18. Do you think the United States should take the (**initiative, dole**) in trying to bring about a compromise peace in the region?

19. The lawyer made the point that her client had been at the scene of the crime before the murder but not (**null and void, subsequent**) to it.

20. If you think that you can get away with selling overpriced products to the people of this town, you are (**deluding, refurbishing**) yourself.

21. He may look like an ordinary man, but he is in fact a figure of real (**panorama, consequence**) in the state government.

22. One of the signs of a truly democratic nation is that it gives protection and freedom to (**initiatives, nonconformists**) who espouse unpopular views.

23. "We must (**formulate, engulf**) a plan to deal with this new situation and carry it out as quickly as possible," the president said.

24. Perhaps he doesn't seem to be very bright, but he has an (**abominable, unerring**) instinct for anything that might make money for him.

25. Many comics get laughs for their (**unerring, bumbling**) antics on the stage.

Choose the word from this Unit that is the same or most nearly the same in meaning as the ***boldface*** *word or expression in the phrase. Write that word on the line. Use a dictionary if necessary.*

1. a contract that is considered **invalid** — null and void
2. to discuss it at our **next** meeting — subsequent
3. **creative** use of recycled materials — resourceful
4. must pass a **demanding** exam — rigorous
5. **prepare** an answer for the defense — formulate
6. a dramatic **vista** of red rock formations — panorama
7. devised a **perfect** plan — unerring
8. a precious **keepsake** of Sally's childhood — memento
9. if we decide to **spruce up** the kitchen — refurbish
10. huge waves that **envelop** the tiny beach — engulf

CCSS Vocabulary: 5. (See pp. T14–15.)

The synonyms and antonyms here do not appear on the Definitions page.

Antonyms

*Choose the word from this Unit that is most nearly opposite in meaning to the **boldface** word or expression in the phrase. Write that word on the line. Use a dictionary if necessary.*

1. declared **valid** by the courts — null and void
2. to **demolish** the old building — refurbish
3. due to my **flawed** sense of direction — unerring
4. **lovely** behavior for a twelve-year-old — abominable
5. waves that **retreat from** the dunes — engulf

Completing the Sentence

From the words in this Unit, choose the one that best completes each of the following sentences. Write the correct word form in the space provided.

1. A truly resourceful administrator always seems to be able to find an effective way of dealing with any problem that may come up.
2. Like so many other young people, he has been deluded into the false belief that there is an easy way to success.
3. Professional baseball players get themselves into shape for the upcoming season by undergoing a rigorous training period each spring.
4. The first meeting will be in the school auditorium, but all subsequent meetings will be held in the homes of our members.
5. You may think that the crude way he has behaved is slightly amusing, but I think it is abominable and inexcusable.
6. Huge clouds of smoke and ash from the active volcano engulfed the sleepy little villages that nestled on its flanks.
7. From the observation deck of the skyscraper one may enjoy a sweeping panorama of the city.
8. What a disappointment to hear that dull and bumbling speech when we were expecting a clear, forceful, and interesting statement!
9. Many an artist whose work has been overlooked in his or her own lifetime has had to trust to posterity for appreciation.
10. All that you will need to refurbish that dilapidated old house is lots of time, lots of skill, lots of enthusiasm, and lots of money.

CCSS Vocabulary: 4.a., 5. (See pp. T14–15.)

11. As a tennis player, Sue doesn't have much speed or power, but she hits the ball with ___**unerring**___ accuracy.

12. Since I was able to prove in court that the salesperson had lied to me, the contract I had signed was declared ___**null and void**___.

13. These old photographs may not look like much, but I treasure them as a(n) ___**memento**___ of the last summer my entire family spent together.

14. During World War II, food became so scarce in Great Britain that the government ___**doled**___ it out to consumers in very small amounts.

15. Anyone who ___**pries**___ into someone else's business runs the risk of opening a can of worms.

16. The alert employee ___**foiled**___ an attempted robbery by setting off the alarm promptly.

17. At the time it occurred, that mistake didn't seem to be too important, but it had ___**consequences**___ that still hurt me today.

18. We must ___**formulate**___ a detailed response that leaves no doubt about our position on this important issue.

19. Rather than sit back and wait for the enemy to attack him, the general took the ___**initiative**___ and delivered the first blow.

20. The term "___**nonconformist**___" was first applied in the 1660s to English Protestants who dissented from the Church of England.

Writing: Words in Action

Answers to both prompts will vary.

1. Look back at "Farewell, Blue Yodeler" (pages 126–127). Suppose that you are a musician who traveled with Jimmie when he was a boy. You want to persuade his father, Aaron Rodgers, that Jimmie should continue to travel with the show and hone his skills as a musician. Write a letter to Aaron Rodgers supporting your position. Use at least two details from the passage and three Unit words.

2. *"Music has charms to soothe a savage breast."—William Congreve*

   It is a common sentiment that music soothes the soul. Do you agree with this statement? Should music always "soothe" the soul, or does it have other purposes? What roles does music play in contemporary life? In a brief essay, support your opinion with specific examples from your observations, studies, the reading (refer to pages 126–127), or personal experience. Write at least three paragraphs, and use three or more words from this Unit.

Writing prompt #2 is modeled on that of standardized tests.

CCSS Vocabulary: 6; Writing: 1.c., 2.d., 3.d., 4. (See pp. T14–15.)

Vocabulary in Context: Informational Text for Unit 10 is available online at **vocabularyworkshop.com**.

The following excerpts are from The Works of Edgar Allan Poe, Volume I *by Edgar Allan Poe. Some of the words you have studied in this Unit appear in* **boldface** *type. Complete each statement below the excerpt by circling the letter of the correct answer.*

1. . . . upon the **subsequent** disposal of the trinkets and jewels . . . it was found that we had greatly undervalued the treasure. ("The Gold-Bug")

A discovery made **subsequent** to an action occurs

a. after **c.** suddenly
b. previously **d.** gradually

2. . . . and I fell down in the bottom of the car, trembling with unmitigated terror. Indeed, I now perceived that I had entirely overdone the business, and that the main **consequences** of the shock were yet to be experienced. ("The Unparalleled Adventure of One Hans Pfaall")

Consequences are a

a. fears **c.** results
b. reminders **d.** memories

3. . . . I should have been unable to accomplish even as much as I had now accomplished, and the wonderful adventures of Hans Pfaall would have been utterly lost to **posterity**, I had therefore every reason to be grateful . . . ("The Unparalleled Adventure of One Hans Pfaall")

Posterity refers to things in the

a. future **c.** basement
b. news **d.** present

Bela Lugosi played the role of the mad scientist in the 1932 film *Murders in the Rue Morgue*, based on Poe's short story.

4. . . . [L]ooking dizzily around, [I] was . . . struck with the idea of our being among breakers; so terrific, beyond the wildest imagination, was the whirlpool of mountainous and foaming ocean within which we were **engulfed**. ("Ms. Found in a Bottle")

Someone **engulfed** by the ocean is

a. fishing in it **c.** floating on it
b. thrilled by it **d.** immersed in it

5. . . . [T]here still remained in his possession a small remnant of his patrimony; and, upon the income arising from this, he managed, by means of a **rigorous** economy, to procure the necessaries of life. ("The Murders in the Rue Morgue")

A **rigorous** economy is definitely NOT

a. energizing **c.** stimulating
b. lenient **d.** invigorating

Snap the code, or go to **vocabularyworkshop.com**

UNIT 11

Note that not all of the 20 Unit words are used in this passage. *Meteoric*, *parody*, *rend*, *replenish*, and *vandalism* are not included.

Read the following passage, taking note of the ***boldface*** *words and their contexts. These words are among those you will be studying in Unit 11. As you complete the exercises in this Unit, it may help to refer to the way the words are used below.*

CCSS Vocabulary: 4; Reading (Informational Text): 4, 6. (See pp. T14–15.)

Here I Am: Galápagos Log

<Log>

Written by Samantha Z. Rosenstern, marine biologist with the Center for Island Research

Wed., Apr. 12 After a delay at the airport, our research team arrived at the Galápagos. I often think that a good **alias** for these islands would be "reptile heaven." No land bridge ever linked the Galápagos with the coast of South America, over 600 miles away. As an unavoidable and **inevitable** consequence, reptiles **prevailed** over mammals in these spots of land straddling the equator. Only reptiles such as the giant tortoise and the land iguana possess the endurance to make long ocean crossings with no fresh water. The **dogged** persistence of these creatures made it possible for them to establish themselves here.

The name Galápagos refers to the islands' most prominent creatures. In old Spanish, *galápago* means "tortoise." Different giant tortoises have different shells. Some are dome-shaped, while others have an arched shell that looks like a saddle.

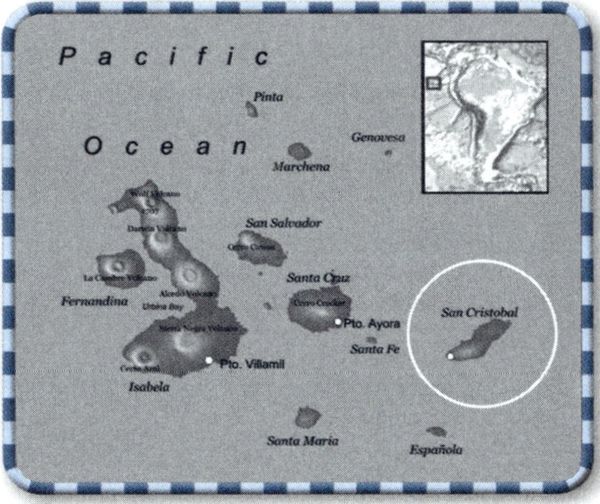

Sat., Apr. 15 My third day of field work on San Cristóbal Island at the eastern edge of the Galápagos archipelago. In mid afternoon, I **amble** down the beach. My leisurely pace would leave most of the Galápagos giant tortoises **dumbfounded**. I calculated that the **burly** giants move at about 0.2 miles per hour. That's barely ten percent of the rate of a human walker!

It really is true that human nature is the same the world over. This morning, I saw tour groups representing seven different nationalities. All were equally in awe of the animals of the Galápagos.

Thurs., Apr. 20 The population of saddlebacks on San Cristóbal has been estimated at 1,800. Long ago, there were tortoises at the southern end of the island. That population is now **extinct**. The **relic** of a specimen of this race poses a new question: Were these tortoises the same as

today's animals, named *Geochelone chathamensis*, or were they a different subspecies of giant tortoise?

One of my goals is to measure the impact of predators on tortoise hatchlings. The first newborns emerged this week after six months of incubation. I cannot help admiring their determination and **grit**. Feral dogs and goats, as well as hawks, are their chief enemies. If youngsters survive, however, they will enjoy a life on an epic scale. When fully grown, the males will weigh up to 800 pounds and measure over six feet from end to end. Amazingly, the tortoises have the longest life span of any creature on Earth—an estimated 150 years. No wonder there are so many gaps in the scientific literature about these animals. It is understandable that scientists' reports might be **distorted**. No one scientist could ever observe the tortoises' entire natural lifespan.

Wed., Apr. 26 Another goal of mine is to document dominance contests among adult saddlebacks. Last night I **rummaged** through my field notes from the last few weeks. Many of the dominance contests take place in plain view. As yet, I have witnessed only a few.

Fri., Apr. 28 Whatever the causes for their **ingrained** hostility, it is clear that superior height gives the winning tortoise its key advantage, as in the sparring contest I witnessed this morning. Saddlebacks can be especially aggressive toward one another. Is this because they have to **skimp** on sparse resources within their habitat, such as food, plants, water, and shade? Some more **sleuthing** during my next month here should answer these questions, as well as a few I haven't yet asked!

Note the spelling, pronunciation, part(s) of speech, and definition(s) of each of the following words. Then write the appropriate form of the word in the blank spaces in the illustrative sentence(s) following. Finally, study the lists of synonyms and antonyms.

1. alias (ā′ lē əs)

(*n.*) an assumed name, especially as used to hide one's identity; (*adv.*) otherwise called

"Mr. Plante" was just one **alias** used by the elusive spy.

Superman, **alias** Clark Kent, began as a comic book character created in 1938.

SYNONYM: (*n.*) pseudonym
ANTONYMS: (*n.*) real name, given name, legal name

2. amble (am′ bəl)

(*v.*) to walk slowly, stroll; (*n.*) an easy pace; a leisurely walk

It's a lovely day to **amble** to work and enjoy the many sights and sounds along the way.

When we woke to see the sun shining, we planned a long **amble** in the park.

SYNONYMS: (*v.*) saunter; (*n.*) ramble
ANTONYMS: (*v., n.*) gallop, dash, sprint, run, race, rush

3. burly (bər′ lē)

(*adj.*) big and strong; muscular

That guy is as **burly** as a lumberjack, so he would be the perfect one to help me move my furniture.

SYNONYMS: strapping, hefty, beefy
ANTONYMS: weak, puny, delicate, frail

4. distort (dis tôrt′)

(*v.*) to give a false or misleading account of; to twist out of shape

A magazine known to **distort** the facts would be an unreliable source of information.

SYNONYMS: disfigure, misshape, falsify

5. dogged (dôg′ əd)

(*adj.*) persistent, stubbornly determined, refusing to give up

The troops fought with **dogged** determination and courage.

SYNONYM: untiring
ANTONYMS: wishy-washy, faltering, irresolute

6. dumbfounded (dəm′ faůnd əd)

(*adj.*) so amazed that one is unable to speak, bewildered

When the shocking news finally reached us, we were completely **dumbfounded**.

SYNONYMS: speechless, stunned, flabbergasted
ANTONYMS: unsurprised, expectant

CCSS Vocabulary: 4.c., 4.d. (See pp. T14–15.)

7. extinct
(ek stiŋkt′)

(*adj.*) no longer in existence; no longer active; gone out of use

The ___**extinct**___ volcano is no longer a threat.

SYNONYMS: died out, vanished
ANTONYMS: still alive, surviving, extant

8. grit
(grit)

(*n.*) very fine sand or gravel; courage in the face of hardship or danger; (*v.*) to grind; to make a grating sound

Cars stall if ___**grit**___ clogs a fuel line.

It upsets me to see Dad get angry and ___**grit**___ his teeth.

SYNONYMS: (*n.*) dirt, mettle
ANTONYMS: (*n.*) timidity, cowardice, faintheartedness

9. inevitable
(in ev′ ə tə bəl)

(*adj.*) sure to happen, unavoidable

Is it ___**inevitable**___ that all comedies have happy endings?

SYNONYMS: inescapable, fated
ANTONYMS: avoidable, escapable, preventable

10. ingrained
(in grānd′)

(*adj.*) fixed deeply and firmly; working into the grain or fiber; forming a part of the inmost being

Biting my lower lip is an ___**ingrained**___ habit.

SYNONYMS: deep-seated, entrenched, indelible
ANTONYMS: superficial, shallow, skin-deep

11. meteoric
(mē tē ôr′ ik)

(*adj.*) resembling a meteor in speed; having sudden and temporary brilliance similar to a meteor's

The young actor's ___**meteoric**___ rise to fame became legendary.

SYNONYMS: brilliant, blazing; ANTONYMS: slow, sluggish, gradual

12. parody
(par′ ə dē)

(*n.*) a humorous or ridiculous imitation; (*v.*) to make fun of something by imitating it

The audience roared with laughter at the comedy troupe's hilarious ___**parody**___.

The new film successfully ___**parodies**___ political life in England.

SYNONYMS: (*n.*) satire, travesty; (*v.*) lampoon, burlesque

13. prevail
(pri vāl′)

(*v.*) to triumph over; to succeed; to exist widely, be in general use; to get someone to do something by urging

We hope to ___**prevail**___ over all obstacles we may encounter on this project.

SYNONYMS: win, rule, overcome, conquer
ANTONYMS: be defeated, go under, succumb

CCSS Vocabulary: 4.c., 4.d. (See pp. T14–15.)

14. relic (rel′ ik)

(*n.*) an object from the past with historical value or interest; a trace of an outdated custom; remaining fragments, ruins

The old Model T in my grandfather's barn is a **relic** of the first American touring cars.

SYNONYMS: (*n.*) artifact, historical object

15. rend (rend)

(*v.*) to tear to pieces; split violently apart (*past tense,* rent)

The abominable tactics of this trial could **rend** public confidence in the legal system.

SYNONYMS: cleave, splinter, tear asunder

16. replenish (ri plen′ ish)

(*v.*) to fill again, make good, replace

Airport crews work quickly to **replenish** a plane's supply of food, water, and safety supplies.

SYNONYMS: restock, refresh, restore
ANTONYMS: empty, drain, sap

17. rummage (rəm′ əj)

(*v.*) to search through, investigate the contents of; (*n.*) an active search; a collection of odd items

It can be an adventure to **rummage** around our garage for remnants of our childhood.

She found an old saddle in the **rummage**.

SYNONYMS: (*v.*) delve into, sift through, poke around

18. skimp (skimp)

(*v.*) to save, be thrifty; to be extremely sparing with; to give little attention or effort to

If you **skimp** on regular meals, you may be tempted to snack on too much junk food.

SYNONYMS: be stingy, scrimp, cut corners
ANTONYMS: be extravagant, splurge, lavish

19. sleuth (slüth)

(*n.*) a detective

A skilled **sleuth** can find hidden clues in unusual places.

SYNONYMS: investigator, gumshoe

20. vandalism (van′ dəl iz əm)

(*n.*) deliberate and pointless destruction of public or private property

The city realizes that it needs to create tougher laws to discourage **vandalism**.

SYNONYM: willful destruction

CCSS Vocabulary: 4.c., 4.d. (See pp. T14–15.)

Choosing the Right Word

*Select the **boldface** word that better completes each sentence. You might refer to the passage on pages 136–137 to see how most of these words are used in context.*

1. The defenders of the Alamo put up a (**burly, dogged**) resistance against the enemy.

2. All I need is a meal, a hot shower, and a good night's sleep to (**replenish, rend**) my energies.

3. Isn't it foolish to think that just because of his (**meteoric, burly**) physique he has no interest in art or music?

4. No, I wasn't (**ingrained, dumbfounded**) to be chosen the most popular member of the class, but maybe I was just a little surprised!

5. Suddenly, the stillness of the early morning hours was (**rent, rummaged**) by a single shot!

Though from Tennessee, Davy Crockett helped to defend the Alamo.

6. To avoid a lot of unwanted attention, the famous rock star registered in the hotel under a(n) (**rummage, alias**).

7. There are several organizations whose goal is to protect endangered species, such as the giant panda, to keep them from becoming (**relics, extinct**).

8. The aging actor trying to play the part of a young man seemed no more than a (**sleuth, parody**) of the great performer he once was.

9. With all of his absences and goofing off in class, it was (**inevitable, meteoric**) that he would not pass the test.

10. Is there anything more romantic than a nighttime (**amble, vandalism**) upon the moonlit decks of a mighty ocean liner?

11. "I'll have two hot dogs with all the fixings," I said to the vendor, "and don't (**prevail, skimp**) on the mustard!"

12. Nikki (**distorted, rummaged**) the truth about her whereabouts in order to conceal her alliance with the defendant.

13. The prejudices of a bigot are sometimes so (**ingrained, burly**) that it is very difficult to get rid of them.

14. When I discovered the abandoned cave that was used for an enemy hideout during WWII, I was amazed with how many war (**aliases, relics**) still remained.

15. I hope to pick up some real bargains at the (**rummage, grit**) sale being held in our civic center.

CCSS Vocabulary: 4.d. (See pp. T14–15.)

16. I know that you don't like the idea of painting the house, but you'll just have to (**replenish, grit**) your teeth and do it.

17. Whether the window was broken accidentally or as an act of (**parody, vandalism**), the fact remains that it is broken and must be paid for.

18. After months of looking for employment, my sister, known for her (**skimpy, dogged**) persistence, finally obtained her dream job as a video game reviewer.

19. An art historian who is trying to verify the authenticity of a painting acts more like a (**sleuth, relic**) than a critic.

20. Although it is sometimes hard, we must have faith that in the long run justice and decency will (**skimp, prevail**).

21. It may be, as you say, that this volcano has been (**extinct, dumbfounded**) for many years, but isn't there some danger that it may come to life again?

22. Since it is possible for nations to settle their disagreements in a reasonable way, we refuse to believe that war is (**inevitable, meteoric**).

23. We scorn all those who would deliberately bend the truth and (**distort, amble**) history in order to suit the political needs of their day.

24. His (**dogged, meteoric**) success at such an early age left him unprepared to handle the disappointments and failures that came to him later in life.

25. Don't you find those TV shows that (**parody, skimp**) famous people hilarious?

*Choose the word from this Unit that is the same or most nearly the same in meaning as the **boldface** word or expression in the phrase. Write that word on the line. Use a dictionary if necessary.*

1. **deep-rooted** sense of right and wrong ______ ingrained
2. ways to **misrepresent** the truth ______ distort
3. tried to **ridicule** the governor ______ parody
4. memoirs of her **dazzling** career ______ meteoric
5. where science **reigns** over superstition ______ prevails
6. greedily **dismember** its prey ______ rend
7. protected by a **brawny** bodyguard ______ burly
8. **refill** the empty bird feeder ______ replenish
9. admiring the **determination** of hardy pioneers ______ grit
10. ruined by **malicious defacement** ______ vandalism

CCSS Vocabulary: 5. (See pp. T14–15.)

The synonyms and antonyms here do not appear on the Definitions page.

Antonyms

*Choose the word from this Unit that is most nearly opposite in meaning to the **boldface** word or expression in the phrase. Write that word on the line. Use a dictionary if necessary.*

1. hoping you will **glorify** our leader ______parody______
2. after **depleting** the ice ______replenishing______
3. **restoration** of an historic statue ______vandalism______
4. reviewing a **lackluster** career ______meteoric______
5. hoping to **unite** the quarrelsome couple ______rend______

Completing the Sentence

From the words in this Unit, choose the one that best completes each of the following sentences. Write the correct word form in the space provided.

1. We saw a bolt of lightning ______rend______ a huge limb from the mighty oak tree.
2. After our furious gallop across the countryside, we allowed our tired horses to ______amble______ back to the stable.
3. The grime on the mechanic's hands was so deeply ______ingrained______ even a thorough scrubbing couldn't entirely remove it.
4. The old custom of celebrating the Fourth of July with a fireworks display still ______prevails______ in many American towns.
5. Isn't it a shame that our School Board must spend thousands of dollars every year just to repair the damage caused by ______vandalism______?
6. The cruise ship stopped at the port both to give the passengers a chance to go ashore and to ______replenish______ the water supply.
7. Isn't it fun on a rainy day to ______rummage______ about in the attic and look for interesting odds and ends?
8. In the late 19th century, Sir Arthur Conan Doyle created one of the most famous ______sleuths______ in literature, Sherlock Holmes.
9. There is an old saying that nothing is really ______inevitable______ except death and taxes.
10. Whenever our team needs a few yards to make a first down, we call on our big, ______burly______ fullback to crash through the line.

CCSS Vocabulary: 4.a., 5. (See pp. T14–15.)

11. We were nothing less than **dumbfounded** when we saw the immense damage that the hurricane had done in so brief a time.

12. Even though so many people were criticizing and ridiculing him, he had the **grit** to continue doing what he felt was right.

13. We greatly admired the **dogged** determination and patience that the disabled veteran showed in learning to master a wheelchair.

14. Her ability to **parody** the words and gestures of prominent Americans makes her an excellent comic impressionist.

15. The old con artist had used so many **aliases** over the course of his criminal career that he sometimes forgot his real name!

16. If you truly want to improve your math grades, you should not continue to **skimp** so often on your homework.

17. The rock singer enjoyed a sudden **meteoric** rise in popularity, but his career faded just as quickly as it had blossomed.

18. As the buffalo began to decrease sharply in numbers, conservationists feared that the species might become totally **extinct**.

19. There are archeological sites in Greece that contain sacred **relics** that the ancients believed held supernatural powers.

20. Her face was so **distorted** with pain and suffering that at first I did not recognize her.

Writing: Words in Action

Answers to both prompts will vary.

1. Look back at "Here I Am: Galápagos Log" (pages 136–137). Suppose that Samantha Rosenstern decides to choose one student to join her in the study of saddlebacks. You are on the short list of candidates. Write a letter to Ms. Rosenstern, convincing her that you are the best person to join her in San Cristóbal. Use at least two details from the passage and three Unit words.

2. If you could choose a place anywhere in the world to visit for scientific research, where would it be? Why? What discovery would you hope to make? In a brief essay, identify your choice and support it with specific examples, details from the reading (refer to pages 136–137), or personal experience. Write at least three paragraphs, and use three or more words from this Unit.

Writing prompt #2 is modeled on that of standardized tests.

CCSS Vocabulary: 6; Writing: 1.c., 2.d., 3.d., 4. (See pp. T14–15.)

Vocabulary in Context: Informational Text for Unit 11 is available online at **vocabularyworkshop.com**.

The following excerpts are from White Fang *by Jack London. Some of the words you have studied in this Unit appear in* ***boldface*** *type. Complete each statement below the excerpt by circling the letter of the correct answer.*

1. And here, in the Klondike, the leader was indeed the leader. The wisest as well as strongest dog was the leader, and the team obeyed him and feared him. That White Fang should quickly gain this post was **inevitable**.

Something that is **inevitable** is NOT

a. avoidable **c.** understandable
b. predictable **d.** sensible

2. So near did the wolves approach, that the dogs became frantic with terror, and it was necessary to **replenish** the fire from time to time in order to keep the adventurous marauders at safer distance.

To **replenish** a fire means to

a. stay near it **c.** let it die out
b. avoid it **d.** build it up

3. The she-wolf stood over against her cub, facing the men, with bristling hair, a snarl rumbling deep in her throat. Her face was **distorted** and malignant with menace, even the bridge of the nose wrinkling from tip to eyes, so prodigious was her snarl.

Something that is **distorted** is

a. shaped **c.** twisted
b. encouraged **d.** confirmed

White Fang, part wolf and part dog, goes from a wild existence to gradual domestication.

4. Kiche licked White Fang soothingly with her tongue, and tried to **prevail** upon him to remain with her. But his curiosity was rampant, and several minutes later he was venturing forth on a new quest.

To **prevail** is to

a. prepare **c.** calm
b. urge **d.** force

5. Public-spirited citizens took down their rifles and went out after him. A pack of bloodhounds followed the way of his bleeding feet. And the **sleuth**-hounds of the law, the paid fighting animals of society, with telephone, and telegraph, and special train, clung to his trail night and day.

A hound that is characterized as a **sleuth** is a(n)

a. tracker **c.** fighter
b. consumer **d.** idler

Snap the code, or go to
vocabularyworkshop.com

UNIT 12

Note that not all of the 20 Unit words are used in this passage. *Abduct*, *compact*, *implement*, *strapping*, and *titanic* are not included.

*Read the following passage, taking note of the **boldface** words and their contexts. These words are among those you will be studying in Unit 12. As you complete the exercises in this Unit, it may help to refer to the way the words are used below.*

CCSS Vocabulary: 4; Reading (Informational Text): 4, 6. (See pp. T14–15.)

Vampires We Have Known

<Humorous Essay>

To the extent that that vampires make appearances in television dramas nowadays, and in movies and novels, too, we can say that we're all quite familiar with these creatures. That's an **indisputable** fact, is it not? And there's nothing **ambiguous** about the claim that there have been reports of vampires for hundreds of years already. The traditional legends of these ominous creatures seem to have **thrived** originally in eastern Europe. One early case stretches back to the year 1672 in old Croatia. There, a legend sprang up around a man named Jure Grando. He had died and been buried and some twenty years later was reportedly back on his feet. It is not precisely clear by what **incalculable** logic the locals derived this knowledge. But it is rather clear that they were convinced that Jure Grando had emerged from the ground as something called a vampire. By secret, **stealthy** tactics and **maneuvers**, the now vampiric Grando was determined to drink the blood of good civilians. He especially liked to trouble his former wife, the poor living widow, Mrs. Grando.

Do you **balk** at believing these strange tales from another age? How can we **confer** now and discuss the case of Jure Grando? Most of the evidence, if there was any, is lost to history. The **scant** traces that remain of any Grando, or of any facts, or of any vampires, show us next to nothing.

Equally well-founded reports of vampires spread through Europe in the century after this episode. By what **earmarks** does one know a vampire?

bloodsucking creature called the chupacabra. It has a taste especially for goats. Needless to say, **intensive** investigations have ensued. And piercing, **strident** calls for action have been voiced in this country by chupacabra believers. They feel an urgent need to find out what is happening to the goats. The results, you ask? Alas, most chupacabras appear to be coyotes with mange.

The fascination with vampire stories will persist, just like our love of other fantasies. To enjoy a fantasy is one thing, and to enjoy a harmless fright is fine. But to believe that every shadow is like a thing alive—that is another thing, entirely.

There are many similarities in vampire tales from around the globe. From Russia to France, **valiant** witnesses leapt forward to relate bold tales about these **frigid** monsters. (Though in France, one wit was heard complaining that the businessmen were the real bloodsuckers.) African tradition informs us of the dread asanbosam. It also thirsts for blood. The thing has hooks for feet and hangs upside-down. The Chinese once feared the jiang shi, which hops along and sucks the life energy out of its victims. The draugs in Scandinavia lingered about graves. They protect buried treasure and drink the blood of trespassers. If their appetite was strong, draugs would eat their victims too. The Bulgarian krvopijacs have only one nostril apiece. They can be **sabotaged** if wild roses are laid around their graves—that will stop them!

We needn't dip far back to old tales in the Western Hemisphere to uncover eyewitness accounts of bloodsucking creatures. In Mexico, Chile, Nicaragua, and Puerto Rico, and by now in other places, there have been thousands of reports in recent decades about the

Audio

For iWords and audio passages, snap the code, or go to **vocabularyworkshop.com**.

Note the spelling, pronunciation, part(s) of speech, and definition(s) of each of the following words. Then write the appropriate form of the word in the blank spaces in the illustrative sentence(s) following. Finally, study the lists of synonyms and antonyms.

1. abduct (ab dəkt′)

(*v.*) to kidnap, carry off by force

Some people with vivid imaginations fear that hostile aliens will come to Earth to **abduct** humans.

SYNONYMS: seize, snatch

2. ambiguous (am big′ yü əs)

(*adj.*) not clear; having two or more possible meanings

The purpose of a test is not to confuse students with **ambiguous** questions, but to determine whether they have learned the material.

SYNONYMS: uncertain, unclear, equivocal
ANTONYMS: obvious, plain, clear, unequivocal

3. balk (bôk)

(*v.*) to stop short and refuse to go on; to refuse abruptly; to prevent from happening; (*n.*) (in baseball) an illegal motion made by a pitcher

My horse **balked** when I urged it to go up the steep mountain slope.

The opposing team scored an additional run because of the pitcher's **balk**.

SYNONYMS: (*v.*) hesitate, block

4. compact (*v.*, *adj.*, kəm pakt′; *n.*, käm′ pakt)

(*adj.*) closely and firmly packed together; small; (*v.*) to squeeze together; (*n.*) an agreement between parties; a small case containing a mirror and face powder; a small car

Computers are much more **compact** now than they were a generation ago.

Workers at the town dump were asked to **compact** the trash to save space.

SYNONYMS: (*adj.*) dense; (*v.*) compress
ANTONYMS: (*adj.*) enormous, humongous, bulky

5. confer (kən fər′)

(*v.*) to consult, talk over, exchange opinions; to present as a gift, favor, or honor

The committee will **confer** before taking any action on the proposed new contract.

SYNONYMS: deliberate, award, bestow
ANTONYMS: withdraw, take away, withhold, deny

CCSS Vocabulary: 4.c., 4.d. (See pp. T14–15.)

6. earmark (ir′ mark)

(*v.*) to set aside for a special purpose; to mark an animal's ear for identification; (*n.*) an identifying mark or feature

Let's ___earmark___ the money we received for the new building fund.

SYNONYMS: (*v.*) reserve; (*n.*) trait, attribute

7. frigid (frij′ id)

(*adj.*) extremely cold; lacking in warmth or feeling

Antarctica has a very ___frigid___ climate.

SYNONYMS: freezing, unresponsive
ANTONYMS: hot, balmy, torrid, warm, friendly

8. implement (im′ plə mənt)

(*n.*) an instrument, tool; (*v.*) to put into effect

The harrow is a farm ___implement___ that is used to pulverize and smooth soil.

The highway patrol will ___implement___ the new speed limit as of July 1 of this year.

SYNONYMS: (*n.*) device, utensil; (*v.*) fulfill, accomplish, achieve, apply, carry out

9. incalculable (in kal′ kyə lə bəl)

(*adj.*) too great to be counted; unpredictable, uncertain

Concerned scientists worry that global warming may cause ___incalculable___ damage to our environment.

SYNONYMS: countless, measureless
ANTONYMS: measurable, countable, predictable

10. indisputable (in dis pyüt′ ə bəl)

(*adj.*) beyond question or argument, definitely true

With such ___indisputable___ evidence, Judge Lee must rule to drop all charges against my client.

SYNONYMS: irrefutable, undeniable, incontestable
ANTONYMS: questionable, debatable, arguable

11. intensive (in ten′ siv)

(*adj.*) thorough, deep; showing great effort; concentrated

It took ___intensive___ physical therapy for the injured athlete to regain her strength and speed.

SYNONYMS: thoroughgoing, heightened, exhaustive
ANTONYMS: relaxed, easygoing, laid-back

12. maneuver (mə nü′ vər)

(*n.*) a planned movement; a skillful plan; a scheme; (*v.*) to perform or carry out such a planned movement

The troops carried out a night ___maneuver___ as part of the training mission.

It takes a steady hand to ___maneuver___ the high-speed power drill.

SYNONYMS: (*n.*) move, tactic; (*v.*) guide, manipulate

13. sabotage (sab′ ə täzh)

(*n.*) an action taken to destroy something or to prevent it from working properly; (*v.*) to take such destructive action

Foreign embassies worry about ___**sabotage**___.

Protesters decided to ___**sabotage**___ the factory.

SYNONYMS: (*v.*) vandalize, cripple, subvert, destroy

14. scant (skant)

(*adj.*) not enough; barely enough; marked by a small or insufficient amount

Somehow, we made the ___**scant**___ supply of food stretch for nearly a week.

SYNONYMS: inadequate, meager, skimpy, bare
ANTONYMS: abundant, plentiful, profuse, excessive

15. stealthy (stel′ thē)

(*adj.*) done in a way so as not to be seen or observed; sneaky, underhanded

The nervous robber took ___**stealthy**___ glances at the cash register.

SYNONYMS: sly, furtive; ANTONYMS: open, direct, aboveboard

16. strapping (strap′ iŋ)

(*adj.*) tall, strong, and healthy

That ___**strapping**___ young man is a good wrestler.

SYNONYMS: sturdy, husky, brawny, athletic, hefty
ANTONYMS: weak, frail, fragile, puny

17. strident (strīd′ ənt)

(*adj.*) harsh, shrill; unpleasant sounding

Her ___**strident**___ laughter showed harsh ridicule.

SYNONYMS: piercing, grating
ANTONYMS: mellow, soothing, musical, honeyed

18. thrive (thrīv)

(*v.*) to grow vigorously; to grow in wealth and possessions

Angie hopes that her business will ___**thrive**___ in today's Internet culture.

SYNONYMS: flourish, blossom, prosper; ANTONYMS: wither, fail

19. titanic (tī tan′ ik)

(*adj.*) of enormous size, strength, power, or scope

The movie plot explores the ___**titanic**___ struggle between the forces of good and evil.

SYNONYMS: gigantic, huge; ANTONYMS: tiny, miniature, diminutive

20. valiant (val′ yənt)

(*adj.*) possessing or acting with bravery or boldness

Sir Galahad was a ___**valiant**___ knight of King Arthur's Round Table.

SYNONYMS: brave, bold, gallant, heroic
ANTONYMS: timid, cowardly, fainthearted, "chicken"

CCSS Vocabulary: 4.c., 4.d. (See pp. T14–15.)

*Select the **boldface** word that better completes each sentence. You might refer to the passage on pages 146–147 to see how most of these words are used in context.*

National Park Service Director Stephen T. Mather, left, urged the U.S. Congress to preserve the redwood forests.

1. Of all the evergreens that tower in America's forests, none can surpass the height and girth of the (**titanic, indisputable**) California redwoods.

2. Truthfulness and sincerity are the (**earmarks, compacts**) of an honest person.

3. The brave defenders of the fort waged a (**scant, valiant**) battle against the enemy's troops.

4. Why is that big, (**strapping, incalculable**) fellow in the advertisement always kicking sand into the face of the 98-pound weakling?

5. When he says that his analysis of the problem is (**valiant, indisputable**), all he means is that he's not willing to listen to anyone else's ideas.

6. The first Pilgrim settlers signed an agreement called the "Mayflower (**Compact, Maneuver**)."

7. What do you think the United States should do when its representatives are (**sabotaged, abducted**) and held for ransom?

8. "It's an (**indisputable, ambiguous**) fact that the finest guitar players in rock music were from the 1970s," Brandon said.

9. Creeping (**stealthily, ambiguously**) through the underbrush, the enemy came within a few yards of the stockade before the guards saw them.

10. Although our club is run more or less democratically, we don't have the time to (**confer, abduct**) about every minor detail.

11. As election day gets closer, the tone of the candidates' political oratory becomes more and more (**titanic, strident**).

12. Aunt Lorna (**conferred, balked**) when the waiter at the seafood restaurant told her that the dinner special—the "catch of the day"—was $41.00.

13. When we made our appeal for funds, their response was so (**incalculable, frigid**) that we realized we would have to find other ways of raising money.

14. The future is indeed (**incalculable, strapping**), but we must face it with faith and confidence.

15. We have worked out a good plan on paper; now we must decide how we are going to (**implement, balk**) it.

CCSS Vocabulary: 4.d. (See pp. T14–15.)

16. The extra money being raised by the band booster club has been (**earmarked, maneuvered**) to fund future band trips.

17. Because her condition was so poor after the operation, she was placed in the hospital's (**stealthy, intensive**) care unit.

18. The Labrador retriever received a medal from the fire department for its (**valiant, compact**) act of saving a drowning man.

19. After straining and sweating in the hot sun for an hour, we realized that we had pushed the stalled car only a(n) (**scant, intensive**) quarter mile.

20. Since *presently* means both "right now" and "in the future," any statement containing it must be considered (**strident, ambiguous**).

21. I don't think democracy can (**balk, thrive**) in an atmosphere of racial and religious hatred.

22. In her floor exercise, the champion gymnast performed some of the most amazing (**earmarks, maneuvers**) I have ever seen.

23. When their pitcher committed the (**balk, earmark**), the umpire advanced our runner from first to second base.

24. When a conquering army overruns a country, the only way the people may have to strike back is by acts of (**ambiguity, sabotage**).

25. Whenever I go out to eat, I (**thrive, sabotage**) my diet by ordering dessert.

Choose the word from this Unit that is the same or most nearly the same in meaning as the ***boldface*** *word or expression in the phrase. Write that word on the line. Use a dictionary if necessary.*

1. may use that **gadget** to move the baggage — implement
2. **resist** because of fear — balk
3. lending us **limitless** support — incalculable
4. its **pocket-size** motor — compact
5. the **inarguable** star of the team — indisputable
6. a most **standoffish** welcome — frigid
7. the king who has been **taken hostage** — abducted
8. to interpret that **vague** remark — ambiguous
9. as they put forth an **immense** effort — titanic
10. a **hearty** young athlete — strapping

CCSS Vocabulary: 5. (See pp. T14–15.)

*Choose the word from this Unit that is most nearly opposite in meaning to the **boldface** word or expression in the phrase. Write that word on the line. Use a dictionary if necessary.*

1. drives an **oversized** car — compact
2. worries about **minor** details — titanic
3. met the **delicate** daughter of the earl — strapping
4. decided to **abandon** the plan — implement
5. expected to **release** the hostages — abduct

Completing the Sentence

From the words in this Unit, choose the one that best completes each of the following sentences. Write the correct word form in the space provided.

1. The millionaire has hired special guards to make sure that his valuable, prize-winning show dog, Lucy, will not be ___abducted___.

2. Even mighty warships were endangered by the ___titanic___ waves that loomed like mountains above them.

3. In Shakespeare's words, "Cowards die many times before their deaths; the ___valiant___ never taste of death but once."

4. At first the zebras did not notice the ___stealthy___ movements of the lions inching their way closer to the herd.

5. The new recruits were rudely awakened from their peaceful sleep by the ___strident___ voice of the sergeant barking commands.

6. I was amazed to see how skillfully Felicia ___maneuvered___ that huge car through the heavy downtown traffic.

7. No doubt our antipollution program will be expensive, but the cost of doing nothing would be simply ___incalculable___.

8. When the winds begin to turn ___frigid___ in November, our thoughts turn to our warm and sunny island off the coast of Florida.

9. Because I'm afraid of heights, I usually ___balk___ at the idea of sitting in the first row of the topmost balcony in a theater.

10. Since the time we have to prepare for the final exams is exceedingly ___scant___, we had better make the best of every hour.

11. Each year a portion of the school budget is **earmarked** for the purchase of new books for the library.

12. As the day of the big game approached, our practice sessions became more and more **intensive**.

13. I prefer the **compact** edition of the dictionary because it is so much lighter and less bulky than the unabridged version.

14. In your training to become a dental assistant, you will become familiar with many of the **implements** that dentists use.

15. The breakdown of all these machines at the same time cannot simply be a coincidence; we suspect deliberate **sabotage**.

16. Why must you always be so **ambiguous** when I want you to give me a straight yes-or-no answer?

17. The president will **confer** well-deserved honors on the retiring ambassador.

18. When our team saw their **strapping** 200-pound defensive linemen, we realized that we would have a hard time running against them.

19. For a person who loves to argue as much as Gene does, there is nothing that is really **indisputable**.

20. The cactus is an example of a plant having natural adaptations that enable it to **thrive** even in a very dry climate.

Writing: Words in Action

Answers to both prompts will vary.

1. Look back at "Vampires We Have Known" (pages 146–147). Imagine you are a reporter. Rumors are spreading about a vampire-like creature attacking animals in your community. Alleviate your community's fears by writing an article that summarizes the history of vampires. Convince readers that there are no vampires. Use at least two details from the passage and three Unit words.

2. What is your opinion about the existence of monsters? Why do you think some people create stories about them? Why do some others believe in them? Write a brief essay, supporting your views with specific examples, observations, the reading (refer to pages 146–147), or personal experience. Write at least three paragraphs, and use three or more words from this Unit.

Writing prompt #2 is modeled on that of standardized tests.

 CCSS Vocabulary: 6; Writing: 1.c., 2.d., 3.d., 4. (See pp. T14–15.)

Vocabulary in Context: Informational Text for Unit 12 is available online at **vocabularyworkshop.com**.

The following excerpts are from Tales of Terror and Mystery *by Sir Arthur Conan Doyle. Some of the words you have studied in this Unit appear in* **boldface** *type. Complete each statement below the excerpt by circling the letter of the correct answer.*

1. The eyes glimmered like two disks of phosphorus in the darkness. They appalled and yet fascinated me. I could not take my own eyes from them. Nature plays strange tricks with us at such moments of **intensity**, and those glimmering lights waxed and waned with a steady rise and fall. ("The Brazilian Cat")

Intensity refers to

a. meekness **c.** fear
b. ignorance **d.** concentration

2. Nothing could be more hearty than his manner, and he set me at my ease in an instant. But it needed all his cordiality to atone for the **frigidity** and even rudeness of his wife, a tall, haggard woman, who came forward at his summons. ("The Brazilian Cat")

People who convey **frigidity** are

a. aloof **c.** dull
b. keen **d.** shy

Sir Arthur Conan Doyle's *Tales of Terror and Mystery* is a compilation of six horror stories and seven mysteries.

3. The court next morning was crammed to overflowing, and a murmur of excitement passed over it when Mr. Humphrey was observed to enter in a state of emotion, which even his trained nerves could not conceal, and to **confer** with the opposing counsel. ("The Black Doctor")

To **confer** with someone is to

a. babble **c.** lie
b. discuss **d.** inspire

4. In the silence of the night I could distinctly hear that someone was coming down the corridor. It was a **stealthy** step, faint and intermittent, as of a man who paused cautiously after every stride. ("The Beetle-Hunter")

Someone trying to be **stealthy** is NOT

a. prepared **c.** obvious
b. crafty **d.** secretive

5. At the time when I was able to fulfill my **compact** I was living in a cottage at Fontainebleau, and as the evening trains were inconvenient, he asked me to spend the night in his house. ("The Leather Funnel")

A person fulfilling a **compact** is honoring a(n)

a. colleague **c.** country
b. host **d.** agreement

Snap the code, or go to **vocabularyworkshop.com**

Vocabulary for Comprehension

*Read the following passage in which some of the words you have studied in Units 10–12 appear in **boldface** type. Then answer the questions on page 157.*

This passage explains why the icy continent of Antarctica is truly an international scientific laboratory.

(Line)

"Science lab" usually means a clean, bright room in which researchers work with high-tech equipment. Antarctica, the fifth largest of Earth's seven continents, is itself an enormous, ice-cold science lab. It has no native population. Few living things can survive in its brutal climate. But scientists are attracted to the rare features of this desolate continent.

Antarctica is more than 95% ice-covered all year long. It has had the lowest air temperature ever measured, as well as some of the highest winds. Because it has no industrial pollution, its ice and snow are pure. All that ice makes it doubtful that any settlement or economic development will ever take place. But many tiny outposts have sprung up since the 1950s.

In that decade, twelve nations set up research stations all over Antarctica. Representatives of those nations got together to draft a **compact** devoting the continent to peaceful study. This pact went into effect in 1961. It forbids military action and nuclear weapons. It promotes a free exchange of ideas.

Antarctic scientists devise and carry out a wide range of tests. They study glaciers, weather patterns and conditions, icebergs, magnetism, volcanoes, the movement of rock plates, and animal and plant biology. They openly share their findings with the global scientific community.

Life in such a difficult place demands planning, special gear, and **grit**. Scientists must figure out how to do their research safely and effectively. They must guard their health and well-being. Internet and satellite technologies surely help. Researchers so far from home can **confer** with the family, friends, and coworkers they left behind. They can stay up-to-date on world events. But they cannot easily come and go. Scientists often arrive before the Antarctic winter, when near-total darkness **engulfs** the area. They typically stay for six to ten long, cold, lonely months.

CCSS Vocabulary: 4.a.; Reading (Informational Text): 2, 4, 6. (See pp. T14–15.)

1. The "rare features" of Antarctica that the author refers to in lines 10–11
   a. have vanished
   b. are never identified
   c. are not so rare or unusual
   d. are identified in paragraph 2
   e. are identified in paragraph 4

2. **Compact** (line 27) most nearly means
   a. speech
   b. dense
   c. small car
   d. reminder
   e. agreement

3. The compact that was drafted had all of the following purposes EXCEPT
   a. to promote peaceful study
   b. to ban all nuclear weapons
   c. to prevent any kind of military action
   d. to divide Antarctica among nations
   e. to share the results of research

4. The meaning of **grit** (line 42) is
   a. courage
   b. gravel
   c. persistence
   d. power
   e. grind

5. **Confer** (line 48) most nearly means
   a. play
   b. argue
   c. consult
   d. study
   e. present gifts

6. **Engulfs** (line 54) is best defined as
   a. avoids
   b. envelops
   c. divides
   d. empties
   e. endangers

7. Paragraph 5 (lines 40–56) focuses on
   a. the future of Antarctica
   b. weather conditions in Antarctica
   c. tests conducted in Antarctica
   d. difficulties of working in Antarctica
   e. research stations in Antarctica

8. Which of the following best states the main idea of the passage?
   a. It is easy to do scientific research in Antarctica.
   b. Antarctica is almost totally covered with ice all year.
   c. Antarctica, the fifth-largest continent, has no native population.
   d. Scientists in Antarctica depend on the Internet for communication.
   e. Scientists from twelve nations share research results about Antarctica.

9. Which of the following conclusions can you draw from the passage?
   a. Antarctica is a difficult place to live.
   b. Antarctica has valuable resources.
   c. There is discord among the nations that signed the 1961 agreement.
   d. In the future, nations will build colonies in Antarctica.
   e. Scientific outposts in Antarctica have damaged native plants.

10. What can you infer about the author's attitude toward the scientists who live and work in Antarctica?
    a. The author envies them.
    b. The author admires them.
    c. The author thinks their life is easy.
    d. The author thinks they are foolish.
    e. The author thinks they disagree.

11. Scientists in Antarctica face all of the following EXCEPT
    a. lack of communication with family
    b. near-total darkness
    c. loneliness
    d. difficulties moving about
    e. extreme cold

12. The author apparently thinks that research taking place in Antarctica
    a. prevents volcanic eruptions
    b. promotes economic development
    c. contributes to climate change
    d. contributes to global knowledge
    e. creates air pollution

CCSS Vocabulary: 4.a.; Reading (Informational Text): 2, 4, 6. (See pp. T14–15.)

Two-Word Completions

Select the pair of words that best completes the meaning of each of the following sentences.

1. When we saw the breathtaking ____________ on that lovely autumn morning, we did not want to miss the stunning vista and decided to ____________ rather than rush.
   a. parody . . . maneuver
   b. panorama . . . amble
   c. relic . . . balk
   d. grit . . . compact

2. I am always ____________ by the amazing powers of observation and deduction exhibited by my favorite ____________, the legendary Sherlock Holmes.
   a. deluded . . . alias
   b. ingrained . . . foil
   c. dogged . . . relic
   d. dumbfounded . . . sleuth

3. When I asked her where I could find the old book, her reply was so ____________ that I had to spend an hour ____________ for it.
   a. indisputable . . . earmarking
   b. bumbling . . . abducting
   c. intensive . . . prevailing
   d. ambiguous . . . rummaging

4. "Although we have devised a plan to deal with the situation," the official said, "we will not be able to ____________ the plan until we receive the funds ____________ by the government for the project."
   a. replenish . . . conferred
   b. implement . . . earmarked
   c. refurbish . . . maneuvered
   d. formulate . . . rummaged

5. The nimble little star quarterback ____________ deftly around the ____________ linebackers attempting to sack him.
   a. engulfed . . . compact
   b. abducted . . . strapping
   c. maneuvered . . . burly
   d. foiled . . . frigid

6. Animals such as the saber-toothed tiger and the woolly mammoth have been ____________ for many thousands of years, but scientists have found the ____________ of these animals of the last Ice Age.
   a. extinct . . . relics
   b. scant . . . earmarks
   c. skimpy . . . foils
   d. indisputable . . . sleuths

7. Kidnappers had made plans to ____________ the official and hold him for ransom. Fortunately, the police were able to ____________ the plot after an informant tipped them off about it.
   a. delude . . . balk
   b. abduct . . . foil
   c. sabotage . . . distort
   d. parody . . . pry

 CCSS Vocabulary: 4.a. (See pp. T14–15.)

In the passage “Farewell, Blue Yodeler” (see pages 126–127), the writer describes Jimmie Rodgers’s last days and states that he was “in a race against time.” The writer means that Jimmie did not have much time to complete his recordings, as he was about to die.

“Race against time” is an **idiom**. Idioms are words, phrases, or expressions based on colorful comparisons. Their meanings should not be taken literally. People usually learn idioms by hearing and using them in everyday speech. Idioms are unique to every language. When you learn a new idiom and its meaning, you are also learning how different cultures, communities, and generations see the world.

Choosing the Right Idiom

Read each sentence. Use context clues to figure out the meaning of each idiom in ***boldface*** *print. Then write the letter of the definition for the idiom in the sentence.*

1. I know I was angry at James for a while, but that is all **water under the bridge** now. ___g___
2. “No matter how much money I save from what I earn babysitting,” Alison complained, “it just seems to be **a drop in the bucket**.” ___c___
3. “I can’t worry about the game tonight,” Sam said. “I’ve got **bigger fish to fry**.” ___j___
4. Tim tried to explain his tardiness to the teacher, but she did not fall for his **old song and dance**. ___a___
5. Marie is very health conscious; **once in a blue moon**, though, she’ll eat something sugary. ___d___
6. We just got a new boss, so this is not the time to **make any waves**. ___e___
7. Garret is still **finding his feet** in his new job as a grocery store cashier. ___b___
8. I couldn’t **believe my ears** when I heard you were moving. ___f___
9. **A little bird told me** that Gwen was getting braces next week. ___i___
10. I don’t mean to **rain on your parade**, but I heard the concert was cancelled. ___h___

a. excuses or lies
b. getting comfortable in
c. a very small amount
d. very infrequently
e. cause trouble; draw attention to yourself
f. believe what I’m hearing
g. a past event that is no longer important
h. spoil your fun
i. A secret source I can’t reveal gave me the information.
j. more important business to attend to

CCSS Vocabulary: 5.a. (See pp. T14–15.)

Writing with Idioms

Find the meaning of each idiom. (Use a dictionary if necessary.) Then write a sentence for each idiom. **Answers will vary.**

1. the cold shoulder **Sample answer: Melinda gave Tom the cold shoulder when he forgot their wedding anniversary.**
2. not my cup of tea
3. to egg on
4. give me a break
5. the cream of the crop
6. over the moon
7. the third degree
8. back to square one
9. shoot the breeze
10. to rake in the dough
11. the big cheese
12. down the road

 CCSS Vocabulary: 5. (See pp. T14–15.)

Denotation and Connotation

A word's dictionary definition is its **denotation**. A denotation is the word's literal meaning, and it conveys a neutral tone.

Words also have connotations. **Connotations** are the emotional associations that people make to certain words. These associations can be either positive or negative.

Consider these synonyms for the neutral word *individualist*:

nonconformist *maverick* *eccentric* *oddball*

Nonconformist and *maverick* have positive connotations, whereas *eccentric* and *oddball* are negative.

Think: People often admire nonconformists and mavericks, because they are usually confident, independent thinkers. People may be wary of eccentrics or oddballs, however, because their ideas may seem too way out or unusual.

Look at these examples of words. Notice how the connotation of each word varies.

NEUTRAL	POSITIVE	NEGATIVE
restore	**refurbish**	**overhaul**
satire	**parody**	**lampoon**
cold	**bracing**	**frigid**

Words can evoke powerful associations in readers. For example, the word *forest* might make some readers think of a beautiful woodland perfect for camping. Others might think of the dark, mysterious forests in fairy tales. Writers must be aware of connotations and choose words carefully so that they can convey the right mood and message.

Shades of Meaning

Write a plus sign (+) in the box if the word has a positive connotation. Write a minus sign (–) if the word has a negative connotation. Put a zero (0) if the word is neutral.

1. compact +	**2.** thrive +	**3.** dumbfounded –	**4.** maneuver 0
5. bumbling –	**6.** vandalism –	**7.** confer +	**8.** scant –
9. subsequent 0	**10.** abduct –	**11.** pry –	**12.** resourceful +
13. delude –	**14.** valiant +	**15.** prevail +	**16.** distort –

CCSS Vocabulary: 5.c. (See pp. T14–15.)

Expressing the Connotation

Read each sentence. Select the word in parentheses that better expresses the connotation (positive, negative, or neutral) given at the beginning of the sentence.

negative 1. It was quite common for outlaws of the wild west to have several (**names, aliases**).

neutral 2. The gymnast achieved (**meteoric, rapid**) fame after her Olympic debut.

negative 3. Our cat (**balked, hesitated**) when I opened the door to let him outside, and he saw that it was raining.

positive 4. We ate our lunch on the veranda and watched the tourists (**amble, trudge**) along the beach.

neutral 5. The movers had a difficult time trying to get the (**titanic, large**) piano into the small loft.

negative 6. The (**strident, loud**) screams from the fans made the security staff a little nervous.

positive 7. After spending the entire summer working out, Ted became a (**beefy, burly**) athlete.

positive 8. Randy saved the program from the ceremony as a (**keepsake, relic**) of the happy event.

Challenge: Using Connotation

Choose vocabulary words from Units 10–12 to replace the ***boldface*** *words in the sentences below. Then explain how the connotation of the replacement word changes the tone of the sentence.* **Answers will vary.**

unerring	**replenished**	**sabotaged**
foiled	**stealthy**	**engulfed**

1. Once again the police were victorious when they **interrupted** ___**foiled**___ the heist of the notorious diamond burglar.
Sample response: The positive connotation of *foiled* makes the action sound more forceful and successful; it suggests that the police had a plan that worked.

2. The unexpected snowstorm **undermined** ___**sabotaged**___ our winter getaway, causing all flights to warmer climates to be cancelled.
Sample response: *Sabotaged* has a more negative tone, suggesting that the snowstorm is like a person deliberately trying to ruin the speaker's vacation.

3. Now that the serious drought has been broken, it will not take long before the lakes will be **refilled** ___**replenished**___.
Sample response: *Replenished* has a positive connotation, suggesting that the drought has not only ended but been reversed.

 CCSS Vocabulary: 5, 5.c. (See pp. T14–15.)

Classical Roots

co, col, com, con, cor—with, together

A form of this Latin prefix appears in **consequence** (page 128), **compact** (page 148), and **confer** (page 148). Some other words in which this prefix appears are listed below.

coincidence	**colleague**	**compute**	**confide**
collaborate	**composure**	**concurrent**	**correspond**

From the list of words above, choose the one that corresponds to each of the brief definitions below. Write the word in the blank space in the illustrative sentence below the definition. Use a dictionary if necessary.

1. to work with others; to aid or assist an enemy of one's country
They agreed to **collaborate** on the science project so they could pool their resources and ideas.

2. to exchange letters; to be in agreement
My cousin and I decided to **correspond** by e-mail after he moved to Montana.

3. occurring at the same time; agreeing
The convicted felon was sentenced to **concurrent** prison terms.

4. the chance occurrence of two things at the same time or place
"What a **coincidence** to bump into you here at the passport office!" she exclaimed.

5. a fellow worker, associate
The proud retiree was honored by her longtime **colleagues** at the library.

6. to tell something as a secret; to entrust a secret
I would never **confide** such details to anyone but a close friend.

7. to determine by arithmetic; to calculate
The mechanic used a calculator to **compute** the total repair bill.

8. calmness of mind, bearing, or appearance; self-control
Even the car alarms wailing outside the auditorium did not ruffle the speaker's **composure**.

CCSS Vocabulary: 4.b. (See pp. T14–15.)

UNIT 13

Note that not all of the 20 Unit words are used in this passage. *Atrocity*, *fluent*, *recitation*, *sulky*, and *supplement* are not included.

Read the following passage, taking note of the ***boldface*** *words and their contexts. These words are among those you will be studying in Unit 13. As you complete the exercises in this Unit, it may help to refer to the way the words are used below.*

CCSS Vocabulary: 4; Reading (Informational Text): 4, 6. (See pp. T14–15.)

Polar Opposites

<Compare and Contrast Essay>

Although they may seem similar, the polar regions of planet Earth are really very different. They **affirm** the old adage that there are two sides to the same coin.

The astonishing climate **traits** of both the Arctic and Antarctica are **stupefying**. Temperatures of –60°F are not unusual. If the harsh winds and vast ice sheets do not **deter** visitors, these strangers will find the elements **disquieting** at the very least. During polar winters, the sun never rises, while during the summers, it never sets. For centuries, explorers had to give careful thought to how to **cope** with these forces of nature. It was essential to **adhere** closely to a more rigorous program of safety precautions than explorers used in more temperate lands.

The Arctic is a region of immense diversity. Although the terrain seems forbidding, many animals **prowl** the land, including polar bears, caribou, wolves, foxes, hares, and weasels. Migrant birds visit from as far away as Central and South America. Possibly the most famous of these birds is the arctic tern. This summer visitor traverses thousands of miles every year, from Antarctica to the Arctic! The ocean **surges** with abundant marine life, especially when warm currents move around some of the Arctic coasts. Surprisingly, vegetation is widespread. Algae, lichens, and dwarf shrubs persist, even in areas of permanent ice.

The Arctic is also home to a broad range of native peoples. For example, the Inuit and Aleuts reside in northern North America and Greenland. The Eurasian Arctic is home to the Sami,

The arctic fox has a thick coat and furred paws to allow for survival in an extremely cold climate.

The emperor penguin, indigenous to Antarctica, is the largest species of penguins.

sometimes called the Lapps, as well as to the Nenets (Samoyed) and the Evenks (Tungus). To suppose that these peoples view their environment as hostile would be a **misapprehension**. According to anthropologists, many Arctic residents are **optimists**. They perceive their surroundings as benevolent and **empowering**, offering an abundant livelihood.

By contrast with the Arctic, which is made up of portions of several continents, Antarctica is a true continent, the fifth largest on Earth. Its landmass covers 5.5 million square miles and lies almost wholly beneath a vast ice sheet. The ice measures 7 million cubic miles—that's about 90 percent of all the ice on Earth. In 1983, the lowest recorded temperature on Earth was measured at an Antarctic research center, Vostok Station: –128.6°F.

Unlike the Arctic, the interior of Antarctica may boast only of invertebrate microfauna, such as nematodes and ciliate protozoans. Seals and birds live on the edges of the land. Probably the most spectacular resident of Antarctica is the emperor penguin, a flightless bird standing between three and four feet tall.

Antarctica is the only continent on Earth without a native human population. Although the North and South Poles were first reached at roughly the same time in the early 1900s, the Arctic and Antarctic regions have had different exploration histories. Study of Antarctica **lagged** for some time, largely because trade routes from North America and Europe to the East seemed much more appealing in the far north.

The 1950s, however, witnessed two important events for Antarctica. First was the development of the tourist industry. Second was the Antarctic Treaty, a breakthrough in international diplomacy. This treaty preserved Antarctica from corrupt or **unscrupulous** exploitation that would **mangle** the environment. The agreement set aside the continent as a scientific preserve.

Despite differences between these two polar regions, both have been an equal source of fascination and inspiration for people throughout the centuries.

Note the spelling, pronunciation, part(s) of speech, and definition(s) of each of the following words. Then write the appropriate form of the word in the blank spaces in the illustrative sentence(s) following. Finally, study the lists of synonyms and antonyms.

1. adhere (ad hēr′)

(*v.*) to stick to, remain attached; to be devoted or loyal as a follower or supporter

Things will work out better if we **adhere** to our original plan.

SYNONYMS: cling, hold fast
ANTONYMS: unfasten, unglue, abandon, betray

2. affirm (ə fərm′)

(*v.*) to declare to be true, state positively; to confirm

Unexpected kindness from a stranger during a time of need can **affirm** one's faith in human nature.

SYNONYMS: assert, ratify
ANTONYMS: deny, disavow, reject, veto, disallow

3. atrocity (ə träs′ ət ē)

(*n.*) an extremely wicked, brutal, or cruel act; something very bad or unpleasant

The Nazis took great pains to keep detailed records of each kind of **atrocity** they committed.

SYNONYMS: enormity, monstrosity
ANTONYMS: good deed, kindness

4. cope (kōp)

(*v.*) to struggle successfully against; to prove to be a match for, deal with satisfactorily; (*n.*) a long religious cloak; a canopy

Education and experience provide us with the skills we need to **cope** with difficult situations.

We exchanged wedding vows under a blue **cope**.

SYNONYMS: (*v.*) make do, get along, handle

5. deter (di tər′)

(*v.*) to discourage, scare off, or prevent through fear or doubt

Traffic jams won't **deter** us from coming to your birthday party.

ANTONYMS: encourage, urge on

6. disquieting (dis kwī′ ət iŋ)

(*adj.*) causing uneasiness or worry

A **disquieting** incident at school put all the teachers and students on edge.

SYNONYMS: disturbing, alarming
ANTONYMS: calming, reassuring, soothing, comforting

CCSS Vocabulary: 4.c., 4.d. (See pp. T14–15.)

7. empower (em paů′ ər)

(*v.*) to give power or authority to; to enable; to permit

Signing this legal paper will ___**empower**___ me to set up my own bank account.

SYNONYMS: authorize, license
ANTONYMS: forbid, prohibit, ban, disqualify

8. fluent (flü′ ənt)

(*adj.*) speaking or writing easily and smoothly, flowing gracefully

Susannah can speak ___**fluent**___ Japanese, French, and Russian.

SYNONYMS: eloquent, articulate, glib
ANTONYMS: tongue-tied, choppy

9. lag (lag)

(*v.*) to move slowly or fall behind; to bring up the rear; (*n.*) a falling behind; the amount by which someone or something is behind; an interval

Please try not to ___**lag**___ behind the others.

There is a three-hour ___**lag**___ from the time I send you an e-mail until you receive it.

SYNONYMS: (*v.*) trail, straggle; (*v., n.*) delay
ANTONYMS: (*v.*) keep up, outstrip, outdo

10. mangle (maŋ′ gəl)

(*v.*) to injure very seriously by cutting, tearing, crushing, etc.; to bring to ruin

Workers could ___**mangle**___ their hands in this equipment if they don't pay attention to what they're doing.

SYNONYMS: mutilate, butcher, disfigure, rend

11. misapprehension (mis ap ri hen′ shən)

(*n.*) a wrong idea, misunderstanding

A lingering ___**misapprehension**___ may cause ill will between friends.

SYNONYM: misconception

12. optimist (äp′ tə mist)

(*n.*) one who expects things to turn out for the best; someone who looks on the bright side of things

An ___**optimist**___ holds a rosy view of life.

ANTONYMS: pessimist, prophet of doom

13. prowl (praůl)

(*v.*) to roam about stealthily in search of something

A panther can ___**prowl**___ freely at night because its dark fur prevents it from being seen.

SYNONYMS: rove, skulk, slink, lurk

CCSS Vocabulary: 4.c., 4.d. (See pp. T14–15.)

14. recitation (res′ ə tā′ shən)

(*n.*) a reading in public of something that is memorized; a memorized poem or piece of prose that is read aloud

Kent was not nervous at all when he gave his Walt Whitman ___**recitation**___ at the school assembly.

SYNONYMS: (*n.*) recital, performance, presentation

15. stupefy (stü′ pə fī)

(*v.*) to make stupid, dull, or groggy; to surprise or astonish

The vet used a powerful tranquilizer to ___**stupefy**___ the animal.

SYNONYMS: stun, daze, shock, amaze, astound
ANTONYMS: awaken, arouse, stimulate, enliven

16. sulky (səl′ kē)

(*adj.*) in a bad or nasty mood, resentful; gloomy

A ___**sulky**___ child does not make a very good playmate.

SYNONYMS: sullen, petulant; ANTONYMS: cheerful, amiable

17. supplement (səp′ lə ment)

(*n.*) something added to complete a thing or make up for a lack; a section added to a book or document; (*v.*) to provide such an addition or completion

The sports ___**supplement**___ is my favorite part of this magazine.

Many people ___**supplement**___ their regular diet by taking daily vitamins.

SYNONYMS: (*n.*) addition, extension; (*v.*) add to

18. surge (sərj)

(*v.*) to have a heavy, violent, swelling motion (like waves); (*n.*) a powerful forward rush

Runners who train hard and who have good stamina often ___**surge**___ ahead of the pack.

A sudden ___**surge**___ of electrical current could make a computer crash.

SYNONYMS: (*v.*) flood, rush, burst, gush; (*n.*) wave
ANTONYMS: (*v.*) recede, ebb; (*n.*) recession, slowdown

19. trait (trāt)

(*n.*) a quality or characteristic (especially of personality); a distinguishing feature

Your most appealing ___**trait**___ is your unfailing sense of humor.

20. unscrupulous (ən skrü′ pyə ləs)

(*adj.*) dishonest; not guided or controlled by moral principles

Avoid dealing with ___**unscrupulous**___ merchants whenever possible.

SYNONYMS: crooked, corrupt, shady
ANTONYMS: fair, honest, trustworthy, aboveboard

CCSS Vocabulary: 4.c., 4.d. (See pp. T14–15.)

Choosing the Right Word

*Select the **boldface** word that better completes each sentence. You might refer to the passage on pages 164–165 to see how most of these words are used in context.*

1. Everything that I have learned about Theodore Roosevelt from history books (**stupefies, affirms**) my reverence for this great president.

2. Who (**prowled, empowered**) you to speak for everyone in our class?

3. A loud groan went through the class when we got the (**unscrupulous, disquieting**) news that there would be a full-period test later in the week.

4. I would love to be half as (**fluent, sulky**) in Spanish as José is in English.

5. All those smooth words and vague promises are not going to (**adhere, deter**) us from doing what we know is needed to improve conditions.

Theodore Roosevelt, the twenty-sixth president of the United States, won the Nobel Prize for Peace in 1906.

6. There is no one (**trait, optimist**) that makes him so likable; it is the overall effect of his personality.

7. When everything went wrong for Stan, and he saw no way out of his troubles, he muttered to himself, "I just can't (**mangle, cope**)!"

8. Come what may, I will (**adhere, affirm**) to the great ideas and ideals for which our ancestors suffered so much.

9. Jonathan was furious when his (**optimistic, unscrupulous**) boss stole his ideas for an advertising campaign.

10. My yoga class helped improve my breathing and (**supplemented, affirmed**) my training for running the marathon.

11. My definition of a(n) (**optimist, misapprehension**) is someone who looks at an almost empty bottle of juice and says, "This bottle is one-quarter full."

12. The City Council has approved funds for a new playground, but we expect a (**lag, surge**) of several months before construction begins.

13. When I saw the (**disquieting, mangled**) vehicle, I thought for sure that the driver had to be seriously injured; amazingly, though, he walked away from the wreck.

14. Even though some animals are ferocious and attack livestock, we should not be (**mangled, deterred**) from protecting their dwindling populations.

15. It is far better to know you are ignorant of something than to act on the basis of wrong information and (**misapprehensions, recitations**).

CCSS Vocabulary: 4.d. (See pp. T14–15.)

16. Shortly after World War II, Japan began the great economic (**surge, trait**) that put it among the world's top industrial nations.

17. My friend took one look at the statue I fashioned from stray pieces of junk and exclaimed, "That's not a sculpture; it's a(n) (**lag, atrocity**)!"

18. The worst way to deal with disappointments is to become (**fluent, sulky**); the best way is to smile and make up your mind to try again.

19. Ms. Edwards is having us listen to professional speakers to help prepare us for our poetry (**recitations, supplements**).

20. Jackals and other scavengers now (**prowl, deter**) through the ruins of what was once a great city.

21. Have all these years of peace and good living (**disquieted, stupefied**) us to such an extent that we are not even prepared to defend ourselves?

22. I agree fully with what the previous speaker has said, but I should like to (**cope, supplement**) his ideas with a few remarks of my own.

23. The play went along smoothly until it came to Mark Antony's funeral oration, which Fred (**empowered, mangled**) beyond all recognition.

24. A true friend would not have been so (**sulky, unscrupulous**) as to take unfair advantage of your trust and confidence.

25. Which stylistic (**traits, surges**) of Van Gogh's paintings do you find most enthralling?

*Choose the word from this Unit that is the same or most nearly the same in meaning as the **boldface** word or expression in the phrase. Write that word on the line. Use a dictionary if necessary.*

1. **damaged** the bicycle's lock while stealing it — mangled
2. did not welcome her **grouchy** attitude — sulky
3. **outrage** that stunned the world — atrocity
4. the most unique **attribute** of the breed — trait
5. hikers who **drop back** to the rear of the group — lag
6. drafting a **smooth and effortless** speech — fluent
7. a special **addendum** to the book — supplement
8. a letter containing some **troubling** news — disquieting
9. his dramatic **delivery** of the poem — recitation
10. unsure how to **manage** without her help — cope

 CCSS Vocabulary: 5. (See pp. T14–15.)

The synonyms and antonyms here do not appear on the Definitions page.

Antonyms

*Choose the word from this Unit that is most nearly opposite in meaning to the **boldface** word or expression in the phrase. Write that word on the line. Use a dictionary if necessary.*

1. comments that **detract from** your main point — supplement
2. witnessed the **spontaneous outburst** on the stage — recitation
3. known for her **sunny** disposition — sulky
4. **halting** public-speaking skills — fluent
5. practicing **caring acts** everyday — atrocities

Completing the Sentence

From the words in this Unit, choose the one that best completes each of the following sentences. Write the correct word form in the space provided.

1. In spite of our best efforts, collections for the Community Fund this year have ___lagged___ far behind last year's figures.
2. Since she has a large family, she finds it necessary to ___supplement___ her income by working at a second job at night and on weekends.
3. Do you think that it is possible to become ___fluent___ in a foreign language without actually living in a country where it is spoken?
4. If you think that I would go to a party without being invited, you are under a complete ___misapprehension___.
5. As the young girl began her ___recitation___, her mouth became dry and her voice began to crack.
6. In World War I, soldiers in the trenches endured one ___atrocity___ after another, such as contaminated food and water, diseases, and gangrene.
7. He is so careless in handling his textbooks that by the end of the term he has practically ___mangled___ all of them.
8. Naturally we were upset when we received the ___disquieting___ news that our uncle had been taken to the hospital.
9. The unfavorable weather reports did not ___deter___ us from holding the picnic that we had planned for so long.
10. In spite of all his talents, he will never gain high public office because so many voters feel that he is ___unscrupulous___ and cannot be trusted.

CCSS Vocabulary: 4.a., 5. (See pp. T14–15.)

11. We were so ___**stupefied**___ by the bad news that for a few moments we just sat there without moving or speaking.

12. When he gets in one of those ___**sulky**___ moods, he is as unreasonable and unpleasant as a cranky child.

13. The Constitution ___**empowers**___ the president to name the people who will fill many of the most important positions in the government.

14. As soon as the doors were opened, the shoppers, eager for the advertised bargains, ___**surged**___ into the store in great waves.

15. Throughout her long and noble career, her outstanding ___**trait**___ has been her deep love for her fellow human beings.

16. If you are having so much trouble with a program of four major courses, how do you expect to ___**cope**___ with a fifth course?

17. It is hard to be a(n) ___**optimist**___ when nothing works out for you.

18. As the robber ___**prowled**___ the streets looking for victims, he was unaware that undercover police officers were watching his every move.

19. Now that the job has been completed, I have finally become skillful in hanging the paper so that it ___**adheres**___ firmly to the wall.

20. The witness solemnly ___**affirmed**___ that the evidence she was about to give was true.

Writing: Words in Action

Answers to both prompts will vary.

1. Look back at "Polar Opposites" (pages 164–165). Using details from the passage, compare and contrast the Arctic and Antarctica. In your conclusion, state which polar region you would rather visit and explain why. Include at least two details from the passage and three Unit words.

2. The author of "Polar Opposites" states that Arctic residents "perceive their surroundings as benevolent and empowering." How do the weather and the environment affect a person's outlook? Write a brief essay, supporting your views with specific examples, observations, the reading (refer to pages 164–165), or personal experience. Write at least three paragraphs, and use three or more words from this Unit.

Writing prompt #2 is modeled on that of standardized tests.

 CCSS Vocabulary: 6; Writing: 1.c., 2.d., 3.d., 4. (See pp. T14–15.)

Vocabulary in Context: Informational Text for Unit 13 is available online at **vocabularyworkshop.com**.

The following excerpts are from Anne of Green Gables *by L.M. Montgomery. Some of the words you have studied in this Unit appear in* ***boldface*** *type. Complete each statement below the excerpt by circling the letter of the correct answer.*

1. Every other Friday afternoon she has **recitations** and everybody has to say a piece or take part in a dialogue. Oh, it's just glorious to think of it.

Recitations are

a. parties
b. readings
c. experiments
d. picnics

2. She said she hadn't time to get sick, watching to see that I didn't fall overboard. She said she never saw the beat of me for **prowling** about. But if it kept her from being seasick it's a mercy I did prowl, isn't it?

The act of **prowling** involves

a. eating
b. swimming
c. sneaking
d. running

3. Marilla felt hot anger **surge** up into her heart again. This child had taken and lost her treasured amethyst brooch and now sat there calmly reciting the details thereof without the least apparent compunction or repentance.

Feelings that **surge**

a. diminish
b. cheapen
c. end abruptly
d. swell rapidly

Megan Follows portrays the resourceful orphan Anne Shirley in this 1985 TV adaptation of *Anne of Green Gables*.

4. . . . Matthew, noting Anne's paleness and indifference and the **lagging** steps that bore her home from the post office every afternoon, began seriously to wonder if he hadn't better vote Grit at the next election.

Someone taking **lagging** steps is

a. lingering
b. forceful
c. hasty
d. skipping

5. "We had a quarrel. I wouldn't forgive him when he asked me to. I meant to, after awhile—but I was **sulky** and angry and I wanted to punish him first. He never came back . . . . But I always felt—rather sorry. I've always kind of wished I'd forgiven him when I had the chance."

A person who is **sulky** is NOT

a. peevish
b. confident
c. friendly
d. energetic

Snap the code, or go to **vocabularyworkshop.com**

Note that not all of the 20 Unit words are used in this passage. *Abstain*, *enumerate*, *extort*, *replica*, and *self-seeking* are not included.

*Read the following passage, taking note of the **boldface** words and their contexts. These words are among those you will be studying in Unit 14. As you complete the exercises in this Unit, it may help to refer to the way the words are used below.*

CCSS Vocabulary: 4; Reading (Informational Text): 4, 6. (See pp. T14–15.)

Madam C.J. Walker and Her Wonderful Remedy

<Biographical Sketch>

Pioneering entrepreneur Madam C.J. Walker was likely both the first woman and first African American self-made millionaire. She achieved her fortune by creating, marketing, and selling a hair tonic for African American women. She **transformed** her life and reached her **exalted** status through hard work, determination, and courage. As she liked to say, "I got my start by giving myself a start."

Madam Walker's real name was Sarah Breedlove. She was born in 1867 into a **glum** world of poverty and hardship. Her parents were newly freed slaves who worked the cotton fields on a Louisiana plantation. They left her an orphan at age seven.

Sarah Breedlove's early life was full of sadness, trouble, change, and **upheaval**. Seeking **sanctuary** from an abusive brother-in-law, she married as a 14-year-old and became a mother as a 17-year-old. She went from picking cotton to washing clothes for $1.50 a day. Despite her lack of formal education and money, she was not content to remain an obedient and **submissive** wife or employee to a tough **taskmaster**. She had other ideas.

To treat her hair loss and a scalp problem caused by poor nutrition, she began mixing homemade hair-care recipes. She hit upon a scalp conditioner and healing formula and dubbed it Madam C.J. Walker's Wonderful Hair Grower. (She used her third husband's name, C.J. Walker, **appending** "Madam" as well for sparkle.) She turned her remedy into a booming business.

Knowing that he who hesitates is lost, Madam Walker quickly took her product on the road. She traveled for years, selling her hair and beauty products successfully door-to-door to a **responsive** and eager audience. Hotels refused to **accommodate** African Americans, so she often stayed instead with local African American parishioners.

After years of struggle, business was so good she was able to hire and train sales agents. They were all African American women seeking a better life. In 1910, Madam Walker moved to Indianapolis and **amalgamated** her different business ventures into The Madam C.J. Walker Manufacturing Company. The Walker compound consisted of a factory, beauty school and salon, and training center for her growing sales force.

A **tally** of Madam C.J. Walker's many accomplishments shows she was not just a successful businesswoman. She was also a philanthropist and arts patron. She used her influence and fortune to help others. She gave large sums to charities and orphanages.

Madam Walker was vocal about social injustice. She spoke out against racist attitudes at a time when it was risky to do so. She petitioned Congress and the President to support federal anti-lynching laws. And she showed her **allegiance** to the National Association for the Advancement of Colored People (NAACP), pledging $5,000 to its anti-lynching campaign. It was the largest single donation the civil rights organization had ever received.

In 1998, the United States Postal Service issued a stamp **commemorating** Madam Walker and her extraordinary accomplishments. Her New York mansion is a National Historic Landmark, as is the former Walker Company building in Indianapolis, which now houses the Madame Walker Theatre Center. There is a street in Manhattan honoring Madam Walker and her daughter, A'Lelia, who was a famous Manhattan society figure.

Harvard Business School recognized Madam Walker as one of the great American business leaders of the twentieth century. It would not be unrealistic or **far-fetched** to say the rags-to-riches story of the little girl who dreamed big has inspired generations.

Audio

For iWords and audio passages, snap the code, or go to **vocabularyworkshop.com**.

Beauty mogul Madam C.J. Walker at the wheel of her Model T Ford

Madam C.J. Walker's Wonderful Hair Grower sparked a beauty empire.

Note the spelling, pronunciation, part(s) of speech, and definition(s) of each of the following words. Then write the appropriate form of the word in the blank spaces in the illustrative sentence(s) following. Finally, study the lists of synonyms and antonyms.

1. abstain (ab stān′)

(*v.*) to stay away from doing something by one's own choice

I find it hard to **abstain** from these tempting and delicious desserts.

SYNONYMS: avoid, decline, resist
ANTONYMS: yield to, give in to, indulge in

2. accommodate (ə käm′ ə dāt)

(*v.*) to do a favor or service for, help out; to provide for, supply with; to have space for; to make fit or suitable

That van is the ideal vehicle for carpooling because it can **accommodate** nine passengers.

SYNONYMS: oblige, lodge, adapt
ANTONYMS: disoblige, inconvenience, trouble

3. allegiance (ə lēj′ əns)

(*n.*) the loyalty or obligation owed to a government, nation, or cause

At a festive yet solemn ceremony, fifty new citizens swore **allegiance** to their adopted nation.

SYNONYMS: obedience, fidelity

4. amalgamate (ə mal′ gə māt)

(*v.*) to unite; to combine elements into a unified whole

Two small companies will **amalgamate** into one large corporation on June 1.

SYNONYMS: merge, consolidate
ANTONYMS: divide, separate, carve up, break up

5. append (ə pend′)

(*v.*) to attach, add, or tack on as a supplement or extra item

We were dismayed when our teacher decided to **append** an additional assignment to our already huge load of homework.

ANTONYMS: detach from, disconnect

6. commemorate (kə mem′ ə rāt)

(*v.*) to preserve, honor, or celebrate the memory of

Each May we **commemorate** Grandpa's life by lighting a special candle for him that burns for 24 hours.

SYNONYM: memorialize
ANTONYMS: dishonor, forget, overlook

CCSS Vocabulary: 4.c., 4.d. (See pp. T14–15.)

7. enumerate (i nü′ mə rāt)

(*v.*) to count; to name one by one, list

These booklets **enumerate** and compare all the high-tech features that new televisions can offer.

SYNONYMS: check off, spell out, specify

8. exalt (eg zôlt′)

(*v.*) to make high in rank, power, character, or quality; to fill with pride, joy, or noble feeling; to praise, honor

Let us now **exalt** the heroes for their courage and character in the face of all this adversity.

SYNONYMS: elevate, raise, uplift
ANTONYMS: lower, cast down, humble, degrade, demote, depose

9. extort (ek stôrt′)

(*v.*) to obtain by violence, misuse of authority, or threats

The kidnappers tried to **extort** a huge sum of money in return for releasing their prisoners unharmed.

SYNONYMS: blackmail, coerce, bilk, "shake down"

10. far-fetched (fär fecht′)

(*adj.*) strained or improbable (in the sense of not being logical or believable), going far afield from a topic

No one will believe the **far-fetched** excuse you just gave!

SYNONYMS: unlikely, hard to swallow
ANTONYMS: likely, probable, plausible, credible

11. glum (gləm)

(*adj.*) depressed, gloomy

The losing team wore **glum** expressions on their faces as the final buzzer sounded.

SYNONYMS: dejected, morose, melancholy
ANTONYMS: cheerful, merry, rosy, sunny

12. replica (rep′ lə kə)

(*n.*) a copy, close reproduction

We visited a life-size **replica** of the *Mayflower*, the Pilgrim ship docked near Plymouth, Massachusetts.

SYNONYMS: duplicate, imitation
ANTONYMS: original, prototype

13. responsive (ri spän′ siv)

(*adj.*) answering or replying; reacting readily to requests, suggestions, etc.; showing interest and understanding

The host of the charming inn was **responsive** to our every wish.

SYNONYMS: sympathetic, open, receptive
ANTONYMS: insensitive, unsympathetic

CCSS Vocabulary: 4.c., 4.d. (See pp. T14–15.)

14. sanctuary
(saŋk′ chə wer ē)

(*n.*) a sacred or holy place; refuge or protection from capture or punishment; a place of refuge or protection

The exhausted refugees found **sanctuary** in a local church.

SYNONYMS: shrine, haven

15. self-seeking
(self sēk′ iŋ)

(*adj.*) selfishly ambitious

That **self-seeking** politician will promise just about anything to win a few more votes.

SYNONYMS: selfish, opportunistic, gold-digging
ANTONYMS: unselfish, selfless, altruistic

16. submissive
(səb mis′ iv)

(*adj.*) humbly obedient; tending to give in to authority, obeying without protest

In some cultures, boys and men still expect girls and women to behave in a totally **submissive** manner.

SYNONYMS: meek, compliant, servile, subservient
ANTONYMS: rebellious, defiant, insubordinate

17. tally
(tal′ ē)

(*v.*) to count up; to keep score; to make entries for reckoning; to correspond or agree; (*n.*) a total or score

They will **tally** the votes after 9:00 P.M.

Our teacher keeps an accurate **tally** of all of our absences.

SYNONYMS: (*v., n.*) total, record

18. taskmaster
(task′ mas tər)

(*n.*) one whose job it is to assign work to others; one who uses his or her power to make people work very hard

The crusty old boss was a harsh **taskmaster** but also an efficient manager.

SYNONYMS: supervisor, slave driver

19. transform
(trans fôrm′)

(*v.*) to change completely in appearance or form; to make into something else

A heavy rain could **transform** the parched yellow fields into a lush green landscape again.

SYNONYMS: alter, convert
ANTONYMS: maintain, preserve

20. upheaval
(əp hēv′ əl)

(*n.*) a sudden, violent upward movement; great disorder or radical change

The sudden change in leadership caused dramatic social and economic **upheaval**.

SYNONYMS: confusion, disruption, chaos
ANTONYMS: tranquility, peace and quiet

CCSS Vocabulary: 4.c., 4.d. (See pp. T14–15.)

*Select the **boldface** word that better completes each sentence. You might refer to the passage on pages 174–175 to see how most of these words are used in context.*

Scottish writer Robert Louis Stevenson was especially known for his adventure novels *Treasure Island* and *Kidnapped.*

1. In Robert Louis Stevenson's classic story, a chemical potion (**tallies, transforms**) the good Dr. Jekyll into the evil Mr. Hyde.

2. He enjoys (**abstaining, enumerating**) all the factors that enabled him to rise from poverty to great wealth, but he always omits the important element of luck.

3. I didn't have time to write a letter to Lucy, but I (**appended, enumerated**) a few sentences to my sister's letter, expressing my congratulations.

4. My trainer wants me to (**abstain, enumerate**) from eating highly processed foods, especially those made with sugar and wheat.

5. We cannot have a peaceful and just society so long as any one group is required to be (**responsive, submissive**) to another.

6. When he felt low, he found that singing (**exalted, amalgamated**) his spirits.

7. Each member of the basketball team was awarded a trophy to (**transform, commemorate**) the championship season.

8. On the weekends, my parents are (**taskmasters, upheavals**), handing out lists of chores for all the children to do.

9. Financiers are planning to (**accommodate, amalgamate**) various businesses in the United States and England into one huge multinational corporation.

10. Ms. Wilentz is the kind of manager who does not try to (**extort, exalt**) cooperation from the people under her, but earns it by being a real leader.

11. Isn't it a little (**far-fetched, self-seeking**) to suggest that the pollution of our environment is mainly caused by creatures from outer space?

12. Nina is not very (**submissive, responsive**) to the idea of hiking up Mt. Kilimanjaro for her honeymoon.

13. Experience has taught me that people who constantly boast about their unselfishness are often secretly quite (**submissive, self-seeking**).

14. After a complete makeover, the scruffy young man was (**exalted, transformed**) into a distinguished-looking gentleman.

15. The detective's suspicion was aroused when the suspect's story failed to (**tally, commemorate**) with the known facts of the case.

16. The mayor had to choose between (**allegiance, tally**) to his political party and his judgment of what was best for the city.

17. The United States has a long history of providing (**upheaval, sanctuary**) to those fleeing persecution abroad.

18. If you look so (**far-fetched, glum**) just because you can't go to the party, how are you going to react when something really bad happens?

19. Unless the poor people of the country see some hope of improving their lives, there will probably soon be a great social (**sanctuary, upheaval**).

20. The new hotel is spacious enough to (**accommodate, extort**) large groups of people attending conventions and banquets.

21. Only seven members of the Security Council voted on the resolution; the others (**abstained, tallied**).

22. Instead of working so hard to prepare (**replicas, allegiances**) of famous works of art, why don't you try to create something original?

23. Because she sets extremely high standards for herself and is always pushing herself to do better, she is her own most severe (**taskmaster, replica**).

24. It remains to be seen how (**glum, responsive**) the students will be to the new method of teaching mathematics.

25. To (**tally, commemorate**) Paul Bunyan's birthday, my uncle made flapjacks.

Synonyms

Choose the word from this Unit that is the same or most nearly the same in meaning as the ***boldface*** *word or expression in the phrase. Write that word on the line. Use a dictionary if necessary.*

1. **acclaimed** as a standard of beauty	exalted
2. as **itemized** on the packing slip	enumerated
3. a **model** of the space shuttle	replica
4. an arrogant and **egotistical** person	self-seeking
5. lit candles in the quiet **place of worship**	sanctuary
6. fear of displeasing the **overseer**	taskmaster
7. has clearly proven his **devotion**	allegiance
8. chose to **refrain** from voting	abstain
9. to **house** an exchange student from Senegal	accommodate
10. how to **threaten** innocent victims	extort

CCSS Vocabulary: 5. (See pp. T14–15.)

The synonyms and antonyms here do not appear on the Definitions page.

Antonyms

*Choose the word from this Unit that is most nearly opposite in meaning to the **boldface** word or expression in the phrase. Write that word on the line. Use a dictionary if necessary.*

1. submitting a **novel idea** — replica
2. **treat yourself to** a banana split — abstain (from)
3. meant to **randomize** the instructions — enumerate
4. never question a **noble** gesture — self-seeking
5. reputation for **donating** money — extorting

Completing the Sentence

From the words in this Unit, choose the one that best completes each of the following sentences. Write the correct word form in the space provided.

1. I love basketball games, but I have decided to ___abstain___ from attending them until I can get my grades up to where they should be.

2. Imagine how ___glum___ we felt when a sudden wave of warm weather melted all the snow and ruined our plans for a winter carnival!

3. Is there anything more despicable than trying to ___extort___ money from innocent people by threatening them with bodily harm?

4. Remember that the Pledge of ___Allegiance___ is not a formula to be repeated mechanically but a summary of our sacred duty to our country.

5. On Memorial Day, Americans gather in ceremonies across the country to ___commemorate___ the nation's war dead.

6. Every entertainer likes a(n) ___responsive___ audience that shows it appreciates and enjoys a performance.

7. I know that Mother has given you all kinds of instructions before you leave for camp, but let me ___append___ some extra advice of my own.

8. Anne usually seems to be quiet and ___submissive___, but she has a way of flaring up when she feels that anyone is being unfair to her.

9. Can you see why it was logical for various labor unions in the clothing and textile industries to ___amalgamate___ into a single organization?

10. Under the U.S. Constitution, officials are never ___exalted___ to a point where they are more important or more powerful than the law.

CCSS Vocabulary: 4.a., 5. (See pp. T14–15.)

11. Good employees don't need a(n) ____**taskmaster**____ to keep them working.

12. In just a few years, she was ____**transformed**____ from an awkward tomboy into a charming young woman.

13. The driving instructor ____**enumerated**____ carefully the bad habits and practices that are likely to lead to accidents.

14. We learned in our science class how ____**upheaval**____ of Earth's crust has resulted in the formation of mountains.

15. Though an injured hand kept Larry from actually bowling, he took part in the tournament by keeping a careful ____**tally**____ of the scores.

16. I enjoyed the first part of the detective story, but the surprise ending was so ____**far-fetched**____ that I couldn't accept it.

17. When we visited New York City, we bought a small ____**replica**____ of the Statue of Liberty as a memento of our trip.

18. I would like to ____**accommodate**____ you, but I don't think it is right to allow you to copy my homework.

19. A portion of the forest has been set aside as a bird ____**sanctuary**____ for the protection of endangered species in the area.

20. When Ben Franklin said, "God helps those who help themselves," he did not mean that the most important thing in life is to be ____**self-seeking**____.

Writing: Words in Action

Answers to both prompts will vary.

1. Look back at "Madam C.J. Walker and Her Wonderful Remedy" (pages 174–175). Suppose you are a sales representative. You want to persuade your company to sell Walker's beauty products. Write a persuasive proposal stating why the products would enhance company sales. Use at least two details from the passage and three Unit words.

2. Madam Walker received many honors for her extraordinary accomplishments. How would you honor a deserving citizen? In a letter to a local commemoration committee, nominate a person. Explain why this person deserves to be recognized and explain how you would like to honor him or her. Highlight the individual's accomplishments and contributions to the community. Support your letter with specific examples from your observations, personal experience, and the reading (refer to pages 174–175). Write at least three paragraphs, and use three or more words from this Unit.

Writing prompt #2 is modeled on that of standardized tests.

 CCSS Vocabulary: 6; Writing: 1.c., 2.d., 3.d., 4. (See pp. T14–15.)

Vocabulary in Context: Informational Text for Unit 14 is available online at **vocabularyworkshop.com**.

The following excerpts are from The Life and Adventures of Nicholas Nickleby *by Charles Dickens. Some of the words you have studied in this Unit appear in* ***boldface*** *type. Complete each statement below the excerpt by circling the letter of the correct answer.*

1. At length, the two money-lenders obtained shelter in a house next door, and, being **accommodated** with a ladder, clambered over the wall of the back-yard—which was not a high one—and descended in safety on the other side.

If a person is **accommodated**, he or she is

a. hidden **c.** shaken down
b. disrespected **d.** helped out

2. "To put him," said Madame Mantalini, looking at Ralph, and prudently **abstaining** from the slightest glance at her husband, lest his many graces should induce her to falter in her resolution, "to put him upon a fixed allowance . . ."

The act of **abstaining** involves

a. escaping **c.** encouraging
b. avoiding **d.** glaring

3. "John, why don't you say something?"

"Say summat?" repeated the Yorkshireman.

"Ay, and not sit there so silent and **glum**."

People who are **glum** are NOT

a. cheery **c.** proud
b. sullen **d.** polite

A scene from a 6.5-hour-long stage version of *The Life and Adventures of Nicholas Nickleby* at the Gielgud Theatre in London, 2010.

4. With such expressions of sorrow, Miss Petowker went on to **enumerate** the dear friends of her youthful days one by one, and to call upon such of them as were present to come and embrace her.

To **enumerate** one's friends, one

a. avoids them **c.** calls on them
b. praises them **d.** counts them

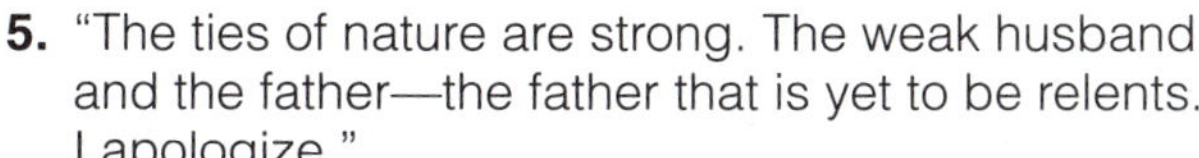

5. "The ties of nature are strong. The weak husband and the father—the father that is yet to be relents. I apologize."

"Humbly and **submissively**?" said Nicholas.

"Humbly and submissively," returned the tragedian, scowling upwards.

An apology made **submissively** is made

a. curtly **c.** obediently
b. enthusiastically **d.** boldly

Snap the code, or go to **vocabularyworkshop.com**

UNIT 15

Note that not all of the 20 Unit words are used in this passage. *Confiscate*, *pantomime*, *pessimist*, and *wistful* are not included.

*Read the following passage, taking note of the **boldface** words and their contexts. These words are among those you will be studying in Unit 15. As you complete the exercises in this Unit, it may help to refer to the way the words are used below.*

CCSS Vocabulary: 4; Reading (Informational Text): 4, 6. (See pp. T14–15.)

Running With the Big Dogs

<Magazine Article>

Throughout history, humans have depended on working guard dogs to protect and herd their animal flocks. For centuries, these dogs have served as **beacons** of protection. A well-trained guard dog is probably the most sensible **precaution** a shepherd or rancher can take to protect his herds against dangerous **encounters** with wolves or bears. The size, strength, and speed of three breeds shed some light on their ability to **retaliate** fiercely against attackers.

First is the Great Pyrenees. This truly massive breed takes its name from the Pyrenees—mountains located between France and Spain. Comparative **data** show that this is one of the largest of the flock guardians. A Great Pyrenees may stand as high as 32 inches and weigh up to 130 pounds. The medium-long, snow-white coat is sometimes shaded with gray or tan. The Great Pyrenees's coat blends in with a flock of sheep or goats and functions as a **sham**. Would-be attackers often do not suspect that the large white shape among the herd animals is really a protector of **epic** courage and strength. A Pyrenees will stop at nothing to **chasten**, or even kill, any invader threatening his flock.

It does not **detract** from the Pyrenees's awesome reputation to note that it is easily trained and especially patient with children. This makes the Pyrenees a **wholesome** household pet. The breed combines safety, affection, and beauty.

Like the Great Pyrenees, the Komondor sheepdog of Hungary enjoys the benefit of camouflage. A Komondor's white coat is doubly protective because it is corded from head to tail. The breed's tangled and woolly coat perfectly enables it to **prosecute** its mission of guarding a flock. Potential predators do not suspect the strength that lurks beneath those ropy cords. In addition, the Komondor's seemingly **uncouth** jacket guards it against the fangs and claws of **berserk** enemies. Finally, a Komondor's coat superbly insulates it against harsh weather.

Great Pyrenees guard sheep and goats.

A Komondor is only slightly smaller than a Great Pyrenees. Males stand up to 28 inches high and may weigh 100 pounds or more. With a large head and a long, agile stride, the Komondor is truly a majestic animal.

The Komondor dog and a Leicester sheep

Farther east in Europe, the Turkish Kangal Dog offers a third canine example of outstanding strength and courage. Largely unknown outside Turkey, the Kangal is prized in its homeland as a national treasure. The photograph below **underscores** several typical characteristics of the breed. Like a Pyranees and a Komondor, a Kangal blends in with the herd. This dog is short-coated and almost always exhibits a black mask and ears. The legs are large-boned and well-muscled, and the tail is curled. The breed's homeland is the rugged steppe, or prairie, of east-central Turkey. Unlike the Great Pyrenees and the Komondor, coated in **celestial** white, the Kangal usually sports a gray or tan-colored coat. The very appearance of a Kangal projects authority. Any illusions that attackers of the herd may harbor will surely be **punctured** if a Kangal is on duty.

Readers can find out more about each of these breeds. Nationally recognized breed associations are located throughout the country.

Inez P. Farquar is a regular contributor to Dog Days *magazine. When she's not playing fetch with her two terriers, Ms. Farquar volunteers at her local animal shelter.*

Audio

For iWords and audio passages, snap the code, or go to **vocabularyworkshop.com**.

The Turkish Kangal Dog guarding goats

Note the spelling, pronunciation, part(s) of speech, and definition(s) of each of the following words. Then write the appropriate form of the word in the blank spaces in the illustrative sentence(s) following. Finally, study the lists of synonyms and antonyms.

1. beacon (bē′ kən)

(*n.*) a light or other signal that warns and guides; a lighthouse; anything that guides or inspires

Sailors returning to port on a dark night search for the glow of a familiar **beacon**.

SYNONYMS: beam, flare

2. berserk (bər sərk′)

(*adj.*, *adv.*) violently and destructively enraged

A **berserk** man terrified the crowd of subway riders.

The wounded lion went **berserk** in his cage.

SYNONYMS: (*adj.*) mad, deranged
ANTONYMS: (*adj.*) sane, rational

3. celestial (sə les′ chəl)

(*adj.*) having to do with the sky or heavens; heavenly; yielding great bliss or happiness

The sun is the brightest **celestial** body in our solar system.

SYNONYMS: ethereal, stellar, blissful
ANTONYMS: earthly, terrestrial, infernal

4. chasten (chā′ sən)

(*v.*) to punish (in order to bring about improvement in behavior, attitude, etc.); to restrain, moderate

Dad knows how to **chasten** the stubborn child with a firm but soothing voice.

SYNONYMS: discipline, temper
ANTONYMS: praise, commend, reward

5. confiscate (kän′ fə skāt)

(*v.*) to seize by authority; to take and keep

The police will **confiscate** that car.

SYNONYMS: commandeer, expropriate
ANTONYMS: return, reinstate

6. data (dā′ tə)

(*pl. n.*) information; facts, figures, statistics

For math class, we collected **data** on the Internet sites students visited during the past week.

7. detract (di trakt′)

(*v.*) to take away from; reduce in value or reputation

Nothing can **detract** from your beauty!

SYNONYMS: subtract from, lower
ANTONYMS: increase, heighten, enhance

CCSS Vocabulary: 4.c., 4.d. (See pp. T14–15.)

8. encounter (en kau̇n′ tər)

(*n.*) a meeting (especially one that is unplanned); a meeting of enemies, battle; (*v.*) to meet or come upon

Remember our ___**encounter**___ with that skunk?

We might ___**encounter**___ other curious animals.

SYNONYMS: (*n.*) confrontation; (*v.*) happen upon
ANTONYMS: (*v.*) avoid, sidestep

9. epic (ep′ ik)

(*n.*) a long narrative poem (or other literary composition) about the deeds of heroes; an event or movement of great sweep; (*adj.*) on a grand scale, vast, titanic

Beowulf, the English ___**epic**___, was written around the year 700.

It describes ___**epic**___ struggles between the forces of good and evil.

SYNONYMS: (*n.*) saga, chronicle

10. pantomime (pan′ tə mīm)

(*n.*) a play or story performed without words by actors using only gestures; (*v.*) to express in this way

The performer included a short ___**pantomime**___.

We ___**pantomime**___ when we're unable to speak.

SYNONYMS: (*n.*) mime show, dumb show

11. pessimist (pes′ ə mist)

(*n.*) one who believes or expects the worst; prophet of doom

A ___**pessimist**___ sees a glass as half empty.

SYNONYM: killjoy; ANTONYMS: optimist, Pollyanna

12. precaution (pri kô′ shən)

(*n.*) care taken beforehand; a step or action taken to prevent something from happening

I advise you to take every ___**precaution**___ necessary to prevent a household fire.

SYNONYMS: foresight, prudence, safeguard
ANTONYMS: recklessness, heedlessness

13. prosecute (präs′ ə kyüt)

(*v.*) to bring before a court of law for trial; to carry out

She was told she would not be ___**prosecuted**___ if she restored the money.

SYNONYMS: put on trial, pursue; ANTONYMS: defend, abandon

14. puncture (pəŋk′ chər)

(*n.*) a small hole made by a sharp object; (*v.*) to make such a hole, pierce

The ___**puncture**___ caused the balloon to explode.

I tried not to wince as the hypodermic needle ___**punctured**___ my skin.

SYNONYM: (*n.*) perforation

CCSS Vocabulary: 4.c., 4.d. (See pp. T14–15.)

15. retaliate (ri tal′ ē āt)

(*v.*) to get revenge; to strike back for an injury

I would ___**retaliate**___ for that cheap insult, but I fear it may only make matters worse.

SYNONYMS: pay back, get even with
ANTONYMS: pardon, forgive, turn the other cheek

16. sham (sham)

(*adj.*) fake, not genuine; (*n.*) something false pretending to be genuine; a pretender; a decorated pillow covering; (*v.*) to pretend

The play includes a ___**sham**___ fight scene.

Her claim that she's a princess is a ___**sham**___.

Don't ___**sham**___ an illness in order to miss a day of school.

SYNONYMS: (*adj.*) phony, counterfeit; (*n.*) fraud
ANTONYMS: (*adj.*) authentic, bona fide

17. uncouth (ən küth′)

(*adj.*) unrefined, crude; awkward or clumsy

Although the quality of his work was good, his ___**uncouth**___ attitude cost him the job.

SYNONYMS: boorish, graceless
ANTONYMS: refined, polished, graceful, genteel

18. underscore (ən′ dər skôr)

(*v.*) to draw a line under; to put special emphasis on; (*n.*) a line drawn under something

The dire situation in the hospital's emergency room ___**underscores**___ the importance of having enough doctors and nurses available.

The word with the ___**underscore**___ is in Spanish.

SYNONYMS: (*v.*) underline, stress, accent
ANTONYMS: (*v.*) downplay, de-emphasize, soft-pedal

19. wholesome (hōl′ səm)

(*adj.*) healthy; morally and socially sound and good; helping to bring about or preserve good health

He always eats ___**wholesome**___ foods.

SYNONYMS: nourishing, beneficial
ANTONYMS: harmful, unhealthy, baneful

20. wistful (wist′ fəl)

(*adj.*) full of melancholy yearning or longing, sad, pensive

Her ___**wistful**___ look made me sad.

ANTONYMS: happy, contented, satisfied

CCSS Vocabulary: 4.c., 4.d. (See pp. T14–15.)

Choosing the Right Word

*Select the **boldface** word that better completes each sentence. You might refer to the passage on pages 184–185 to see how most of these words are used in context.*

1. Laura Ingalls Wilder wrote a series of children's books that describe the (**celestial, epic**) story of Western migration.

2. Is it right to (**retaliate, confiscate**) against an evil act by performing evil acts of one's own?

3. The youth center was a (**precaution, beacon**) to young people seeking help and guidance.

4. My first (**encounter, data**) with the new neighbors was amicable, and I believed we were all going to become good friends.

5. As I watched through the soundproof hospital window, the skaters on the pond seemed to be carrying out a colorful (**pantomime, epic**).

6. The news that I had been dropped from the football squad (**detracted, punctured**) my dream of becoming a great gridiron hero.

7. Parents who fail to (**chasten, detract**) their children for rude, impolite behavior may regret their lenient attitude later.

Laura Ingalls Wilder's "Little House" books are beloved by several generations of readers.

8. My grandmother becomes (**wistful, detracted**) when she recalls her childhood in the Swiss Alps.

9. Marie is not really pretty, but her sparkling personality and (**berserk, wholesome**) charm make her very attractive.

10. She had such a (**celestial, sham**) expression on her face that I thought she'd seen a vision of heaven.

11. I, for one, was extremely offended by the teen's (**underscored, uncouth**) behavior and foul language.

12. Many a perfectly healthy employee has been known to (**retaliate, sham**) illness to avoid going to work.

13. It does not (**prosecute, detract**) in the least from his reputation as a great player to say that all the team members deserve equal credit.

14. For some strange reason, the photocopier suddenly went (**berserk, wistful**) and started spewing vast quantities of paper all over the floor.

15. Although I do not get seasick, I am going to take some anti-motion sickness medication just as a (**precaution, puncture**).

CCSS Vocabulary: 4.d. (See pp. T14–15.)

16. The report that he sent to the president of the company (**underscored, retaliated**) the need for better planning and more careful use of funds.

17. I knew that it would be difficult to raise funds for the recycling program, but I never expected to (**chasten, encounter**) so many tough problems.

18. During the long years of defeat, Lincoln searched for a general who would (**prosecute, underscore**) the war fearlessly until the Union was saved.

19. The trouble with being a(n) (**underscore, pessimist**) is that you are so taken up with what is going wrong that you are unaware of what is going right.

20. Before we can plan properly for the upcoming school year, we must have accurate (**beacons, data**) on the results of last year's programs.

21. If you try to smuggle goods into this country without paying the customs duties, the inspectors may (**puncture, confiscate**) the goods and fine you.

22. Our driving instructor has emphasized that the use of seat belts is not a "silly" (**encounter, precaution**) but a surefire way of saving lives.

23. The child gazed (**wistfully, wholesomely**) at the shiny toys in the store window.

24. Her writing style is a little (**pessimistic, uncouth**), but what it lacks in polish and refinement is more than made up for by its wonderful humor.

25. When I want a(n) (**epic, wholesome**) snack, I eat a handful of almonds.

Choose the word from this Unit that is the same or most nearly the same in meaning as the ***boldface*** *word or expression in the phrase. Write that word on the line. Use a dictionary if necessary.*

1. such a **naysayer** pessimist
2. a crowd that is **out of control** berserk
3. should **emphasize** its safety features underscore
4. crowds enjoying the **charade** pantomime
5. sure to certify the **numbers** data
6. a convincing, yet **made-up** excuse sham
7. a small **pinprick** in the leather puncture
8. with a strong desire to **avenge** retaliate
9. staring with such **heartbreaking** eyes wistful
10. might **impound** our property confiscate

CCSS Vocabulary: 5. (See pp. T14–15.)

The synonyms and antonyms here do not appear on the Definitions page.

Antonyms

*Choose the word from this Unit that is most nearly opposite in meaning to the **boldface** word or expression in the phrase. Write that word on the line. Use a dictionary if necessary.*

1. anticipated your **sensible** behavior — berserk
2. to convey ideas through **talking** — pantomime
3. the greeter's **cheerful** demeanor — wistful
4. **idealists** who always share their views — pessimists
5. forced to **restore** the leather case — confiscate

Completing the Sentence

From the words in this Unit, choose the one that best completes each of the following sentences. Write the correct word form in the space provided.

1. Little did I realize when I **encountered** that old man on a lonely beach that this chance meeting would change my life.
2. In the old days, whippings and other forms of physical punishment were used to **chasten** student misbehavior, even in college.
3. In polite society, it is considered **uncouth** to balance peas on your knife at the dinner table.
4. Before we use the blowtorch in our industrial arts class, we are required to take the **precaution** of wearing goggles.
5. The workbook directions instruct the user to **underscore** the subject of each sentence in red and the predicate in blue.
6. My definition of a(n) **pessimist** is someone who worries about the hole in the doughnut and forgets about the cake surrounding it.
7. Over the years, a great many ships have been saved from destruction by that tall **beacon** standing on the rocky coast.
8. Though many people doubted that the new program would do any real good, I thought it was a very **wholesome** development.
9. Now that we have gathered a vast number of **data**, it is up to us to draw some useful conclusions from all this information.
10. When she said she would "turn the other cheek," she simply meant that she would not **retaliate** for the injury done to her.

11. So there I was with a(n) ___**puncture**___ in one of my rear tires, on a lonely road, on a dark night, and during a violent rainstorm!

12. The police have done their job in arresting the suspect; now it is up to the district attorney to ___**prosecute**___ him and prove his guilt.

13. Late that afternoon, one of the inmates went ___**berserk**___ and totally wrecked the infirmary.

14. With a(n) ___**wistful**___ expression on his face, the prisoner looked through his cell window at the patch of sky that meant freedom to him.

15. Although he could speak no English, he made us understand by the use of ___**pantomime**___ that he was extremely thirsty.

16. Isn't it remarkable that a(n) ___**epic**___ poem such as *The Iliad*, written almost 3,000 years ago, still has interest for readers today?

17. Nothing can ___**detract**___ from the fact that he stood by us in our hour of greatest need.

18. After the war, all the property that had been ___**confiscated**___ by the government was turned back to its former owners.

19. In ancient times, people gazed at the sky and studied the planets and other ___**celestial**___ bodies to predict the future.

20. Freedom of speech is a(n) ___**sham**___ and a mockery if it does not apply to people whose opinions are very unpopular.

Writing: Words in Action

Answers to both prompts will vary.

1. Look back at "Running with the Big Dogs" (pages 184–185). Suppose that you are a herder who must choose one of the three dog breeds discussed in the essay—Great Pyrenees, the Komondor, or the Kangal—to protect your herd. You must convince your family that your choice is correct. Write a letter to your family in which you support your choice of herding dog using at least two details from the passage and three Unit words.

2. Dogs have held important jobs over the years. They herd and protect farm animals; they help guide the blind; they serve in the military and assist fire fighters and police officers; and they rescue people after disasters. Write a brief essay about how dogs help humans. Include specific examples, observations, studies, the reading (refer to pages 184–185), or personal experience. Write at least three paragraphs, and use three or more words from this Unit.

Writing prompt #2 is modeled on that of standardized tests.

 CCSS Vocabulary: 6; Writing: 1.c., 2.d., 3.d., 4. (See pp. T14–15.)

Vocabulary in Context: Informational Text for Unit 15 is available online at **vocabularyworkshop.com**.

The following excerpts are from "The Legend of Sleepy Hollow" by Washington Irving. Some of the words you have studied in this Unit appear in ***boldface*** *type. Complete each statement below the excerpt by circling the letter of the correct answer.*

1. Such was one of the favorite haunts of the Headless Horseman, and the place where he was most frequently **encountered**.

Whenever someone is **encountered**, he or she is

a. surprised **c.** come upon
b. inspired **d.** taken down

2. What fearful shapes and shadows beset his path, amidst the dim and ghastly glare of a snowy night! With what **wistful** look did he eye every trembling ray of light streaming across the waste fields from some distant window!

A **wistful** look is one that is

a. satisfied **c.** ashamed
b. brooding **d.** mischievous

Schoolteacher Ichabod Crane being pursued by the Headless Horseman in an illustration by Frances Brundage.

3. How often did he shrink with curdling awe at the sound of his own steps on the frosty crust beneath his feet; and dread to look over his shoulder, lest he should behold some **uncouth** being tramping close behind him!

Something that is **uncouth** is NOT

a. coarse **c.** courageous
b. clumsy **d.** cultured

4. All this he called "doing his duty by their parents"; and he never inflicted a **chastisement** without following it by the assurance, so consolatory to the smarting urchin, that "he would remember it and thank him for it the longest day he had to live."

A **chastisement** is a(n)

a. suspicion **c.** affection
b. punishment **d.** weakness

5. Could that girl have been playing off any of her coquettish tricks? Was her encouragement of the poor pedagogue all a mere **sham** to secure her conquest of his rival?

A **sham** is

a. deception **c.** lesson
b. collection **d.** fashion

Snap the code, or go to **vocabularyworkshop.com**

CCSS Vocabulary: 4.d.; Reading (Literature): 4. (See pp. T14–15.)

Vocabulary for Comprehension

*Read the following passage in which some of the words you have studied in Units 13–15 appear in **boldface** type. Then answer the questions on page 195.*

This passage discusses a theory that modern scientists use to explain why the great Spanish painter Francisco de Goya was often ill.

(Line)

The masterful Spanish painter Francisco de Goya (1746–1828) **coped** with strange bouts of illness at various times in his life. Might his illness have explained the dramatic changes in his work? His early paintings were gentle and bright. His graceful portraits were lovely. But over time, his work grew dark and moody. He began to paint angry scenes in thick, dark colors. Art historians have long debated the reasons for this shift in Goya's style. Could it have been his health?

Modern science has evidence to suggest that Goya may have had a severe case of lead poisoning. High levels of lead in the bloodstream can cause muscle and joint pains, headaches, hearing loss, dizziness, mental distress, nausea, deranged conduct, personality changes, and finally, death. This list **tallies** with the list of symptoms that Goya suffered.

Goya's **disquieting** symptoms forced him to take breaks from painting. When he felt well enough to return to painting, he would rush back to his studio. There he would grind pigments again and paint enthusiastically to make up for the **lag** in his output.

Like most artists of the past, Goya made his paints himself. Grinding the pigments put him at risk of inhaling lead dust and getting it in his eyes, mouth, and ears and on his skin. Goya was known to use an unusual amount of a pigment called *lead white*. It gave his works their characteristic pearly glow. But it also made him sick. Although other artists risked lead poisoning, few used as much lead white as Goya did.

It no longer seems **far-fetched** to think that Goya's physical condition changed his artistic vision. One can only wonder how modern medical knowledge might have prevented his illness and allowed him to express his later genius.

CCSS Vocabulary: 4.a.; Reading (Informational Text): 2, 4, 6. (See pp. T14–15.)

1. The author's primary purpose is to prove that
   a. Goya is Spain's greatest genius
   b. Goya was an inferior artist
   c. Goya had many physical symptoms
   d. Goya's later paintings are superior to his early work
   (e.) Goya's severe lead poisoning caused great changes in his work

2. The meaning of **coped** (line 3) is
   a. avoided
   b. discovered
   (c.) dealt with
   d. laughed at
   e. suffered from

3. The two rhetorical questions in paragraph 1 (lines 4–6 and line 14) provide the focus for
   (a.) the entire passage
   b. paragraph 1
   c. paragraph 2
   d. paragraph 3
   e. paragraph 4

4. In paragraph 1, the sentence about art historians (lines 11–13) implies that
   a. art historians are argumentative
   b. the theory stated is definitely true
   c. the theory stated is definitely false
   (d.) there are other theories to explain Goya's change in style
   e. not everyone believes there was a definite shift in Goya's style

5. **Tallies** (line 23) is best defined as
   (a.) agrees
   b. totals
   c. merges
   d. conflicts
   e. degrades

6. The main purpose of paragraph 2 is to
   a. make readers feel sorry for Goya
   b. describe Goya's various symptoms
   c. show conflict between modern science and art historians
   d. show symptoms of lead poisoning
   (e.) prove that Goya's symptoms are those of severe lead poisoning

7. The meaning of **disquieting** (line 25) is
   a. surprising
   (b.) disturbing
   c. unusual
   d. painful
   e. hidden

8. **Lag** (line 32) most nearly means
   a. glut
   b. belief
   (c.) delay
   d. inconsistencies
   e. disappointment

9. **Far-fetched** (line 45) is best defined as
   a. selfish
   b. plausible
   c. sympathetic
   (d.) improbable
   e. shocking

10. The author's attitude in this passage is
    a. disbelieving
    (b.) matter-of-fact
    c. optimistic
    d. humorous
    e. outraged

11. Which of the following best outlines the organization of this passage?
    a. Goya's biography, lead poisoning
    b. grinding pigments, lead poisoning
    c. art historians' views, modern science's views
    d. Goya's later work, lead poisoning, Goya's symptoms
    (e.) changes in Goya's work, symptoms, grinding pigments, lead poisoning

12. Which of the following would the author most likely agree with?
    a. Goya's health has no bearing on a discussion of his artistic works.
    (b.) The circumstances of an artist's life can impact his or her style.
    c. Scientists will one day discover the cause of Goya's change in style.
    d. Experts in science and art history are at odds with one another.
    e. The story behind the changes in Goya's style will never be known.

CCSS Vocabulary: 4.a.; Reading (Informational Text): 2, 4, 6. (See pp. T14–15.)

Two-Word Completions

Select the pair of words that best completes the meaning of each of the following sentences.

1. In the opening of *The Iliad*, Homer's famous ____________ poem about the Trojan War, the hero, Achilles, who has not been accorded the proper reward for his brave deeds, is ____________ moodily in his tent.

a. celestial . . . prowling
b. disquieting . . . shamming
(c.) epic . . . sulking
d. berserk . . . lagging

2. To say our new boss is a(n) ____________ is one thing. But you are wrong to say that you believe she is making us work very hard to ____________ for past wrongs that were done to her.

a. sham . . . prosecute
b. atrocity . . . mangle
c. pessimist . . . extort
(d.) taskmaster . . . retaliate

3. The ____________ who had been lurking very suspiciously around the neighborhood was caught in the act of breaking into our house. The police ____________ the set of burglar's tools that he had with him as evidence to back up the charges against him.

(a.) prowler . . . confiscated
b. optimist . . . underscored
c. sham . . . mangled
d. pessimist . . . enumerated

4. "The only way we are going to ____________ people from driving a car while drunk," the speaker observed, "is to impose stiff penalties on such behavior and ____________ offenders to the full extent of the law."

a. empower . . . accommodate
b. detract . . . chasten
c. exalt . . . puncture
(d.) deter . . . prosecute

5. There's a wise old saying that a(n) ____________ will see a partially filled glass of water as half full, while a ____________ will see the same glass of water as half empty.

a. taskmaster . . . sham
(b.) optimist . . . pessimist
c. replica . . . tally
d. trait . . . beacon

6. It's difficult to ____________ all the reasons I like him, especially because he has exhibited so many excellent ____________.

(a.) enumerate . . . traits
b. pantomime . . . epics
c. puncture . . . beacons
d. amalgamate . . . lags

7. The young, newly discovered actor has such ____________ good looks that adding any makeup would ____________ from her natural beauty.

a. uncouth . . . append
b. sulky . . . transform
(c.) wholesome . . . detract
d. empowering . . . abstain

 CCSS Vocabulary: 4.a. (See pp. T14–15.)

The author in the passage about Madam C.J. Walker (see pages 174–175), describing Walker's incentive to sell hair products, uses the old saying "he who hesitates is lost." This proverb means that if someone spends too much time thinking about what action to take, the opportunity will vanish.

A **proverb** is a short saying that conveys a simple truth about life. Proverbs offer wise, everyday advice, and they can be used in many contexts. Many proverbs originate from the Bible, Shakespeare's plays, and other classic literature.

Choosing the Right Proverb

Read each sentence. Use context clues to figure out the meaning of each proverb in ***boldface*** *print. Then write the letter of the definition for the proverb in the sentence.*

1. **Lightning never strikes twice**, so stop worrying that you're going to fall down on stage again! __e__
2. **It's often said that when the cat's away, the mice will play**, but our class always stays on task when our teacher has to leave the room. __j__
3. "**Don't change horses in the middle of the stream**, Marie," I said. "Stick to your original topic and finish the report you started writing." __g__
4. Joyce lost the debate, but **there's no point in crying over spilt milk**. __f__
5. They **never do things by halves** in my uncle's auto repair shop. __a__
6. I know you want to blame Eric, but **it takes two to make a quarrel**. __b__
7. John should reconsider giving Monique a loan; **lend your money and lose your friend**. __h__
8. I'm not upset that Katie's business card looks just like mine; **imitation is the sincerest form of flattery**. __i__
9. Knowing that **he who pays the piper calls the tune**, Claude ordered for everyone at the table. __c__
10. You should **learn to walk before you run** and stop expecting to paint a masterpiece in your first art class. __d__

a. Undertake tasks wholeheartedly.

b. In an argument, both sides share blame.

c. The person who pays the bill decides how to spend the money.

d. Master a skill patiently, step by step.

e. The same misfortune is unlikely to occur twice to the same person.

f. Don't fret over something that has already happened.

g. Avoid making a change after an activity has begun.

h. Lending money to friends can ruin the relationship.

i. Copying someone is an unintended compliment.

j. People take advantage of a situation when there's no supervision.

CCSS Vocabulary: 5.a. (See pp. T14–15.)

WORD STUDY

Writing with Proverbs

Find the meaning of each proverb. (Use a dictionary if necessary.) Then write a sentence for each proverb. **Answers will vary.**

1. Cross the stream where it's shallowest. **Sample response: Find the easiest way; Cross the stream where it's shallowest--just use a cake mix instead of baking from scratch.**
2. Give credit where credit is due.
3. Make the best of a bad situation.
4. Practice what you preach.
5. Even a cat may look at a king.
6. A bad penny always turns up.
7. The best fish swim near the bottom.
8. Don't shut the barn door after the horse has gone.
9. Home is where the heart is.
10. One tree doesn't make a forest.
11. When it rains, it pours.
12. Where there's smoke, there's fire.

CCSS Vocabulary: 5. (See pp. T14–15.)

Denotation and Connotation

Words have two kinds of meanings. **Denotation** refers to the word's literal meaning, which you'll find in a dictionary entry. The denotation conveys a neutral tone.

Connotations are the emotional and cultural associations that people make to words. These associations are the "shades of meaning" we perceive in words that have similar, but not identical, denotations. A connotation can have a positive or negative tone.

Consider these synonyms for the word *copy:*

replica *facsimile* *sham* *fraud*

Replica and *facsimile* have neutral connotations, while *sham* and *fraud* have deeply negative connotations.

> **Think:** A museum might display a replica or a facsimile of a famous artwork or document, but it would never exhibit a work considered to be a sham or fraud.

Look at these examples of words that are similar in denotation but have different connotations.

NEUTRAL	POSITIVE	NEGATIVE
pronounce	**affirm**	**dictate**
satisfied	**proud**	**self-seeking**
meet	**encounter**	**confront**

Remember that writers choose their words deliberately. They understand that people associate feelings with words. Writers know how to influence their audiences, and thus readers should be mindful of the specific connotations carried by certain words.

Shades of Meaning

Write a plus sign (+) in the box if the word has a positive connotation.
Write a minus sign (–) if the word has a negative connotation.
Put a zero (0) if the word is neutral.

1. mangle [–]

2. pantomime 

3. submissive [–]

4. optimist  

5. empower 

6. glum 

7. data [0]

8. beacon [+]

9. commemorate 

10. recitation 

11. berserk 

12. atrocity [–]

13. fluent 

14. unscrupulous 

15. celestial 

16. uncouth [–]

CCSS Vocabulary: 5.c. (See pp. T14–15.)

WORD STUDY

Expressing the Connotation

Read each sentence. Select the word in parentheses that better expresses the connotation (positive, negative, or neutral) given at the beginning of the sentence.

positive **1.** The office manager kept (**promoting, exalting**) her resourceful young assistant, hoping to procure a large raise for her in the next fiscal year.

neutral **2.** Rhonda wants to become a (**taskmaster, manager**) at the hotel when she graduates from school.

positive **3.** I'd like to (**commemorate, remember**) my father with a special gathering on the anniversary of his death.

positive **4.** The professor shared all of her knowledge with her graduate students, hoping to (**empower, help**) them in their future careers.

neutral **5.** In order to (**inflate, supplement**) his income, my uncle took a second job that he could do from home.

negative **6.** Brandi was amused when her host (**mangled, stumbled over**) the pronunciation of her last name.

negative **7.** Several homeowners were suspicious of the man (**wandering, prowling**) around their neighborhood.

negative **8.** Don't let the price (**frighten, deter**) you; this house is really a very good deal, and you won't regret buying it.

Challenge: Using Connotation

*Choose vocabulary words from Units 13–15 to replace the **boldface** words in the sentences below. Then explain how the connotation of the replacement word changes the tone of the sentence.* **Answers will vary.**

sulky	**uncouth**	**abstain**
exalt	**lag**	**responsive**

1. During Lent, many Catholics **withdraw** abstain from eating meat on Fridays.
Sample response: *Abstain* makes the tone of the sentence sound more formal and the action seem more intentional and serious.

2. Those young actors are very **sensitive** sulky when the director offers suggestions on how they can improve their performances.
Sample response: *Sulky* creates a negative tone by suggesting that the actors are thin-skinned and liable to pout rather than accept the criticism.

3. Although Bernie thought that eating with his mouth open was funny, family members found his behavior to be **ill-mannered** uncouth.
Sample response: *Uncouth* suggests a degree of crudeness and therefore injects a more negative tone.

 CCSS Vocabulary: 5, 5.c. (See pp. T14–15.)

pre—before

This Latin prefix appears in **precaution** (page 187). Some other words in which this prefix appears are listed below.

prearrange	**prefer**	**preliminary**	**preoccupy**
precise	**prehistoric**	**premature**	**preside**

From the list of words above, choose the one that corresponds to each of the brief definitions below. Write the word in the blank space in the illustrative sentence below the definition. Use a dictionary if necessary.

1. coming before the main business or action; introductory; something that comes before the main event, a curtain-raiser

   Although the young boxer lost the **preliminary** bout, knowledgeable fans could readily see that he had promise.

2. to like better, choose over something else; to put forward, press

   Although many customers **prefer** to order healthy appetizers and main courses, restaurant owners report an increased interest in rich desserts.

3. unexpectedly early in development; coming too soon

   The expectant mother was alerted to the possibility of a **premature** birth, so she took extra good care of herself.

4. to absorb one's attention completely or at the expense of other things

   She was so **preoccupied** with the novel that she forgot to return my phone call.

5. very definite or clear, exact; very careful; strict

   The doctor left **precise** instructions on how to clean the wound.

6. to arrange ahead of time

   One important task of a travel agent is to **prearrange** transportation and accommodations so that the client can focus on enjoying the trip.

7. belonging to the period before written history

   The museum has a fascinating new exhibit that explains how scientists identify and classify the bones of **prehistoric** animals.

8. to have authority over, oversee

   Tomorrow is the first opportunity our principal will have to **preside** at the community school board meeting.

CCSS Vocabulary: 4.b. (See pp. T14–15.)

FINAL MASTERY TEST

Synonyms

Select the two words or expressions that are most nearly the same in meaning.

1. a. limber	**b.** numb	**c.** celestial	**d.** nimble
2. a. vacate	**b.** encounter	**c.** tally	**d.** confront
3. a. pry	**b.** empower	**c.** authorize	**d.** accommodate
4. a. compact	**b.** waylay	**c.** compress	**d.** stupefy
5. a. confer	**b.** induce	**c.** billow	**d.** surge
6. a. memento	**b.** pacifist	**c.** oracle	**d.** keepsake
7. a. immense	**b.** titanic	**c.** stealthy	**d.** meteoric
8. a. replenish	**b.** amble	**c.** saunter	**d.** balk
9. a. allegiance	**b.** synopsis	**c.** fidelity	**d.** consequence
10. a. queue	**b.** deluge	**c.** enigma	**d.** cascade
11. a. douse	**b.** prowl	**c.** besiege	**d.** immerse
12. a. compliant	**b.** submissive	**c.** rigorous	**d.** contemporary
13. a. liberate	**b.** engulf	**c.** maneuver	**d.** manipulate
14. a. supplement	**b.** gloat	**c.** relish	**d.** infuriate
15. a. famished	**b.** outright	**c.** sheepish	**d.** ravenous

Antonyms

Select the two words that are most nearly opposite in meaning.

16. a. acquit	**b.** wither	**c.** thrive	**d.** depict
17. a. innovation	**b.** trait	**c.** replica	**d.** sham
18. a. append	**b.** confiscate	**c.** detract	**d.** enumerate
19. a. optimist	**b.** responsive	**c.** incalculable	**d.** pessimist
20. a. acute	**b.** bumbling	**c.** optional	**d.** taut
21. a. expend	**b.** retrieve	**c.** denounce	**d.** idolize
22. a. ruffle	**b.** dole	**c.** vow	**d.** prevaricate
23. a. immobile	**b.** jovial	**c.** smug	**d.** glum
24. a. maximum	**b.** giddy	**c.** mortal	**d.** minimum
25. a. motivate	**b.** cringe	**c.** bluster	**d.** deter

Analogies

Select the item that best completes the comparison.

26. inhabitant is to **settled** as
- **a.** citizen is to abominable
- **(b.)** vagabond is to wandering
- **c.** orphan is to disinterested
- **d.** homebody is to gory

27. fear is to **intimidate** as
- **a.** dirt is to scour
- **b.** trust is to discredit
- **(c.)** force is to quash
- **d.** argument is to verge

28. vegetable is to **perishable** as
- **(a.)** iron is to durable
- **b.** pet is to gullible
- **c.** clown is to sinister
- **d.** argument is to logical

29. exalt is to **higher** as
- **a.** persevere is to lower
- **b.** lag is to higher
- **(c.)** debase is to lower
- **d.** deem is to higher

30. thankful is to **ingratitude** as
- **a.** ambiguous is to uncertainty
- **b.** belligerent is to strife
- **c.** eternal is to duration
- **(d.)** unrepentant is to remorse

31. serene is to **stormy** as
- **a.** petty is to trifling
- **b.** martial is to warlike
- **c.** global is to universal
- **(d.)** boisterous is to quiet

32. chain saw is to **topple** as
- **a.** bulldozer is to befuddle
- **b.** pickax is to irk
- **(c.)** fungus is to blight
- **d.** trowel is to scan

33. inept is to **bungle** as
- **a.** amiable is to insult
- **(b.)** frugal is to conserve
- **c.** aggressive is to pacify
- **d.** sensitive is to strand

Two-Word Completions

To complete the sentences, select the best word pair from among the choices given.

34. Taking the ____________ to make friends with new students at school can really help them ____________ the changes happening in their lives.
- **a.** onset . . . repent
- **b.** illusion . . . tarry
- **(b.)** initiative . . . cope with
- **d.** terrain . . . abstain from

35. The new principal has begun ____________ stricter rules about the use of ____________ materials in school.
- **a.** designating . . . wholesome
- **(b.)** implementing . . . illicit
- **b.** foiling . . . resourceful
- **d.** commemorating . . . burly

36. It is a bad idea to ____________ breakfast in the morning, because you will probably find yourself ____________ and tired later in the day.
- **a.** rummage through . . . sulky
- **b.** cede . . . inflammatory
- **b.** dissect . . . strapping
- **(d.)** skimp on . . . sluggish

37. Doesn't it make you a(n) ____________ to expect that she pay you back right away when it often takes you a month to ____________ someone?
- **(a.)** hypocrite . . . reimburse
- **b.** sage . . . constrain
- **b.** atrocity . . . refurbish
- **d.** nonconformist . . . prosecute

Supplying Words in Context

To complete each sentence, select the best word from among the choices given. Not all words in the word bank will be used. You may modify the word form as necessary.

refute	**facet**	**prevail**	**culprit**
encompass	**devastate**	**arid**	**beacon**
delude	**variable**	**maze**	**debut**
puncture	**retaliate**	**subordinate**	**epic**

38. The story of the men who first climbed to the top of Mount Everest is a(n) ______**epic**______ of human courage and strength.

39. Only a tiny ______**puncture**______ in the skin showed where the doctor had made the injection.

40. Now that the two candidates have finished their long, hard campaigns, it is up to the voters to say which one will ______**prevail**______.

41. I am grateful to my parents, who have always ______**subordinated**______ their own interests and desires to the well being of their children.

42. You are just ______**deluding**______ yourself if you think you can do well in school without regular, systematic study.

43. His arguments were so soundly based and so well presented that no one could ______**refute**______ them.

taskmaster	**pantomime**	**misrepresent**	**unerring**
groundless	**pathetic**	**dumbfounded**	**instantaneous**
sabotage	**rendezvous**	**sleuth**	**eerie**
fray	**valiant**	**dispatch**	**far-fetched**

44. In the days of silent movies, actors and actresses had to express ideas and emotions by means of ______**pantomime**______.

45. My long-awaited ______**rendezvous**______ with Eileen turned out to be a disappointment when she got sick and could not make it.

46. We have learned by experience that she is so shrewd that her judgments of people are almost ______**unerring**______.

47. What a(n) ______**eerie**______ feeling it gave us to listen to ghost stories as we sat around the flickering campfire!

48. I cannot believe that these repeated breakdowns of the machinery are no more than "accidents"; I suspect ______**sabotage**______.

49. Coach Robinson is a strict ______**taskmaster**______, who expects instant obedience and 100 percent effort from all his players.

*Select the word or expression that best completes the meaning of the sentence or answers the question, with particular reference to the meaning of the word in **boldface** type.*

50. A person who is wearing **manacles** is probably a

a. prisoner
b. model
c. judge
d. teacher

51. You would seek **sanctuary** if you were

a. hungry
b. being pursued
c. in the dark
d. rich

52. A habit that is deeply **ingrained** is

a. a bad one
b. hard to change
c. easy to get rid of
d. of no great importance

53. If you receive news that is **disquieting** you will probably be

a. delighted
b. calm
c. pleased
d. upset

54. A student who is lost in a **reverie**

a. has taken a wrong turn
b. has a toothache
c. is daydreaming
d. is well prepared for final exams

55. A school course dealing with **vocations** will help you

a. plan for a career
b. become a good dancer
c. become a "math shark"
d. develop your speaking ability

56. A study program might properly be called **intensive** if it

a. is a lot of fun
b. is open to everyone
c. calls for hours of hard work
d. will help you get a summer job

57. A person who **reminisces** a great deal might be criticized for

a. living in the past
b. insulting other people
c. using foul language
d. borrowing money

58. A person who **abducts** another will probably

a. receive a prize
b. be arrested for kidnapping
c. get picked for a team
d. go to the hospital

59. You will **affirm** your mastery of the words taught in this book if you

a. spell them incorrectly
b. forget what they mean
c. never use them in class
d. score 100% on this Final Test

60. Which of the following would be a **chastening** experience?

a. winning a scholarship
b. going to a party
c. spending the day at the beach
d. doing poorly on this exam

61. A basketball player who lacks **stamina** would be likely to

a. miss foul shots
b. tire quickly
c. argue with the referee
d. show a lack of team spirit

Choosing the Right Meaning

Read each sentence carefully. Then select the item that best completes the statement below the sentence.

62. The report provided the **data** I needed to finish my research paper.
The word **data** most nearly means
(**a.**) information **b.** money **c.** assistance **d.** equipment

63. Although she usually acted meek, during tough times she showed more **grit** than anyone else.
The word **grit** most nearly means
a. judgment **b.** fear (**c.**) courage **d.** restlessness

64. He spent so much time **dawdling** over which movie to see that by the time he made a decision, both films had already started.
The word **dawdling** most nearly means
(**a.**) loafing **b.** working **c.** fighting **d.** napping

65. As punishment for failing the exam, his father **restricted** his after-school activities.
The word **restricted** most nearly means
(**a.**) limited **b.** widened **c.** guided **d.** ended

66. Those who had been following the case closely thought the "not guilty" verdict a **parody** of justice.
The word **parody** most nearly means
(**a.**) mockery **b.** example **c.** cause **d.** fear

67. After our ill-fated first meeting I had many **misgivings** about the new team member, but I've found I like her very much after taking time to get to know her.
The word **misgivings** most nearly means
a. setbacks (**b.**) doubts **c.** victories **d.** presents

68. The **inevitable** result of procrastination is a lot of stress the night before an exam.
The word **inevitable** most nearly means
a. sudden (**b.**) unavoidable **c.** regrettable **d.** unexpected

69. The teacher corrected the **misapprehension** that the rule "I before E except after C" applies in all cases.
The word **misapprehension** most nearly means
a. plan **b.** formula **c.** examination (**d.**) misunderstanding

70. Her dream is to turn her talent as a skilled **mimic** into a career as an actress.
The word **mimic** most nearly means
a. athlete **b.** politician **c.** speaker (**d.**) imitator

WORD LIST

The following is a list of all the words taught in the Units of this book. The number after each entry indicates the page on which the word is defined.

abduct, 148
abominable, 128
abstain, 176
accommodate, 176
acquit, 52
acute, 62
adhere, 166
adverse, 24
affirm, 166
affluence, 100
agenda, 72
alias, 138
allegiance, 176
amalgamate, 176
ambiguous, 148
amble, 138
amiable, 72
apparel, 14
append, 176
arid, 24
arrears, 100
assailant, 24
atrocity, 166
authorize, 90
avenge, 110

balk, 148
barrage, 34
beacon, 186
befuddle, 72
berserk, 186
besiege, 14
bigot, 34
billow, 24
blight, 72
bluster, 62
boisterous, 72
bumbling, 128
bungle, 62
burly, 138

cascade, 100
cede, 110
celestial, 186
chasten, 186
clarity, 72
commemorate, 176
commentary, 62
compact, 148
compliant, 73
compress, 14
confer, 148
confiscate, 186
confront, 24
consequence, 128
conserve, 73
constrain, 24
contemporary, 25
cope, 166
cringe, 100
crotchety, 100
culprit, 90

data, 186
dawdle, 90
debut, 73
deem, 52
delude, 128
deluge, 110
denounce, 14
depict, 25
designate, 34
deter, 166
detract, 186
devastate, 52
discredit, 52
discretion, 110
disinterested, 25
dispatch, 14
disquieting, 166
dissect, 90
distort, 138
diversity, 34
dogged, 138
dole, 128
douse, 14
dumbfounded, 138
duration, 62

earmark, 149
eerie, 62
elusive, 52
empower, 167
encompass, 25
encounter, 187
engulf, 128
enigma, 34
enumerate, 177
epic, 187
exalt, 177
expend, 90
expressly, 15
extinct, 139
extort, 177

facet, 63
famished, 15
far-fetched, 177
fatality, 90
fidelity, 63
fluent, 167
foil, 129
formulate, 129
forsake, 15
fray, 63
frigid, 149

gainful, 15
generate, 52
giddy, 110
gloat, 34
global, 35
glum, 177
gory, 73
grit, 139
gross, 73
groundless, 25
gullible, 91

headstrong, 63
hypocrite, 25

idolize, 53
illicit, 91
illusion, 35
immense, 15
immerse, 91
immobile, 100
impact, 110
impassable, 100
implement, 149
incalculable, 149
incomprehensible, 25
indisputable, 149
induce, 73
inept, 15
inevitable, 139
inflammatory, 91
infuriate, 35
ingenious, 15
ingrained, 139
ingratitude, 53
inhabitant, 63
initiative, 129
innovation, 101
instantaneous, 16
intensive, 149
intimidate, 111
irk, 16

jovial, 101

keepsake, 53

lag, 167
leeway, 73
libel, 16
liberate, 111
limber, 74
logical, 111

manacle, 101
maneuver, 149
mangle, 167
manipulate, 26
martial, 101
maximum, 26
maze, 74
memento, 129
memorandum, 91
meteoric, 139
mimic, 26
minimum, 101
misapprehension, 167
misgiving, 16
misrepresent, 111
mortal, 53
motivate, 35

nimble, 101
nonconformist, 129
null and void, 129
numb, 63

oaf, 16
onset, 102
optimist, 167
optional, 111
oracle, 74
outright, 111
ovation, 53

pacifist, 35
pacify, 63
panorama, 129
pantomime, 187
parody, 139
partisan, 74
partition, 102
pathetic, 91
perishable, 102
persevere, 91
pessimist, 187
petty, 53
plight, 53
posterity, 130
precaution, 187
prevail, 139
prevaricate, 92
prosecute, 187
prowl, 167
pry, 130
puncture, 187

quash, 92
queue, 35

ravenous, 64
recede, 16
recitation, 168
refurbish, 130
refute, 64
reimburse, 74
relic, 140
relish, 92
reminisce, 92
remorse, 64
rend, 140
rendezvous, 111
repast, 16
repent, 54
replenish, 140
replica, 177
resourceful, 130
responsive, 177
restrict, 35
retaliate, 188
retrieve, 102
reverie, 54
revocation, 54
rigorous, 130
rotund, 112
ruffle, 26
rummage, 140

sabotage, 150
sage, 36
sanctuary, 178
saunter, 112
scan, 54
scant, 150
scour, 92
self-seeking, 178
serene, 26
setback, 64
sham, 188
sheepish, 26
sinister, 102
skimp, 140
slake, 36
sleuth, 140
sluggish, 112
smug, 64
stamina, 26
stealthy, 150
strand, 54
strapping, 150
strident, 150
strife, 54
stupefy, 168
submissive, 178
subordinate, 112
subsequent, 130
sulky, 168
supplement, 168
surge, 168
synopsis, 64

tally, 178
tarry, 64
taskmaster, 178
taut, 102
template, 102
terrain, 36
testimonial, 92
thrive, 150
tint, 112
titanic, 150
topple, 54
trait, 168
transform, 178

uncouth, 188
underscore, 188
unerring, 130
unscrupulous, 168
upheaval, 178

vacate, 74
vagabond, 74
valiant, 150
vandalism, 140
variable, 112
verge, 112
vocation, 36
vow, 36

waylay, 36
wholesome, 188
wistful, 188
wither, 36
writhe, 92

INDEX

Affixes, 8
Analogies, 11
Context Clues, 7
Literary Text, 21, 31, 41, 59, 69, 79, 97, 107, 117, 135, 145, 155, 173, 183, 193
Online Resources, 13, 21, 23, 31, 33, 41, 51, 59, 61, 69, 71, 79, 89, 97, 99, 107, 109, 117, 127, 135, 137, 145, 147, 155, 165, 173, 175, 183, 185, 193
Reading Passages, 12–13, 22–23, 32–33, 50–51, 60–61, 70–71, 88–89, 98–99, 108–109, 126–127, 136–137, 146–147, 164–165, 174–175, 184–185
Vocabulary and Reading, 9
Vocabulary Strategies, 7
Word Structure, 8
Word Study
- **Adages**, 121
- **Classical Roots**, 49, 87, 125, 163, 201
- **Connotation and Denotation**, 47–48, 85–86, 123–124, 161–162, 199–200
- **Idioms**, 45, 83, 159
- **Proverbs**, 197
- **Shades of Meaning**, 47, 85, 123, 161, 199